THE TEACHER'S GUIDE TO INCLUSIVE EDUCATION

750 STRATEGIES FOR SUCCESS

A GUIDE FOR ALL EDUCATORS

PEGGY A. HAMMEKEN

Peytral Publications

Minnetonka MN

The Teacher's Guide to Inclusive Education – 750 Strategies for Success. A Guide for All Educators
Peggy A Hammeken
Copyright © 2007 Peytral Publications, Inc.
10 9 8 7 6 5 4 3 2
Printed in the United States of America

The material cited in this publication is credited to the source whenever possible. Many of the ideas and suggestions have been submitted by practicing educators and every attempt has been made to determine the original source. If you have questions or concerns about the material please contact the publisher and every attempt will be made to correct the information in future printings. All names of people and places used in this book have been changed. Any similarity to individuals or situations is coincidental and no implications should be inferred.

At the time of this book's publication, all of the telephone numbers and Web site URLs are accurate and active; all publications, organizations, Web sites, and other resources exist as described in this book; and all have been verified. The author and Peytral Publications, Inc. make no warranty or guarantee concerning the information and materials given out by organizations or content found at the Web sites, and we are not responsible for any changes that occur after this book's publication. If you find an error or believe that a resource listed here is not as described, please contact Peytral Publications, Inc.

This book was previously published as *Inclusion: 450 Strategies for Success* (1995 ISBN 0-9644271-7-6 and 2000 1-890455-25-3). Due to the amount of material and extensive updates to this publication, it is published as a new publication instead of a revised edition.

Cover Illustration: Maria del Mar Chapa Hammeken
Editor: Peggy Henrikson

Publisher's Cataloging-in-Publication
(Prepared by Quality Books, Inc.)

Hammeken, Peggy A.
    The teacher's guide to inclusive education : 750 strategies for success : a guide for all educators / Peggy A. Hammeken.
        p. cm.
    Includes bibliographical references.
    LCCN 2007928583
    ISBN-13: 9781890455101
    ISBN-10: 1890455105

    1. Inclusive education--United States. 2. Children with disabilities--Education--United States. 3. Special education--United States--Planning. I. Title.

LC1201.H265 2007   371.9'046'0973
                          QBI07-600138

Peytral Publications, Inc.
PO Box 1162
Minnetonka, MN 55345
Tel: 952.949-8707
www.peytral.com

Table of Contents

Acknowledgements

This book is a collaborative effort on the part of many educators, students, parents and administrators. The ideas have been compiled from actual experiences in inclusive education settings.

I would like to acknowledge the Eden Prairie School District (Eden Prairie, Minnesota) for providing support and encouragement to all staff involved in inclusive education settings. Their contributions and ideas were the foundation for this book. For the revised, updated edition, I want to thank all of the dedicated educators, consultants, service providers and parents nationwide who have shared their ideas, comments and suggestions.

I also would like to acknowledge my family. My daughters, Vanessa and Melissa, provided encouragement and contributed ideas, and the book would not have been possible without my husband, Roberto. His enthusiasm and support have always been apparent, even during the most difficult stages.

Finally, I dedicate this book to my mother, Marlene (1934-1992), who taught me at an early age that all people are equal, regardless of their ethnic background, religion or disability.

"When the world seems large and complex, we need to remember that great world ideals all begin in some home neighborhood."

Konrad Adenauer

A Word from the Author

The passage of the Education for All Handicapped Children Act of 1975 (P.L. 94-142) mandated a free, appropriate public education for all children with disabilities. This law also guaranteed due process rights, mandated IEPs and became the core of funding for special education. With P.L. 94-142, the educational system faced the challenge of including all students with disabilities in the general education setting. The law also declared that all students were to be educated in the least restrictive environment.

In spite of the law, two educational systems emerged. One educational system was called "regular" and the second "special." As students returned to their home schools, the resource room—often separated from the general education classroom—became the most widely used placement alternative. In reality, the majority of programs were still separate but were now located within the same building. During this time period, many students were mainstreamed into the general education setting for classes such as home economics, physical education and the arts, during lunch and recess, or when specific educational criterion were mastered.

Since 1975, the educational system has made enormous strides in providing appropriate education for people with disabilities. The law has been revised many times over the years, and our nation's special education law is now called IDEA (Individuals with Disabilities Education Act). Nevertheless, a great deal still needs to be accomplished.

In today's schools, the practice of educating all children with and without disabilities together in heterogeneous classrooms often is referred to as inclusive education, or simply inclusion. The terms *inclusion, full inclusion,* and *mainstreaming* are frequently interchanged, even though, in reality, they do not mean the same thing. The first placement option is usually the classroom. Mainstreaming was actually the reverse. Students received service is the special education "room" and only returned to class for non academic subjects. Inclusive education entitles the student to exercise the basic right to be educated in the least restrictive environment. Special education is not a place, but a set of services that enable every student to experience success and participate to the greatest extent possible in the general education environment. The set of services developed for individual students is created with the understanding that there is no single "one size fits all" standard. A full continuum of service options is available, but the general education classroom is the first placement option, even when the student's individual goals are different from those of his or her peer group. If a student is removed from the classroom environment, the school district must be able to justify the reason that the student is unable to participate in that environment.

Nationwide, our society is becoming more diverse. This societal change is reflected in the school districts as well. As students in the general education setting become increasingly diverse, current curriculum and materials must be adapted to accommodate all students.

Throughout the United States, school districts differ in their acceptance, commitment and implementation of inclusive practices. School districts must define their philosophies. General and special education teachers must plan together for the participation and social integration of students with disabilities. It is no longer a choice of whether or not to include a student. It is the law!

This book is based on the author's belief that:

- *Inclusive education can improve the current educational system.* With inclusive education, the accommodations directed toward students with disabilities are beneficial to other students in the general education setting as well. These strategies help to improve and individualize the curriculum for all students. The focus of the educational system is placed on the student instead of the curriculum.

- *Inclusive education helps students become more accepting and sensitive to one another.* When students with special needs are included in the general education setting, all students benefit. Students learn to accept one another as contributing members of society, regardless of abilities or limitations.

- *Inclusive education encourages collaboration.* Both general and special education teachers possess a wealth of information due to their education and experience. Yet, in the past, rarely was time allowed to share this knowledge. With inclusive education, the current educational system is no longer two disconnected systems with separate curricula and goals. With inclusive education, all members of the educational team work together and share knowledge, while striving towards a common goal.

Inclusive education is not a passing trend. It is the law! Persons with disabilities often have been undervalued in our society. A great amount of time and energy is spent testing, sorting and labeling, oftentimes so we can justify serving, separating, and excluding. There is a great deal to learn from one another. By combining knowledge and expertise, and by creating partnerships between families and school personnel, the result will be an improved educational system for all.

"We can do anything we want if we stick to it long enough."

Helen Keller

"Let us be a proud nation that takes responsibility for all our children."

Judy Heumann

Introduction

When *Inclusion: 450 Strategies for Success* was first published in 1995, inclusive education was in its infancy. Students with disabilities were primarily included in the general education setting for music, the arts and physical education, and to acquire socialization skills. The remainder of the day was often spent in a separate educational setting.

Many years later, inclusive education continues to evolve. Some districts are just beginning, whereas others have many years of experience. For educators now experienced in teaching in inclusive settings, inclusive education is simply best practice. But for those just beginning, the phrase "inclusive education" may evoke a wide range of feelings. Some educators may feel anxious, as the transition to inclusive education requires a system-wide change and often involves venturing into new and unknown territory. Educators who embrace change may feel elated and ready to change the status quo! But no matter what the feelings are, rest assured, all educators have experienced, or will experience, an extensive range of emotions during the transition stage.

The feelings associated with the concept of inclusive education often are not directly related to the integration of students into the general education setting. Most educators believe that students with disabilities belong in the classroom setting and are entitled to a free and appropriate education with their peers. *The strong feelings generally directed toward the inclusive education movement often are related to the process of transition and the effort to manage the transition effectively.* The dual educational systems that have been in existence for so many years are merging, but it is a slow process and does not occur automatically. It takes time, an abundance of energy, the willingness to change and, most of all, an internal belief that inclusive education is truly the best for all students.

So how is an inclusive program developed? Federal law provides the guidelines but allows individual schools the flexibility to develop programs that meet the individual needs of the students. Proper implementation of a program takes time, preparation and extensive planning.

This book was developed to help educators implement inclusive practices for students in the general education setting. With the implementation of inclusive education programs and the development of curriculum adaptations, all students benefit. The accommodations made for the students served in special education will also benefit students who receive service under Title One, Section 504, students with limited English language, and students who have no "label" but simply need additional support for success.

The first three chapters of this book contain ideas and guidelines to help professionals develop and implement an inclusive education program. The implementation phase is crucial to the success of the program, yet this area is often overlooked. For those who have an existing program, the book includes an abundance of ideas to help improve or expand the current inclusive education setting.

The rest of the chapters have hundreds of ideas and strategies for adapting the curriculum and specific information to help educators work with the students in the classroom. Not only will these ideas help students with special needs, but they will benefit many other students in the classroom as well. Often the ideas listed are applicable for all curriculum and subject areas.

In the Appendix are reproducible forms to assist you with each aspect of inclusive education. The forms may be used as they appear in the book or may be adapted to meet the individual needs of students or the program.

The Resources section at the end of the book includes books and websites full of additional ideas and lists of organizations that specialize in specific areas. Explore the websites of these organizations. Often they provide inexpensive (and sometimes free) materials.

As with the *Inclusion: 450 Strategies for Success*, the ideas and strategies are conveniently numbered. Due to the extensive revisions and additional content in this book will no longer correspond with the previous editions therefore the book has been retitled and completely rewritten. When planning for an individual student, the numbered items allow educators to quickly reference a strategy, if needed, and to keep an accurate record of the strategies implemented and the results. When adapting the curriculum and implementing change into a student's program, it is important to remember that all students are unique, and a strategy that may benefit one student will not necessarily be effective for another. As a new strategy is implemented, or when a change occurs in the student's program, it is important to allow ample time for adjustment before trying to determine the effectiveness of the strategy. Often when too many changes are implemented simultaneously, it is difficult to document which strategy or combination of strategies has benefited the student the most. Some students readily adapt to the change, while others need additional time.

Whenever the curriculum is adapted or modified, files should be created and the materials saved for future use. Often a school will designate a central location where copies of materials can be catalogued and stored. At the building level, this central location becomes a resource area for both general and special education teachers. Some districts have a central resource area that can be accessed by educators throughout the school district. Before modifying and adapting material, search to see whether or not it is currently available. Call the publisher, or look in the current teacher's guides of the adopted curriculum. Often there are supplemental resources appropriate for students with special needs and ESL students, and frequently, these resources may be used for other students as well.

Good luck with your inclusive program! You will make a difference in the lives of many.

Notes:

_____

_____

_____

_____

_____

_____

_____

_____

_____

_____

_____

_____

_____

"If you think you're too small to make a difference, you obviously have never been in bed with a mosquito!"

Michele Walker

Chapter One

Inclusive Education

Special education is a service that provides support for qualifying students. The law requires that students who receive special education services participate with their peers in academic and nonacademic activities unless there is a justifiable reason and this reason is documented in the student's Individual Education Program (IEP). The IEP must address all aspects of the student's life, including academics, social and emotional issues, the student's transportation and even extracurricular activities. In order to exclude the student from the academic areas in the classroom, the IEP Team must consider the benefits of related services, modifications, adaptations and additional school supports. Some of the supports and services provided to a student may include curricular and environmental changes, team teaching, use of technology and alternative instructional strategies, to name only a few. Not all students will be included in the classroom environment, but with additional support and services, many more students will. A continuum of services is still available, but no longer is a student automatically placed into a separate classroom or resource room when the student qualifies for special education services.

Chapter Note:
On page 31, you will find a complete list of the reproducible forms referred to throughout this chapter. The reproducible forms are located in the Appendix.

So how is an inclusive program created? Federal law provides the guidelines, but schools have the flexibility to develop a program that fits the individual environment. There is no blueprint for an inclusive education program, as the program is developed based on the services required. Therefore, since each individual student has specific documented needs, the compilation of the type and amount of service (direct or indirect minutes) and additional support (paraprofessionals) is what determines the structure of the program. Proper implementation takes time, preparation and extensive planning. Whether you are in the preliminary planning stage or have an inclusive program in place, you will find information in this chapter to help with your stage—and all stages—of the program development.

Ideally, inclusive education programs are developed during the spring for the upcoming school year. When planned in the spring, some schools opt to develop a Leadership Team. This team usually includes administrators, teachers and support staff. The role of this team is to oversee the initial planning stage and present the findings to the remainder of the staff. During the planning stage, the general and special educators can group and place students into the classrooms, and when the new school year begins, all systems are in place and ready! This is the ideal situation—but often not the reality. A more realistic scenario is that when teachers return to school in the fall, they are asked to implement an inclusive program and to provide service to students. Often the students have already been randomly placed into classrooms. The students have been scattered between so many different classrooms that it is physically impossible for the special education teachers to provide the direct service that is documented in the IEP. In order to provide the documented direct service to students, the students often end up back in a resource room or learning center, as it is the only way to meet the required documented minutes listed in the IEP. When educators find themselves in this situation, they do the best they can and try to stay in compliance with the IEP but often are unable to do so.

Often when inclusive education is new to a school, a leadership team is developed to lay the foundation for the program. If this approach is taken, it is crucial that the special education teachers have a strong and realistic overview of the students, their needs and the support currently available when working through the details. This is important, as a program is designed not only with the needs of the students in mind but also within the context of the number of educators and paraprofessionals available. In an ideal world, schools would have unlimited budgets, staff and support services available. But, in the real world, this is not the case. Therefore, the initial "pilot" group of students is often determined by the special education department and administration. The reason for this is simple. General education teachers are familiar with the amount of direct/indirect service provided in their individual classrooms but usually do not have a panoramic view of the entire program—nor would we expect them to. Therefore, the initial data is frequently gathered and compiled by the special education department. Once the information has been compiled, the special education department will have specific data as to the number of classroom teachers needed to accommodate the students in the general education setting.

As mentioned previously, there is no required blueprint for program development, but this chapter will outline a basic plan from which to work. Some schools may select and implement several of the ideas, others will follow it step-by-step and some will decide to modify the entire plan. Some schools decide to create a Leadership Team, whereas in others, the teachers involved group students and create workable schedules. The ideas presented in this chapter are only guidelines and should be modified and adapted to meet your current situation.

Planning for Inclusive Education

Every school is unique. Whether your school is large, small or somewhere in the middle, a plan is needed. The most common transition scenarios are as follows. In heavily populated schools with large special education departments, several special education teachers generally volunteer to transition the first year, while the others continue to teach in a self-contained environment and to provide service to the students who will transition the upcoming year. Other schools opt to transition all students at the same time. A number of schools prefer to initiate the transition during a natural break in the school calendar. Natural transition times may include third grade (as many students are referred and placed in second grade), the first year of middle school or the first year of high school. The program continues as the student enters fourth grade or the second year of middle school or high school. As students transition between schools, it is a perfect time to create a transition IEP and prepare for the new school year. Often, administration is willing to work with the special education department to determine the best timing.

Whether inclusive education is implemented on a small scale or with the entire special education population, the time to begin is now! The following section provides a basic outline to use. As mentioned earlier, some schools will opt to follow this plan step-by-step, others will select the components they feel will work in their environment, and some may simply use it as an outline and will develop everything on their own.

Restructuring the Special Education Department

One of the greatest changes with inclusive education is the restructuring of the special education department. Therefore, it is important for the special education team to sit down together to discuss the individual views related to inclusive education. Some teams prefer to develop a set of questions in advance so each member will have time to think about it previous to the meeting. Other teams develop the questions together and work through them together. To get started, a list of questions is provided here. **Form #1, Planning for Inclusive Education: The Special Education Team,** is found in the Appendix along with the other forms referenced in this chapter, also lists the questions and may be reproduced for those who would like to provide the questions in advance.

As a special education team, discuss the following questions to obtain the various viewpoints related to inclusive education.

- How many special education students are currently in the program? Approximately how many students are at each grade level or subject area?

- As a team, what is our preference? Should the program be implemented with a small group of selected students, or would it be better to transition students by grade level? Should the entire special education population transition at the same time? Is there a target group of students that we would like to transition first? Do we have a choice?

What is our rationale for selecting the previous transition method?

- Do we have sufficient support staff (paraprofessionals)? For the upcoming school year, do we anticipate a growth or decrease in support staff?

- Considering the amount of support staff we currently have, are we using these vital members of the team to the fullest extent? Do the support staff have blocks of downtime in the current schedule? Do the support staff arrive too early or too late in the day to maximize student support? Is there flexibility in the schedules so they can be staggered and have some paraprofessionals arrive earlier and others later in the day to maximize student contact?

- As a team, how can we provide a continuum of services for students? Do we have sufficient special educator staff to provide service to students, both in a pull-out program (if needed) and in the general education setting?

- If the decision is made to transition a percentage of the students, which special education teachers would like to work in an inclusive classroom the upcoming year? Do we have a choice?

- After discussing the previous questions, what are the biggest obstacles that we will encounter?

- Additional comments and concerns.

At this time, it will be difficult to answer all of the previous questions, but it is important to discuss them. If the decision is made to develop a Leadership Team, it is possible that one or two teachers will represent the entire special education department, so it is important to receive input from everyone.

Some school districts will delegate money for consultants to assist in the development of individual programs, which offers certain advantages. First, a consultant is able to provide examples of various models developed in similar settings. Issues can be addressed objectively, as the consultant is not directly involved with the school system. But, in the end, the most successful programs are developed by individual schools, after visiting area schools, working with consultants and compiling all of the data. The real inclusive education "experts" are the people who work in the school environment and are involved with the students on a day-to-day basis. The reason for the success of these programs is simple. The administration, educators, support staff and parents understand the needs and the unique dynamics of the building climate, which strongly influence the program. So whether you are involved as an individual or part of a committee, you are now an "expert." No one knows or understands the school climate, the students or the staff dynamics better than the people working within the building.

Establishing a Leadership Team

Schools approach inclusive education in many ways. Prior to the initiation of the program, often schools will establish a Leadership Team. This team may include general and special education teachers, administrators and parents. Some schools also include specialists, such as counselors, psychologists or other staff members who are able to provide a broad perspective of the special education population. For example, the music and physical education teachers have always worked in inclusive settings, as students consistently have been included in these areas. These teachers are able to provide insight relating to how specific children work together in large group settings and can often provide insight into specific situations.

Once established, the Leadership Team oversees the development of the inclusive education program. If the school decides to develop a Leadership Team, some members of the team (such as a general education teacher, special educator, paraprofessional and administrator) may want to take time to visit other sites in the district or neighboring schools with inclusive programs. The rationale of sending a team of people is so each person is able to discuss the program with their program counterpart. Administrators can ask questions directly of administrators, teachers can speak with teachers and the support staff can get feedback from other support staff. Therefore, the information gathered will be comprehensive and will encompass a complete overview of the program. This is very helpful, especially for those who are not sure what inclusive education is or involves. When observing, the team will gather a vast amount of information, both positive and negative. The negative feedback obtained is important, as one can learn a great deal from the experiences of others and often avoid making the same mistakes.

The Role of a Leadership Team. The role of the Leadership Team is to: develop the vision of how inclusive education will look in the school; determine possible barriers and discuss possible solutions; develop some of the long- and short-term goals of the program; and compile and present the recommendations to the entire staff. Following are steps that the Leadership Team may take.

Step 1 – Develop a vision.
The first step of the Leadership Team is to develop a vision. A vision will help the team to focus the "ideal program." Although everything discussed for the ideal program is not always obtainable, often by brainstorming, many of the suggestions become a starting point for more realistic ideas. Use a white board or large piece of paper to record the ideas of the team members. Encourage participation and write down all ideas. Some of the questions to discuss may include the following:

- How will the ideal program look?

- How can an environment be created to promote success for all students?

- What resources are currently available in our school, in the school district and in the community?

- What steps do we need to take to create this type of program?

- What are our goals as a team? Where would we like to be in one month, three months, six months and by the next school year? What are some of the short-term objectives that will help us to reach these goals?

It is also important at this time to determine the long-term goals of the Leadership Team. **Form #2, Leadership Goals,** can be used to compile this information. Goals of the Leadership Team may include the deadlines for meeting with the staff, dates for follow-up meetings, etc.

Step 2 – Determine the benefits and barriers of inclusive education.
List the benefits and possible barriers to obtaining the vision within the building. **Form #3, Sample Benefits and Barriers,** provides a list of commonly compiled benefits and barriers. **Form #4, Benefits and Barriers,** is a blank worksheet that can be made into a transparency and used with the group or distributed to team members so they can list their own ideas before discussing them as a team. Often the lists are quite long, so it is advisable to have several additional blank transparencies available if this activity is completed as a group.

Step 3 – Develop the goals and objectives of the inclusive education program.
Some Leadership Teams develop specific long- and short-term goals for the program. For example, a long-term goal may be to select one or more target groups of students that will be placed into inclusive classrooms for fall of the upcoming school year. The short-term goals may include items such as: "The students will be grouped in May for the upcoming school year;" "classroom teachers will be selected prior to the end of the school year;" and "in-service workshops for participating teachers will be scheduled for fall." **Form #5, Sample Goals and Objectives,** includes some examples of long- and short-term goals. **Form #6, Goals and Objectives,** is a blank worksheet that can be used to write the specific goals and objectives of the Leadership Team.

Step 4 – Share the information with all staff members.
Once the initial Leadership Team meetings have finished, it is time to share the information with the entire school staff. A member of the Leadership Team will present the information that has been compiled to this point. If time permits, all of the previous activities (Steps 1-3) can also be completed with the staff. Once completed, the Leadership Team and staff results can be compared. More often than not, the responses, concerns, goals and objectives of both groups will be very similar.

- At the staff meeting, the goals and tentative timelines for implementation can be presented. The staff may have additional suggestions.

- At the end of this meeting, all of the results should be compiled and distributed to all staff members.

Step 5 – Hold follow-up meetings.

Follow-up meetings should not be scheduled until the notes from the initial staff meeting have been disseminated and the staff members have had time to think about the upcoming changes and to formulate questions. Within two weeks, a follow-up meeting should be scheduled to answer general questions about inclusive education. If a specific grade level or subject area has not yet been selected, questions will continue to be general. If a target group of teachers and students has been identified, the grade level and/or subject area teachers should also be notified at this time. Since classroom teachers have not yet been determined, it will be a general announcement. For example, the staff may be told that all students entering grades three and four and also all students who receive math service will be included in the classroom for the upcoming school year.

Step 6 – Make additional preparations.

All interested educators should be allowed time to visit schools in the area that have inclusive education programs and observe the programs in action. Perhaps the Leadership Team has already visited sites, but the opportunity should also be provided at this time to all interested staff members. By talking with colleagues, service providers and the paraprofessionals involved in these programs, great lessons can be learned. Often colleagues will share what they have learned from experience. Keep in mind that a negative experience can be made positive with a few changes. Learn from the experience of others and modify the ideas to meet the individual school climate. Site visitation often alleviates many of the fears that teachers have related to inclusive education, because often the greatest fear is the fear of the unknown.

The State Department of Education often has valuable resources available. Some Departments of Education have funded pilot programs and provided grants to help with the training and implementation of programs. These schools are frequently available for site visits. Local universities that receive grant money to help develop training programs often provide this information free of charge as partial fulfillment of their grant requirements.

At this time, there is an abundance of research and many journal articles and books related to inclusive education. Search the Internet for information. Some key words for the search include: *Special Education, ERIC* or *Inclusive Education*. Or, you may search by a specific disability. When searching by a specific disability, frequently you will access the national organization related to the disability. These organizations have vast amounts of information and often have links to related websites. Additional information can be accessed through the United States Department of Education or the Department of Education in your state.

Grouping Students

At this time, the foundation has been developed, the benefits and barriers have been listed and some short- and long-term goals have been addressed. This preliminary information has been presented to all staff members, and everyone is aware that changes will occur in the future. The staff is also aware that the change will affect some staff members more than others. Since students will be grouped, not all general education teachers will have students with special needs in their classrooms. Now it is time to select a target grade level or levels, or subject area(s). Since classroom teachers have not been determined, simply label the groups—e.g., Grade 2: Classroom #1, Classroom #2, Classroom #3 and so forth. At the secondary level, the groups will be labeled by subject area, such as Grade 10 Math: Classroom #1, Classroom #2 and Grade 10 English: Classroom #1, Classroom #2, Classroom #3 and so forth.

Due to the increasing number of students in special education and the limited resources, both human and monetary, grouping the students is the most feasible option. Students will receive an increased amount of direct service when grouped. It is more efficient for one special education teacher to teach a large number of students at one grade level than many small groups at various grade levels.

- Divide the students by grade level, and count the number of students who need to be placed.

- If the entire special education team is moving toward inclusive education, determine how to divide the caseloads. If dividing by grade level, the caseloads for each teacher will not be equal. However, it will be less difficult to accommodate 15 students at one grade level (with only one curriculum to master) than 10 students in three different levels or in different subject areas. Also, as the special education teacher is assigned to more grade levels and more classrooms, the scheduling becomes more difficult.

Inclusive programs are difficult to manage when students are placed individually into classrooms. With one student per classroom, there is inadequate time to consult, to provide appropriate accommodations or to meet the direct amount of service predetermined by the IEPs. Grouping of students is not for the convenience of educators, which some critics believe. Students must be grouped to some extent, as school districts do not have sufficient money to hire the staff to support students one-on-one, nor is it beneficial to students to have a special education teacher or paraprofessional hovering over them the entire school day. When grouping students, it is also important that students not be grouped by handicapping conditions. Students should be placed into classrooms based on their individual needs, which are determined by the IEP.

To facilitate the process of grouping the students, write each student's name on a sticky note. Multicolored notes may be used to indicate handicapping conditions, such as yellow for learning disabilities, blue for behavior disabilities and perhaps a separate color to indicate students who have paraprofessionals assigned. When using individual notes for each student, the names can be rearranged easily on a white board. Experiment with various groups of students. Keep in mind that neither the special nor general education populations will ever fit into perfect groups, so look for manageable groups. When grouping, place yourself in the position of the classroom teacher. If a combination of students is difficult to manage in a resource room setting, it will be more difficult to manage in a classroom setting.

Grouping students is a challenge! Creating the initial groups is the most difficult. As the students move into the second year of the program, some students will need additional support, whereas for others, the support may decrease, and the groups can be adjusted and rearranged accordingly.

Read the following suggestions for various ways to group students. The following section includes suggestions for grouping students cross-categorically, academically, according to learning styles and in other ways.

Cross-Categorical Groups. Cross-categorical groups are one placement option. Students should not be placed by handicapping condition, as the goal is not to create a resource room within a classroom. By analyzing each student's level of service and his or her strengths and areas of service, cross-categorical placement provides many different options. Following are some possibilities:

- A student with high needs, such as a student with a cognitive delay or a behavior disorder (with documented paraprofessional time), could possibly be placed with students who need curriculum accommodations and minimal support. The paraprofessional is able to assist the high-need student and provide supplemental support, while monitoring the other students in the classroom.

- A student with a cognitive delay (who requires an alternate or parallel curriculum) may be grouped with students who require minimal academic support. Often, as the academic discrepancy increases, the paraprofessional time is also increased for students with cognitive delays. Therefore, students who require a minimal amount of service can receive support from the special education teacher or paraprofessional also. At times, a student with a behavior disorder responds well in a situation where the student can help others, so this is another possible option.

- A student with a learning disability who experiences difficulty with auditory processing possibly can be grouped with students who have difficulty concentrating or following directions. Both types of students often require simplified verbal instruction, together with supplemental written or visual material. All of these students would benefit from a quiet, structured environment.

- Students with language difficulties (either expressive or receptive) that have documented service in the IEP may be a possible group. Students with receptive language difficulties may not understand multiple-meaning words and oral directions or be able to follow class lectures. Students with expressive language difficulties may have difficulty explaining the thought process used to solve a problem, whereas others may not be able to organize and sequence their thoughts. The speech/language clinician can work directly with the classroom teacher or in the classroom to provide support to these students.

- Several students who receive service in a specific area, such as math, could be grouped.

- Students who receive dual services, such as support with academics combined with help processing spoken language, may be grouped. The speech/language clinician would be able to work with the students together in the classroom, and the classroom teacher can provide supplemental vocabulary lists and materials for the clinician.

- Students who receive service from an occupational therapist could possibly be grouped with students who also need additional support for general classroom assignments. Students who receive service for OT often need extra time to complete assignments, as they may write slowly, inaccurately and illegibly, so these students can be combined with students who also need extra support to complete assignments. These students may have difficulty copying problems, filling in small spaces, completing worksheets or cutting and pasting. The occupational therapist will be able to provide modifications, adaptations and special materials as well as work with the students in the classroom.

- Students who need adaptive therapy could be grouped into a classroom, and the specialist often can team teach a class such as physical education. The student's IEP goals could possibly be met in the physical education setting.

- For students with severe memory difficulties, an appropriate placement option may be with students who have learning disabilities. Although students who experience difficulties with short- or long-term memory do not qualify under a stand-alone handicapping condition, students with memory difficulties have their own set of needs that are often similar to students with learning difficulties. These students may need additional review before tests and special organizational aids, and they may need to have homework books and/or check-in and check-out systems.

Academic Groups. Students may also be grouped by academics. As you read through this list, think about the currently identified students. Do certain students work especially well together? Are there students that will be easy to accommodate in the classroom setting? Could the number of these students be increased to four or five per classroom since there are no behavior issues? Here are some options to consider when grouping students:

Academic needs	Reading levels	Work habits
Math placement	Organizational skills	Subject area
	Problem-solving skills	

Learning Styles. Identifying a student's learning style may also help with grouping. Most teachers are familiar with Anthony Gregorc's work. Gregorc combined the ideas of abstract and concrete thinking with sequential and random order to create four different learning styles: abstract-sequential (AS), concrete-sequential (CS), abstract-random (AR) and concrete-random (CR). Some students will work better in environments that are suited to their personal learning styles, whereas other students are more flexible and can handle almost any classroom environment. Classroom teachers also teach according to their own styles. For example, some teachers have very quiet, orderly classrooms. For the concrete-sequential (CS) learner, this environment is perfect. However, if an abstract-random (AR) student is placed in a quiet, orderly classroom, this student may not do as well, because the AR student needs to move around and learns in a different manner.

Following is a simplified description of the four learning styles. If you would like further information or more complex inventories, Anthony Gregorc's website is listed in the Resources section.

The abstract-sequential (AS) student tends to lean toward an environment that is orderly and mentally stimulating. This student may prefer to work independently in a quiet environment that is free of distractions. The student relies on "thinking" to reach conclusions and often prefers to work independently.

The concrete-sequential (CS) learner performs best in a quiet environment, where expectations and rules are clearly defined. The environment should be quiet and ordered. These students prefer a "hands-on" approach to learning. They tend to like rewards and feel good when they have accomplished a task. They prefer to finish one task before beginning another.

The abstract-random (AR) learner focuses more on feelings and emotions. These children tend to get caught up in their environment, and often, time is an issue. The AR student will work best in an environment that is flexible and allows the student to move around, rather than an environment with restrictive rules and regulations.

The concrete-random (CR) learner tends to be flexible and inventive and enjoys taking risks and trying new things. Concrete-random children tend to be creative and love to explore the environment as a way of learning. They like an environment with a lot of activity. The CR student can handle multiple projects at one time.

Form #7, Learning Styles Checklist, is a checklist adapted from the book *Inclusion: A Practical Guide for Parents* by Lorraine O. Moore. (See Resources section.) This simple checklist can be given to students 10 and older to help determine what type of environment best meets their needs. Once this information is gathered, it may be useful when placing students with specific classroom teachers.

Additional Grouping Strategies. Following are some additional approaches that can be considered when grouping students.

- When appropriate, group students who receive adaptive physical education, speech/language service, occupational therapy, physical therapy or other related services. Often these services are provided in a separate location. When students are grouped, coordination of related services is easier, as the general education teacher often is able to schedule the academics around the related support services. When possible, the related services should be incorporated into the general education setting. For example, OT service may be incorporated into the English block or, at the elementary level, into the written language block, handwriting block or perhaps art class. Is it possible for the adaptive physical education teacher to lend support to the regular physical education teacher? Perhaps the two teachers will opt to team teach the class. The speech and language clinician may support the student during language arts by helping the student organize thoughts or lending support to specific vocabulary exercises.

- Group students who require daily monitoring of organizational skills or who participate in a daily check-in or check-out program. Some students are required to meet with a counselor, social worker or psychologist during or at the end of the day. Perhaps there is a possibility of grouping some of these students so the support professional is able to come to the classroom and meet with a small group of students with similar needs.

- Some school districts group a large number of students in a classroom, and the special education teacher spends the majority of the day team teaching. All classes are co-taught. The parents are advised of the co-teaching arrangement in spring of the previous year.

- Students who are in the due process system (referral or assessment phases) should be grouped into a classroom, if the preliminary data suggests the student may qualify.

Compiling the Student Data

It is time to compile the student data. **Form #8, Sample Student Data Sheet,** is an example of a spreadsheet for 14 different students at one grade level. The information in this example was extracted from the IEPs. Direct minutes are divided into the various areas for each student in the program. Please note that the direct minutes of service equal the total amount of service provided per week. Additional support services are also included. **Form #9, Student Data Sheet** is a blank spreadsheet that can be used to compile the information for the target group of students in your school. Use a separate sheet Student Data Sheets for for each grade level and also each subject area) as documented in the IEP.

Group students at each grade level into the smallest number of classrooms possible. When grouping by reading levels, keep in mind that students who need minimal accommodations may be able to work with a paraprofessional, if no teaching is required. When the students are grouped, communication increases, as will the amount of direct service. Fifteen minutes in a classroom with one student is less beneficial when compared to one hour with four students. The larger time block allows more flexibility for both general and special education teachers. **Form #10, Sample Student Groups,** demonstrates how the students were grouped into four separate classrooms and provides an explanation as to why the students were grouped in this manner. **Form #11, Student Groups,** is a blank worksheet you can use to group the students. Form #11 provides various sections to experiment with grouping students by learning styles, math and problem solving skills and related services.

- Review placement files for new students. If there are questions related to a file, call the previous school before assigning the student to a classroom. Be sure all of the files have arrived and the student has no special needs that have to be addressed.

Scheduling the Paraprofessional

At this point, students have been tentatively grouped. Even though classroom teachers have not been selected, the number of general educators required per grade or subject area has now been determined. As paraprofessional time is also documented on the students' IEPs, you know that certain classrooms will receive additional support and services, not only from paraprofessionals but from other service providers as well.

A comment heard frequently is, "We simply do not have enough paraprofessionals to provide adequate support for the students." If the students have not been grouped, the paraprofessional is often assigned to various classrooms for short periods of time, and in some cases, the allotted time may be as little as 20 minutes. In a situation such as this, the paraprofessional often arrives at the class and the general education teacher is teaching, giving instructions, completing a group lecture or conceivably answering questions. Therefore the paraprofessional is unable to interrupt and help the student and often spends the time waiting for the general education teacher to finish. A few extra minutes must be built into the paraprofessional's schedule to allow for some flexibility.

When students are grouped and paraprofessionals are placed strategically within these groups, more direct service can be provided, resulting in increased support for the student. Also, there must be planning time for special education teachers to collaborate with both paraprofessionals and general education teachers daily. The fewer people involved in each component of the program, the more efficient the program becomes. Communication is the key to successful inclusion.

Paraprofessionals are vital to inclusive education. In many districts, the number of paraprofessionals exceeds the number of teachers. These hardworking adults provide service to many of the most complex and challenging students in the school, yet often they are unsupervised and receive limited training. The role of the paraprofessional is to provide service and support to individual students or groups of students under the direct supervision of a licensed teacher. This may include re-teaching a previously learned skill, providing academic, social and emotional support, and helping students with personal care. The role of the paraprofessional is not that of a surrogate teacher.

Often districts have several types of paraprofessionals on staff. Some may be "program support staff." These people are often used in many situations, including working with a variety of students regardless of the types of disabilities involved and handling administrative duties, such as maintaining databases. A second type of paraprofessional provides "pupil support." This person may be assigned to a specific student in the program.

When determining the amount of service for paraprofessionals, keep the following in mind:

- Consider the paraprofessionals' allotted minutes very carefully. Strategically place paraprofessionals assigned to specific high-need students in classrooms where other students will also benefit. If a paraprofessional is assigned to a very high-need student, there may be no other option but to have this paraprofessional in a one-on-one situation.

- Students who need daily accommodations for assignments, curriculum support or re-teaching may be grouped with a paraprofessional. The paraprofessional cannot provide direct initial instruction, but this person is able to re-teach and reinforce the previously taught skills, make curriculum adaptations (under the direction of the general or special education teacher) and provide support with daily assignments.

- If there are blocks of open time in the paraprofessional's schedule, mark it as "flexible time." Once the program is implemented, general education teachers may use this time for additional support for the students as needed. This small amount of time may allow support to be extended to other curriculum areas. For example, often students only receive reading support during the reading or language arts block, although reading occurs in every subject.

- Some schools have designated a room where students can go if they need additional support. Staffing of this room often is voluntary. Some schools rotate the duties between teachers and paraprofessionals. Other schools have staffed this area with parent volunteers. Any student who needs additional support with academics or needs to have a test read aloud may use the room. This helps all students, not only those who receive special education services.

- Allowing paraprofessionals to have some flexible time works in some school districts. The paraprofessional is employed for a specific number of hours per week. The hours are used as needed and may change on a daily basis. This increases the flexibility of the program. It works well for paraprofessionals who are employed two to three hours per day. Some schools allow the paraprofessional "comp" time, if needed, for special projects or field trips. Some of the more fortunate districts have money set aside to increase hours when necessary. Check with the district to see if there are any options for scheduling.

- Schedule a minimum of 10 minutes per day for the classroom teacher and the paraprofessional to meet and to plan. The paraprofessional is a vital member of the team, and training is often overlooked. *Inclusion: An Essential Guide for the Paraprofessional* is the paraprofessional component of this series. (See Resources section.)

- Develop a tentative schedule for the paraprofessional(s). The schedule should include the total number of hours required for the program. These minutes are directly correlated to the Individualized Education Plan. If there are additional hours available, determine as a group where more service is needed. Remember to include consultation time in the schedule. **Form #12, Paraprofessional Minutes,** will help with the calculation of paraprofessional time.

Scheduling the Special Education Teacher

Now let's look at the daily structure of the program. Gather the master schedules for the target grade level. Read through the following ideas about scheduling several times before beginning. As a group, discuss the types of scheduling that may work for your individual environment. Look at **Form #13, Sample Schedule for the Special Education Teacher,** for ideas. **Form #14, Schedule for the Special Education Teacher,** is a blank worksheet. It provides a basic outline from which to work.

- The majority of students qualify and receive service for reading and written language. It is important to stagger the teaching blocks on the schedule so special education teachers are available to provide direct service to the inclusive classrooms. Here are some additional examples:

  If two general education teachers have the same reading and language arts blocks, consider grouping the students who work with the paraprofessional into one of the blocks, and schedule the special education teacher into the other. If paraprofessional time is not available, the two general education teachers and the special education teacher will need to stagger the time blocks so the special education teacher is able to work within all classrooms. For example, on **Form #13, Sample Schedule for the Special Education Teacher,** all four of the classrooms had their reading and language arts block during the first academic block of the morning. In order for the special education teacher to serve all the students, two of the general education teachers were required to move their language arts blocks to mid-morning so the teacher and paraprofessional would be able to serve all the students in this entire grade level.

- At the secondary level, reading and written language affect the majority of subject areas. The academic time slots may need to be staggered. If this is not possible, one option is for one of the general education teachers to begin a class with a group activity and move on to independent work, while the other classroom teacher begins the class with independent work and moves to a group activity, allowing the special education teacher to provide service to both classrooms during the same class period.

- It is very important that the special education teacher or paraprofessional be present during the initial instruction. Often, staff members feel this is wasted time, and so they do not schedule in these additional minutes. However, this time is beneficial for several reasons. It allows the general education teacher maximum flexibility to monitor and adjust assignments. When lesson changes occur, they do not have to be explained to the special education person at a later time. The special education teacher is also able to determine the style of instruction and formulate ways to re-teach or clarify the instruction if needed. It is also an optimum time for direct observation of students.

- Determine the number of students who receive service for math. If the students are grouped for math instruction, it may be possible to place the students with math goals into one classroom and team teach the subject. If the students are not grouped for math, there are several options: divide the special education time between two classrooms; group the students with math IEPs into the same homeroom; or use paraprofessional time to assist with the coverage of the various groups. At the secondary level, often students with IEPs take a fundamental math course. If this is an option, this course could be team taught.

- Determine the students' needs for the entire school day. Previously, students have been served mainly in the isolated areas of reading, written language, math and speech/language. These four areas impact the entire day. Incorporate service into the appropriate academic blocks.

- Create a flexible time slot in the schedule. It does not need to be a large block of time. The general education teachers may use this time block to incorporate special projects, lessons or alternate testing procedures as needed. This time block may also be used as a preparation, observation or testing block. Oftentimes, special education teachers do not schedule lunch breaks, as they need to accommodate many different schedules. A lunch break is needed during the day. If this is the case, speak with the general education teachers and decide how schedules can be altered or rotated to provide a specific break in the schedule. Grade levels have specific lunch blocks, and special education professionals need to do the same.

- Schedule time each day, before or after school, for the special education teacher to meet with each general education teacher. This may be an informal arrangement. Changes in daily lesson plans can be made during this time. Since many special education meetings occur before school, be sure there is a definite ending time so this meeting does not overlap with the time scheduled to meet with the general education teachers. A lack of communication will cause the program to deteriorate rapidly.

- With inclusive education, educators are expected to collaborate in new ways that previously have not been expected. Not only is finding the time to talk important, but the way in which ideas and requests are communicated is very important. Most educators have not been trained to supervise other adults, yet with inclusive education, educators are often responsible not only for supervising, but for evaluating the paraprofessionals. This may be an area where staff development is needed.

- Staff involvement is important! Look for additional ways to incorporate the special education teachers into the classroom environment. Some simple ideas may include reading aloud to the class several times a week or participating in special projects, class rewards or field trips. As involvement increases, students see special education as an integral part of the classroom.

- Schedule a daily preparation time. This time is easier to schedule at the middle and secondary levels, as classes meet during specific time blocks. At the elementary level, it is more difficult, as the school day does not have natural divisions. If the special education teacher is unable to schedule a preparation and testing block, ask general education teachers to advise the special education teacher in advance when there are open breaks in the schedule. Often unplanned events occur, and special education service is not needed. When notified in advance, special education teachers can allocate this time as a preparation or testing block. Additional preparation and testing times often occur during group activities, movies, speakers, field trips, art activities or special programs.

Presenting the Inclusion Plan

Congratulations! The plan is now complete. A large amount of information has been gathered, and it is time to determine what information is relevant to share. The items that have been gathered may include:

- The school's vision of inclusive education
- The benefits and barriers to inclusive education
- The long- and short-term goals, with the expected completion dates
- The target group of students, listed by grade level. For example:

Grade 2. Classroom #1 – four students

Grade 3. Classroom #1 – six students, with paraprofessional time
        Classroom #2 – four students
        Classroom #3 – five students, with minimal service

- Classroom schedules for the grade levels or subject areas selected
- Any additional information or special situations

Now for the big question! Is participation voluntary, or are the general education teachers selected by the administration? Although it is done both ways, attitude plays an important role in the success of the program. A positive attitude is crucial to the success of systematic change. Oftentimes, when negative attitudes are encountered with inclusive education, these attitudes are not related to providing service for the students, but are related to how an individual responds to and accepts change. There are a small percentage of people who thrive on change and embrace the chance to implement a new program. These people enjoy the challenge and excitement of trying something new and different. Others may have a "wait and see" attitude. These individuals prefer to observe first and make sure that the program is effective and is in the best interest of the students before investing their time and energy. They prefer to come on board once they have seen the movement of the program. Still others do not want to implement a change, often due to upcoming retirement, career change or personal reasons that have not been shared.

From this point forward, the staff members directly involved in the program will meet together and work together to define their individual programs. The type of program will vary depending upon the unique styles of the individual teachers.

Inclusive education is not a passing trend. It is the law! A great amount of time and energy has been spent testing, sorting and labeling, only so we could justify serving, separating and excluding the students from the classrooms. There is a great deal to learn from one another. When teachers combine their knowledge and expertise, creating partnerships between families and school personnel, the result is an improved educational system for all.

In-Service and Training

Attitude plays an important role in the success of the program. In order to be successful, all educators must be enthusiastic and ready to implement the change. Often the fear associated with any change is the fear of the unknown. Therefore, as with any system change, training is an important component.

In-service and training may be implemented in many ways. The majority of universities now offer specific courses for general and special education teams and for paraprofessionals. As a result of the No Child Left Behind (NCLB) Act, numerous training courses are also offered at community colleges and online for paraprofessionals and support staff. In addition, hundreds of staff development videos are available. Although videos require a substantial initial investment, they can be used again and again for large and small group presentations and for new staff members. Following are some ideas to think about related to in-service and training.

- Develop a district-wide special education resource area. This area may include some of the following material.

    ✓ Copies of individual training materials used by schools throughout the district or found on websites.

    ✓ Staff development training videos that can be checked out by individual schools or people interested in acquiring additional knowledge about a specific topic

    ✓ Material no longer used by individual students so they are available to others, such as: computer programs, laptops, assistive technology devices, special equipment, etc.

- In order to provide appropriate training, survey the school staff to determine what sort of training is needed. **Form #15, Staff Survey of In-Service Needs,** is a simple form that can be used. Training at the building level should include both topics that are specific to the needs of the teaching staff and some topics that are appropriate for the entire staff, such as "Disability Awareness." If one teacher has a student who is visually impaired, it is important that the staff members who work with that student receive relevant training, but there is no need to provide an in-service on this topic for every staff member in the school.

- Some staff development concerns may affect the entire building, whereas others may affect only a specific classroom. Following are some frequently asked questions that may be used as guidelines in developing in-service training.

Overview of Inclusive Education

What is inclusive education? How does it differ from mainstreaming?

Why is inclusive education important?

What are federal and state guidelines related to inclusive education?

What is the district philosophy?

How do we include special education students in the general education environment and yet meet all of their needs?

Special Education

How is a student referred to special education?

What is the general education teacher's role in the special education process?

What is the general education teacher's responsibilities in relation to the student's IEP?

What is a 504 Plan and how does it differ from the IEP?

Collaboration

What is an effective team?

How can we work together to form effective teams?

What are the roles and responsibilities of each person in an effective inclusive setting?
What are various teaching models that can be used in a collaborative setting?

How can we creatively find additional time to plan together?

How can we increase the communication in a collaborative setting?

Modifying and Adapting Curriculum

What are accommodations?

How do we modify and adapt the curriculum?

What is the difference between an accommodation and an adaptation?

How can curriculum be adapted when a large discrepancy exists between the classroom curriculum and the students' current levels of performance?

Who is responsible for making the accommodations and modifying the curriculum?

Paraprofessionals in the Classroom

What is the role and responsibility of the paraprofessional in the classroom?

Who is responsible to guide the paraprofessional?

Who is responsible for disciplining a student in the general education setting when a paraprofessional is present?

If the paraprofessional's student is absent from class, what is the paraprofessional's responsibility?

How can additional planning time be incorporated into the paraprofessional's day?

Should the paraprofessional be included in the evaluation of the students?

Who is responsible to evaluate the performance of the paraprofessional?

In-service is an important part of all inclusive education programs and should be provided whenever needed. All in-services do not need to be directed towards the entire staff. Many can be presented in small-group sessions as the need arises.

Program Follow-Up

Once the program is established, it is important to obtain feedback from the teachers, paraprofessionals, parents and students. Questionnaires are a simple way to assess the program. When such surveys are used frequently, small problems are discovered before they become serious. These surveys may also help determine staff development needs. The following survey forms at the end of this chapter can be used:

Form #16, Student Survey
Form #17, All about School!
Form #18, Parent Survey
Form #19, Paraprofessional Survey
Form #20, Staff Survey

Once these surveys have been completed, it is important to follow up:

- Compile the information received from the surveys. Highlight any areas that need attention.

- Analyze the student surveys. Talk to students individually about their concerns.

- If a parent indicates a concern, share the concern with the classroom teacher. Once discussed, call the parent to discuss it further. If the concern is related to an individual student, it can be dealt with by the involved parties. If it is a program concern, it should be discussed as a team.

- Determine the needs of the paraprofessionals and decide whether each concern is isolated or whether it affects all of the paraprofessionals. Determine whether or not further in-service is needed.

Chapter One Conclusion

Chapter One has offered a suggested approach to establishing an inclusive education program that your school can adapt to fit its specific needs. Although nothing is set in stone, this approach has proven to be effective. First, the staff becomes clear about what inclusive education involves. Sometimes a Leadership Team is established to determine particulars. The staff involved may visit other schools who have inclusive programs to get ideas and see what's working and what's not. A list of benefits and barriers is drawn up, and the barriers are addressed. The Leadership Team or relevant staff formulate a vision of what the inclusive education program at their particular school will look like.
Short- and long-term goals for the program are written and specific objectives are established. Students are grouped according to chosen criteria, paraprofessional time is scheduled, and it is determined how the general education teachers, special education teachers and paraprofessionals can best work together to meet the students' needs.

Surveys are very helpful, both in determining in-service and training for staff and in determining necessary adjustments to the program after it has begun, based on feedback from staff, students and parents.

On the next page is a list of all the forms referenced in this chapter. The 20 reproducible forms are found in the Appendix. You can use these forms to help you plan, organize and specify details for the inclusive education program in your school.

Appendix Forms for Chapter One

#1	Planning for Inclusive Education: The Special Education Team
#2	Leadership Goals
#3	Sample Benefits and Barriers
#4	Benefits and Barriers
#5	Sample Goals and Objectives
#6	Goals and Objectives
#7	Learning Styles Checklist
#8	Sample Student Data Sheet
#9	Student Data Sheet
#10	Sample Student Groups
#11	Student Groups
#12	Paraprofessional Minutes
#13	Sample Schedule for the Special Education Teacher
#14	Schedule for the Special Education Teacher
#15	Staff Survey of In-Service Needs
#16	Student Survey
#17	All about School!
#18	Parent Survey
#19	Paraprofessional Survey
#20	Staff Survey

There are two primary choices in life: to accept conditions as they exist, or accept the responsibility for changing them.

Denis Waitley

Notes:

_____

_____

_____

_____

_____

_____

_____

_____

_____

_____

_____

_____

_____

"The past cannot be changed. The future is yet in your power."

Mary Pickford

Chapter Two

Working Together in the Inclusive Classroom

In order for a team to function successfully, the team members should hold the belief that team teaching provides a more effective teaching environment, which in turn benefits all students, not only those with special needs. Several traits will help professionals work together collaboratively. These important traits include flexibility, professionalism, the desire to work with others, respect for one another and, of course, a sense of humor. Educators in a team situation must be able to listen to one another, communicate effectively and hold common goals and expectations for students.

Collaboration is very important with co-teaching. Collaboration is an interactive process that enables teachers with expertise in various academic areas to provide service to a group of students with a wide range of needs. Effective co-teachers are flexible and tolerant; they accept responsibility for all students in the classroom; and they maintain positive relationships and open lines of communication.

> **Chapter Note:**
> On page 44, you will find a complete list of the reproducible forms referred to throughout this chapter. The reproducible forms are located in the Appendix.

A significant part of co-teaching is the ability to incorporate the perspectives of both the general and special educators into a classroom lesson. Special education teachers tend to approach instruction and the management of students by focusing on the individual needs, accommodations and analysis of the instruction, whereas general educators teach to the middle due to the diverse needs of the students in the classroom. When teachers co-teach, each professional brings a different perspective to the classroom. Professionals can learn from one another.

Two Teachers – One Classroom

Several types of teaching occur in inclusive settings: team teaching, supportive teaching, supplemental teaching and parallel teaching. There are hundreds of variations to these models, and depending upon the resource, they may be referred to by different names. For the purposes of this publication, the terms *team*, *supportive*, *supplemental* and *parallel teaching* will be used. These terms are simple and self-explanatory. Professionals may decide to use one teaching style or fluctuate between the various models, depending upon the outcome and the type of lesson. In all types of co-teaching, both teachers plan the lessons, determine their individual roles and assess the outcomes.

- **Team Teaching:** In a team teaching environment, two (or more) staff members work to plan, develop and teach the lesson. The roles and responsibilities are determined by those involved. Just as general education teachers often co-teach a lesson or class, general and special education teachers can do the same. The teaching responsibilities are predetermined and shared.

- **Supportive Teaching:** In a supportive teaching environment, one teacher leads and the second adult provides support. The students receive the basic instruction from the lead teacher. The general or special education teacher may take the lead and the roles may change depending upon the lesson. Modifications and instructional support are provided to the student within the classroom setting by the supporting adult. If a paraprofessional is the supporting adult, the support to the student must be provided under the direction of the general or special education teacher.

- **Supplemental Teaching:** With supplemental teaching, the groups may vary in size. In this environment, the lesson may be presented to the class as a whole and then the class divided into smaller groups to reinforce, re-teach or provide enrichment. Supplemental teaching may also be used prior to the lesson, allowing time for the teacher to pre-teach specific material before it is presented to the entire class. For some students, a separate curriculum may be implemented at this time.

- **Parallel Teaching:** In this teaching environment, the general and special education teachers plan together to ensure consistency in the instruction between the two groups. Each teacher delivers the lesson to a group of the students. There may be times when each teacher instructs with a separate curriculum, but the final goal is the same. For example, both groups may be working on a main idea and supporting details, but the reading curriculum used may be at different levels.

Most lesson plan books are not conducive to team teaching. **Form #21, Daily Lesson Activities and Objectives,** includes a reproducible lesson plan format that can be used to plan and document daily lessons. This form includes space to document the lesson with objectives, to check off the type of teaching that is most appropriate for the lesson (team teach, supportive, supplemental or parallel) and to make notes about specific accommodations for students. There is also a space to include additional notes for both teachers. If this lesson plan format works for you, reproduce as many copies as needed and place them in a three-ring binder.

Once teams have been established, it is important to reflect on certain questions. These questions are just a starting point for some of the important issues that will need to be discussed. At the end of the chapter, you will find **Forms #22** to **#26**, which can be reproduced and used for discussion guidelines during planning sessions and filled out as a team. They include the following discussion questions, which cover the areas of planning and teaching, discipline, grading, classroom environment and working with parents.

Planning and Teaching – Form #22:

- When and how much time do we need to allocate for planning? Daily? Weekly?

- Do we prefer formal or informal sessions?

- What is the best time to schedule these sessions within our current schedules?

- What will our individual roles be when planning lessons?

- How will the teaching be structured in the classroom? Will classes be team taught? Will supportive teaching, supplemental teaching or parallel teaching better serve the students in the classroom?

- If we will be co-teaching the majority of the day, how should we communicate this to parents?

- When problems occur, how will we solve them?

- What do we see as personal, individual strengths that will contribute to the classroom teaching structure? What are the strengths that we see in each other?

Discipline – Form #23:

- What is the classroom discipline plan?

- Will all students be expected to follow the same plan?

- Are rewards and consequences part of the classroom discipline plan?

- Who will be responsible for classroom discipline? How will we deal with specific behaviors, and who will do what?

- Will all students be expected to follow the same rules?

- If rules are different for different students, how do we work out issues of fairness in the class, and how do we explain the different standards for different students to the class?

Grading – Form #24:

- Who will be responsible for grading the students?

- What type of grading system will be used?

- Will adaptations and modifications affect the students' grades?

- If modified grading is used, what should the guidelines be?

- Should we evaluate a student's progress using a variety of ways in addition to testing?

- Will students receive credit for participation?

Classroom Environment – Form # 25:

- What is the daily classroom routine? What about pencil sharpening, bathroom breaks and moving around the classroom?

- Will there be designated areas in the classroom to turn in assignments and store home/school notes, assignment books, curriculum materials, etc.?

- Will we be sharing a teaching space? If so, what is the best way to physically structure the classroom to meet our needs?

- Is there a space that confidential information, such as IEPs and behavior plans, can be stored so we can both have access when necessary?

- Does sharing a space include sharing supplies and materials?

- What are our greatest concerns about sharing a teaching space?

Working with Parents – Form #26:

- When problems arise, who will be responsible for contacting the parents of the shared students?

- How will parent/student conferences be handled?

- How should we introduce ourselves to the parents and students on the first day of school?

Form #27, My Profile as an Inclusive Teacher, is a questionnaire for the special education teacher. This personal checklist will help determine individual areas of strength and also the areas that may need further development. This checklist has been adapted and reprinted with permission from the book *The Teacher's Guide to Intervention and Inclusive Education* by Glynis Hannell. (See Resource section.) **Form #28, My Profile as a Paraprofessional,** is a questionnaire especially for the paraprofessional. Although the paraprofessional is usually not included in team planning, this person is a vital member of the team and will be in the classroom for a large amount of time.

Collaboration

Collaboration is important! Special and general educators frequently view situations differently because of their educational backgrounds and experiences. This is important in an inclusive setting! The special educator is an advocate for the student with special needs, and the general educator is an advocate for all of the students in the classroom. In order for the program to be successful, educators must collaborate effectively. One of the greatest benefits of inclusive education is the knowledge acquired from working together!

The previous section provided discussion questions that can be used to help strengthen the newly formed team. The team begins to develop as educators work together to determine the teaching style that will work best, how to discipline students, how to grade shared students and how to work with the parents. This is the first step in the process.

The second step is to look at the various areas of communication and analyze the individual strengths and weaknesses of each team member. Dr. Patty Lee, author of *Collaborative Practices for Educators – Six Keys to Effective Communication,* (see Resources section) defines the six areas of communication that will result in more effective collaboration. This recommended book is based on the premise that educators are often more collaborative with students than with adult colleagues. For example, when working with students in the classroom, teachers tend to listen closely and ask meaningful questions, attempt to understand where students are coming from, put energy into explaining themselves and watch students for indications of misunderstanding. On the other hand, with adult colleagues, teachers are habitually more casual in their communication. They often interrupt their colleagues more, put energy into getting a personal point across rather than attempting to understand theirs, listen halfheartedly at meetings and do not really give much thought to how they express themselves. These habits truly interfere with effective communication. It's not that educators do not know how to communicate, but they simply tend be more casual in conversations with colleagues.

Dr. Lee's book covers the six main areas of communication: developing expectations, preparing ahead, understanding perspectives, asking questions, listening and speaking clearly. It also provides simple practice activities to develop skill in each of these six areas. The simple activities may be completed alone, with a colleague or as a team.

The following chart is adapted from charts in Dr. Lee's book. It provides an interesting comparison between some of the communication strategies frequently used with students in the classroom and what sometimes occurs when teachers communicate with adult colleagues.

WHAT WE OFTEN DO WITH KIDS	WHAT WE SOMETIMES DO WITH ADULTS
DEVELOPING EXPECTATIONS	
Set high expectations for our students	Set few expectations for our work with our peers
Explain/co-create classroom rules and standards of behavior	Conduct our meetings in ways they have always been conducted, with no agreed upon code of conduct
Predict that we will need to accommodate for individual learning differences	Expect everyone to process the information in the same way we do
PREPARING AHEAD	
Decide and think about what to say	Say the first thing that comes to mind
Plan what questions to ask	Prepare what we will say—not what we will ask
Expect to monitor and respond to feedback from students so we can improve the lesson	Persist in conducting business in the habitual ways regardless of feedback
UNDERSTANDING PERPECTIVES	
Accept that their emotional states will affect their productivity	Expect about the same productivity across time
Cut them some slack when we know of difficult circumstances in their lives	Expect them to leave their difficulties at home
See it as a positive challenge when they disagree with us	Take it personally when they disagree with us
ASKING QUESTIONS	
Wait until we have their attention	Ask when we are ready
Ask a lot of questions	Make more statements than inquiries
Welcome most of their questions	Become defensive in response to some of their questions
LISTENING	
Give appropriate eye contact	Attempt to look at them and something else simultaneously
Attend well enough to ask questions related to what they just asked	Attend enough so that we can make our next point
Give them our full attention	Attend to many things at once
SPEAKING CLEARLY	
Use "I" messages	Use "you" or "they" messages
Vary our pace according to the situation	Proceed at a similar pace most of the time, often in a hurry
See it as a positive challenge when they disagree with us	Take it personally when they disagree with us

Adapted and reprinted with permission. *Collaborative Practices for Educators – Six Keys to Effective Communication 2006* by Dr. Patty Lee.

There is a false assumption that teachers automatically know how to collaborate and work together—but in reality, it is a learned skill. Most educators will admit that they work more collaboratively with their students than they do with their colleagues. After all, most teachers entered the education field to teach kids! But collaboration skills must be learned in order to work together effectively in teams. Whether the team consists of two teachers or an entire department, the personalities that members bring to the table have an impact on how the team will function. Some educators are not comfortable speaking up, whereas others have a strong need for control. Some people like to solve everything as a group, whereas others simply want to finish, delegate tasks and move on. Sometimes one member ends up doing all of the work, whereas other team members are noncommittal. When working in teams, it is easy for misunderstandings to occur and collaboration to slowly cease to exist. Working together in an inclusive setting requires good collaboration and communication skills.

Finding Time to Work Together

Finding the time to plan and prepare for instruction is always a major obstacle in inclusive settings. Teachers already must attend curriculum meetings, grade level meetings, staff meetings, parent meetings, IEP meetings and more. Following are some suggestions to consider.

- Use support staff (teaching assistants, paraprofessionals) to monitor the classroom when students are viewing a movie or when they are working independently or in small groups, where teaching is not taking place.

- Often students have special classes such as music, art or physical education. This time may periodically be used for planning.

- Hire a floating substitute as part of the inclusive education program. This substitute can work in various classes to free up general and special educators.

- If the school employs long-term substitutes at the building level, utilize these employees when no teachers are absent.

- Grade level (or subject area) teachers can combine lesson activities such as large group presentations, videos, labs and the like. By combining, it may possibly free up one of the classroom teachers to plan.

- Schedule lunchtimes together.

Setting Up the Inclusive Classroom

The design of the classroom environment will depend upon the type of teaching conducted there, which of course is determined by the needs of the students. The following list provides some ideas to help with setting up the classroom and creating an environment more conducive to team teaching.

- Determine which teaching environment meets the needs of the selected group of students. Some teachers co-plan and teach the lesson, others prefer to have one teach while the other provides support, and yet others prefer to divide the class into two smaller groups. The teaching strategies vary throughout the day depending upon the structure of the class, the lesson and the individuals (both students and teachers) involved.

- If you anticipate large amounts of supportive, supplemental or parallel teaching to occur, establish two teaching areas in the classroom. A table in one corner of the classroom with an area to store teaching supplies is appropriate. If table space is not available, a quiet area of the classroom with an ample supply of clipboards may be the only option.

- Some teachers find a teaching space outside the classroom is beneficial, such as a table in a hallway or perhaps another classroom where class is not in session. Some students prefer to work in small groups outside the classroom, as it may be less distracting.

- A study carrel is useful. Portable study carrels made of corrugated cardboard can be easily stored when not in use. These benefit students who are easily distracted.

- When designing the class seating charts, students who receive support service should be seated in an area that allows the special education teacher or paraprofessional to access the students without disturbing the rest of the class.

- Designate a specific area for teachers to leave notes, schedule changes and other pertinent information. This allows teachers to easily find these changes without disrupting the classroom teacher during a lesson.

- Maintain a box of necessary supplies in each classroom. In addition to the basic supply of pencils, pens, markers and highlighters, include folders to organize copies of lesson plans, personal copies of the teacher's guides and additional supplemental materials.

- A portable cart is another way to organize. Special educators can organize the cart in the morning with materials for the day. When special educators travel between various classrooms throughout the day, the cart will help to keep teacher's guides, lesson plans and supplies in one place. Time is saved, as the teacher no longer needs to return to the special education office for materials between classes. Another option is keep one cart in each classroom.

- A file cabinet in the classroom helps keep materials and files close at hand. This is especially important for copies of confidential student information. Most teachers will reorganize a space or provide a drawer in their individual cabinets. If no space is available, the most economical method is to use a file box or inexpensive file folder purchased from a local office supply store.

- It's important to have special education teachers and paraprofessionals post their schedules in both the general and special education areas. This allows colleagues to reach them if necessary.

- A pager provides a practical solution for teachers of students with severe behavior difficulties who work in inclusive settings. If a crisis occurs in another classroom, the teacher can be paged immediately. It is important to have a back-up contact plan in case the teacher is teaching or working directly with a group of students and cannot leave the classroom. The principal, social worker or psychologist may be an appropriate back-up person in case a situation arises. **Form #29, Emergency Back-Up Plan,** can be used as a template.

- During the school day, it is important for the special education teacher to be in the classroom area. A desk may be placed in or near the classrooms at the elementary level. If you are a secondary teacher and work in a specific area, such as English, consider placing a desk or worktable in the English department. For a successful inclusive education program to occur, educators need to be in close proximity to the classrooms during the school day. The more visible you are, the better the communication between the adults.

- Maintain a file of modified materials and ideas. The supplemental units and audiocassettes can be stored in this file. This enables the general education teacher to find the materials if needed. It is a good idea to make two copies of everything— one for special education and one for general education. Some educators send copies of the materials to the special education administration office so they are accessible to teachers throughout the district.

- Develop a centrally located professional library of materials. The library may include books, videos, reference materials and lists of community services. There are many exceptional staff development videos available on the market. Staff development videos are an excellent way to learn more about a specific subject area without having to read an entire textbook. For example, not all teachers will have students with autism or dyslexia, and therefore it is not appropriate to provide in-service training on these subjects for the entire school. Staff development videos provide support for small-group training. Be sure to have a sign-out sheet so materials can be easily located if needed by another professional.

- As new students are enrolled, the placement folders should be reviewed by the special education department before determining classroom placement. Carefully check the files for special education data. If the student has an IEP or has experienced academic or behavior difficulties in the past, place the student into an inclusive classroom. Sometimes the general and special education folders arrive separately, so be sure to review the folders carefully.

- As new students are added during the school year, the program becomes more complex and schedules must be coordinated between more people. This is difficult, but not impossible. On a positive note, the majority of new students qualifying for special education often are not placed until January. By this time, the existing program is in operation and running smoothly! Students are more responsible and comfortable with their placements and have become more independent. Of course, if luck is really on your side, the qualifying student will be in a classroom where a program is already in place.

Professionalism

Educators spend hours each week meeting with parents, colleagues and other adult professionals in the educational system. When the school day begins, teaching takes on real meaning. The classroom becomes an animated stage with one adult performer and an active participating audience of students. When a special education teacher or paraprofessional is added to the group, the dynamics of the entire group may change.

Not all adults are comfortable with other adults in the classroom. Trust takes time to develop. The working dynamics of the inclusive program will change as the comfort level between the educators increases. In the majority of situations, new friendships and bonds are formed, although this is not always the case. It is important to remember the ultimate goal of the educational merger is to provide a successful educational experience for the student. As adults, it is important to respect one another as professionals and strive to reach the common goal. With time, an educational team will evolve in place of the two separate educational systems.

If you are a special education teacher, here are some guidelines to consider. (Many of these guidelines apply to the general education teacher and paraprofessional as well.)

- Do not tolerate "put-downs" of any student, parent or colleague. These statements immediately create an "us" and "them" atmosphere. Comments should always be professional, respectful and nonjudgmental, whether they are made outside your department or within it.

- Create a personal "I can!" philosophy. When challenges arise, if you have a positive attitude, it will be easier to find a positive solution.

- Follow through on what has been delegated and agreed upon as a team. During planning sessions, if deadline dates have been determined and you KNOW that you will not be able to meet the deadline, change the date immediately. It is very frustrating for those who have met the deadlines to have everything put on hold because one person did not do his or her part.

- No one is an expert on everything. If you do not know the answer to a specific question, do not be embarrassed to say so. Offer to find the answer and follow up with the team.

- If you feel you are pulled in too many directions and just can't get anything done—or can't meet the needs of all the students—ask for help. There are times when an inclusive program has been planned out on paper, but in reality, it just doesn't work. Sit down and talk with the team about your concerns, and ask for help. Since you are working with many teachers, often the classroom teacher is not aware of the demands on your time.

- Remember that everyone has both good and bad days. Often, with two teachers in the classroom, the extra support is appreciated. There are times when situations may be observed such as a teacher losing his or her temper with a student. Unless a situation continually occurs, puts a student in danger or is totally unprofessional, focus on the positive. The fastest way to damage a relationship with a co-teacher is to damage a reputation.

- All teachers have distinct teaching and discipline styles. When working in a specific grade level or subject area, you may observe strategies and techniques that will help others teaching the same unit. Before sharing, ask the teacher for permission.

- Be sure to schedule time to meet with the classroom teachers. This time can be used to make changes in lesson plans and schedules. Extreme flexibility is very important! This time should be listed as a priority. In order for inclusive education to work, teachers must talk daily. A program can quickly fall apart if teachers do not honor and respect this time.

- If possible, work at the same grade level or in the same subject area for at least two years. The first year is a learning experience for everyone. You create a new team, experiment with new teaching strategies, implement training for staff and spend many hours adapting and modifying the curriculum. You learn a tremendous amount from trying new ideas, adapting the old ones and teaching together. The first year in an inclusive setting is comparable to the first year in a new school system. Everything is new! The second year is much easier for the educational team. You are now an active participating member of the general education team, in-service is minimal, the roles are defined, and the modifications and adaptations can be reused.

Teaching is a very demanding job. There are always new initiatives and programs to learn. Be supportive and understanding of one another, especially when someone is having difficulties at work or at home. In a successful inclusive education program, all educators and paraprofessionals benefit from trying to see the others' points of view, and being flexible and respectful.

Chapter Two Conclusion

This second chapter has presented some ideas that will facilitate the collaboration between general and special education teachers and paraprofessionals who work together in an inclusive classroom. Whether it is a team, supportive, supplemental or parallel teaching environment, planning and communication are vital. Deciding ahead of time how to deal with matters such as discipline, grading, class organization and interfacing with parents will help build a solid collaboration. Acting with respect, understanding and professionalism will result in a more harmonious situation for everyone concerned.

Following is a list of the nine forms referenced in this chapter. These reproducible forms are located in the Appendix. You can use these forms to help get your collaboration off to a good start.

Appendix Forms for Chapter Two

#21	Daily Lesson Activities and Objectives
#22	Discussion Questions: Planning and Teaching
#23	Discussion Questions: Discipline
#24	Discussion Questions: Grading
#25	Discussion Questions: Classroom Environment
#26	Discussion Questions: Working with Parents
#27	My Profile as an Inclusive Teacher
#28	My Profile as a Paraprofessional
#29	Emergency Back-Up Plan

"Coming together is a beginning, staying together is progress, and working together is success!"

Henry Ford

"We see a future where young people learn in different ways but all are expected to learn to higher standards."

Judy Huemann

Chapter Three

General Information About Special Education

Every year children with disabilities receive special education services under the federal law known as IDEA. In order for the student to receive service, a specific procedure is followed to determine the student's eligibility. The referral process often begins after the classroom teacher has tried to help the student by providing additional support, changing the environment, modifying the curriculum and perhaps providing additional instruction. Sometimes the pre-referral intervention strategies work and a student referral is not made. Other times, the classroom teacher will try multiple strategies and the area of concern continues to be problematic. When this happens, the general education teacher often makes a referral to the special education team. The steps for possible special education placement are described here. This is only a simplified guide. School districts may add additional steps or require additional documentation. The current law in its entirety can be found on the website for the Department of Education.

Chapter Note:
On page 60, you will find a complete list of the reproducible forms referred to throughout this chapter. The reproducible forms are located in the Appendix.

Special Education Placement

Referral to Special Education: The referral to special education is initiated when a classroom teacher (or parent) has specific concerns related to a student's classroom achievement. Often the classroom teacher has implemented specific, documented classroom interventions, and these interventions have not helped the student. When this occurs, the classroom teacher may request that the student be evaluated by the special education team. Before this can occur, the classroom teacher needs to contact the parent or guardian and discuss the possible referral. The parent must sign a consent form before the referral can take place. The referral team may consist of general and special education teachers, counselors, psychologists, administrators and other specialists who may be able to provide insight regarding the individual student. Upon review, the team may decide to proceed with the evaluation or to postpone it until further intervention has occurred.

Evaluation: If a decision is made to evaluate the student, a comprehensive evaluation is scheduled. The evaluation procedures and assessments vary depending upon the areas of concern. The tests may include cognitive ability tests, academic testing, behavior rating scales, speech and language assessment and so forth.

Eligibility: Once the assessment is complete, the team reconvenes to compile the data and discuss the results and to determine whether or not a student meets the federal guidelines to qualify for special education services. If the student does not qualify, the team may offer suggestions to the classroom teacher, and the classroom teacher is responsible to meet the student's needs without additional support. If a student is determined eligible for service, the special education team has 30 school calendar days to reconvene and develop the Individual Education Plan (IEP). The school must notify the parents (in writing) of the outcomes from the eligibility meeting. Parents have the right to challenge the decision.

IEP Meeting: The school must notify and invite the parent(s) to the upcoming IEP meeting. The parents (and student if appropriate) attend this meeting and help to develop and write the IEP. After the IEP is written, all team members sign this document before the student is able to receive services.

Service: After the IEP has been signed, special education service may begin. Teachers, parents and other service providers receive a copy of the IEP. The IEP lists the student's current level of performance, specific goals and objectives for the student, strategies to be implemented, accommodations and amount of service the student will receive and how the student's progress will be measured. This legal document is reviewed and updated at often as necessary (with a minimum of once per year), and the student is re-evaluated every three years.

Disability Categories

Currently, IDEA lists 13 separate disability categories for which students may receive service. Often teachers are concerned, as they are unfamiliar with the characteristics of the various disabilities. NICHCY (National Dissemination Center for Children with Disabilities) has created fact sheets for each of these categories. Each fact sheet defines the disability, describes its characteristics and offers tips for teachers and parents. Each ends with a very helpful list of resources and disability organizations that can offer more information and assistance.

Following is a summary from the NICHCY Fact Sheets of various disability categories with some additional information. Complete disability definitions can be found in the *Code of*

> **NICHCY FACT SHEETS**
> These NICHCY Fact Sheets can be reproduced and handed out as long as the source is cited. The NICHCY Fact Sheets can be found at:
> *www.nichcy.org/disabinf.asp*

Federal Regulations. When reading, it is important to remember that every student with a disability is unique, and each disability has a range of mild to severe characteristics.

Disability Definitions

1. Autism: Autism and Pervasive Developmental Disorder (PDD) are developmental disabilities that share many of the same characteristics. Autism is defined as "… a developmental disability significantly affecting verbal and nonverbal communication and social interaction, generally evident before age 3, that adversely affects a child's educational performance." Other characteristics often associated with autism are engagement in repetitive activities and stereotyped movements, resistance to environment change or change in daily routines, and unusual responses to sensory experiences. Spectrum Disorders, Asperger's syndrome, Rett's syndrome and Childhood Disintegrative Disorder are diagnostic terms that fall within this category. Children with autism or PDD vary widely in abilities, intelligence and behaviors.

Classroom Implications: The classroom environment should be structured, and the education program and daily routine should be consistent and predictable. The student should always be made aware in advance of changes to the school day or routine. This student will learn better when information is presented visually as well as verbally. This student may have difficulty interpreting facial expressions, body language and voice tone. It is important to create opportunities for the student to have structured social and collaborative interactions and to provide lots of opportunities for practice.

2. Deaf-Blindness: Deaf-blindness is defined as "... concomitant [simultaneous] hearing and visual impairments, the combination of which causes such severe communication and other developmental and educational needs that they cannot be accommodated in special education programs solely for children with deafness or children with blindness."

Classroom Implications: The student will need specialized services that will be specifically listed and described in the student's IEP. See #3 Deafness and #13 Vision Impairment including blindness.

3. Deafness: Deafness is defined as "... a hearing impairment so severe that a child is impaired in processing linguistic information through hearing, with or without amplification, that adversely affects a child's educational performance." Hearing loss is generally described as slight, mild, moderate, severe or profound, depending upon how well a person can hear the intensities or frequencies most greatly associated with speech. Generally, only children whose hearing loss is greater than 90 decibels (dB) are considered deaf for the purposes of educational placement.

Classroom Implications: Hearing loss or deafness does not affect a student's intellectual capacity or ability to learn. However, these students will generally require some form of special education services in order to receive an adequate education. In the classroom, the student will receive specialized services from various specialists, depending upon the student's needs. The student should be provided with specialized seating (such as a swivel chair), allowing the student to see the faces of the students, teachers and interpreter. The student will need assistance with oral directions, note-taking and any information that is presented verbally. It is important to provide as much information visually as possible. Captioned films and videos are a must.

4. Emotional Disturbance: Emotional disturbance is defined as "... a condition exhibiting one or more of the following characteristics over a long period of time and to a marked degree that adversely affects a child's educational performance—an inability to learn that cannot be explained by intellectual, sensory or health factors; an inability to build or maintain satisfactory interpersonal relationships with peers and teachers; inappropriate types of behavior or feelings under normal circumstances; a general pervasive mood of unhappiness or depression; and a tendency to develop physical symptoms or fears associated with personal or school problems." Some characteristics may include hyperactivity, aggression (towards self and others), withdrawal, immaturity and learning difficulties.

Classroom Implications: The educational program for this student needs to include attention to providing emotional and behavioral support as well as helping the student to master academics, develop social skills, and increase self-awareness, self-control and self-esteem. The student may need intervention plans and behavior contracts. This student may also have additional services documented in the IEP. These related services may be provided by behavior specialists, counselors and psychologists

5. Hearing Impairment: Hearing impairment is defined as "... an impairment in hearing, whether permanent or fluctuating, that adversely affects a child's educational performance." Deafness is defined as "a hearing impairment that is so severe that the child is impaired in processing information through hearing, with or without amplification." A child with a hearing impairment generally can respond to auditory stimuli.

Classroom Implications: Hearing loss or deafness does not affect a student's intellectual capacity or ability to learn. However, these students will generally require some form of special education services in order to receive an adequate education. In the classroom, the student may receive specialized services, such as speech and language services and auditory training from a specialist. If the student uses sign language, an interpreter will be required. The classroom teacher will need to be trained to use an amplification system. The student should be provided with specialized seating (such as a swivel chair), allowing the student to see the faces of the students, teachers and interpreter. The student will need assistance with oral directions, note-taking and any information that is presented verbally. It is important to provide as much information visually as possible. Captioned films and videos are a must.

6. Mental Retardation: Mental retardation is defined as "... significantly subaverage general intellectual functioning, existing concurrently with deficits in adaptive behavior and manifested during the developmental period, that adversely affects a child's educational performance." To diagnose mental retardation, professionals look at the student's mental abilities (IQ) and compare it to the student's adaptive skills. Mental retardation varies from mild to severe. Students who are within the mild range will take longer usual to learn new information. These students will be able to live independently as adults. Students with severe mental retardation will need more intensive support throughout their lives.

Classroom Implications: Students with mild mental retardation may not be diagnosed until they reach school age. As the student becomes older and the academic demands become more strenuous, often paraprofessional support is increased. The student will need accommodations to the curriculum and perhaps a parallel curriculum. Large tasks should be broken into smaller steps, and information should be presented visually, along with hands-on activities and manipulative materials. For students with more severe mental retardation, the classroom focus is on self-help, communication, socialization and vocational skills.

7. Multiple Disabilities: Multiple disabilities is defined as "… concomitant [simultaneous] impairments (such as mental retardation-blindness, mental retardation-orthopedic impairment, etc.), the combination of which causes such severe educational needs that they cannot be accommodated in a special education program solely for one of the impairments. The term does not include deaf-blindness." Educational programming is likely to begin from infancy. The main focus for many of these students will be to increase their independence.

Classroom Implications: In order to be effective, educational programs need to incorporate a variety of components to meet the considerable needs of these students. Multiple educational and medical staff may be involved in the student's educational programming, including speech and language therapists, physical and occupational therapists and medical specialists. Students may also have a need for medication and special equipment. Students may require communication devices, wheelchairs and a variety of assistive technology devices.

8. Orthopedic Impairment: Orthopedic impairment is defined as "… a severe orthopedic impairment that adversely affects a child's educational performance. The term includes impairments caused by congenital anomaly (e.g., clubfoot, absence of some member, etc.), impairments caused by disease (e.g., poliomyelitis, bone tuberculosis, etc.), and impairments from other causes (e.g., cerebral palsy, amputations, and fractures or burns that cause contractures)."

Classroom Implications: Students with orthopedic impairments have a wide range of disabilities. First, read as much as you can about the specific disability. These students are able to learn, but they will need accommodations in the classroom environment. Some of the students will need special medical attention, for which training will be provided. A great deal of assistive technology is currently available, such as communication boards and communication devices. A great deal of special computer technology may be used, such as keyboards or switches. With the advances of technology, new equipment and technologies are continually being created and improved.

9. Other Health Impairments: Other health impairments is defined as "… having limited strength, vitality, or alertness, including a heightened alertness to environmental stimuli, that results in limited alertness with respect to the educational environment, that is due to chronic or acute health problems such as asthma, attention deficit disorder or attention deficit hyperactivity disorder, diabetes, epilepsy, a heart condition, hemophilia, lead poisoning, leukemia, nephritis, rheumatic fever, and sickle cell anemia; and adversely affects a child's educational performance."

Classroom Implications: Students with other health impairments have a wide range of disabilities. It is important to educate yourself and read as much as you can about the specific area. Due to health issues, some students may be absent for large amounts of time, which will affect their academic performance and may require special education support to maintain academically in the classroom.

10. Specific Learning Disability: Specific learning disability is defined as "… a disorder in one or more of the basic psychological processes involved in understanding or in using language, spoken or written, that may manifest itself in an imperfect ability to listen, think, speak, read, write, spell, or do mathematical calculations, including conditions such as perceptual disabilities, brain injury, minimal brain dysfunction, dyslexia, and developmental aphasia." However, learning disabilities do not include, "… learning problems that are primarily the result of visual, hearing, or motor disabilities, of mental retardation, of emotional disturbance, or of environmental, cultural, or economic disadvantage)." There is no one sign that will indicate that a student has a learning disability. A student could possibly have a learning disability if some of the following characteristics are present. The student has difficulty with rhyming words and connecting letters to sounds or difficulty spelling words; reads fluently but has difficulty understanding what was read; struggles with handwriting and getting ideas down on paper; has a limited vocabulary and uses the same words over and over; reverses letters; has trouble distinguishing between sounds; confuses letters and numbers; has difficulty taking turns or reading body language; or seems very intelligent but is not learning at the expected rate. All children experience some of these, but if a student exhibits multiple characteristics, it could indicate a learning disability.

Classroom Implications: The classroom implications vary greatly. The student may need tasks broken into small steps, textbooks read aloud, help taking notes, testing modifications and additional support with organization and study skills. Since learning disabilities may occur in isolated areas such as math, reading, language or writing, the types of accommodations are too numerous to list—but will be listed in the student's IEP.

11. Speech and Language Impairment: Speech and language impairment is defined as "… a communication disorder such as stuttering, impaired articulation, a language impairment, or a voice impairment that adversely affects a child's educational performance."

Classroom Implications: Students with language delays may experience difficulties with speech such as stuttering, hesitations, repetitions or difficulty pronouncing words. Other students may have voice disorders where they experience inappropriate pitch, tone or quality. Allow these students extra time to express themselves and alleviate pressure to speak in a group. These students will receive direct service from the speech teacher, and the classroom teacher may be asked to listen for and assist the students with various speech areas throughout the day. Some students will have a language disorder, which may include the inability to express their ideas, or they may use a limited vocabulary. Some students may have a language delay. Students should always be encouraged to use their speech and language skills, while educators provide appropriate wait time, genuine praise and encouragement.

12. Traumatic Brain Injury: Traumatic brain injury is defined as "... an acquired injury to the brain caused by an external physical force, resulting in total or partial functional disability or psychosocial impairment, or both, that adversely affects a child's educational performance. The term applies to open or closed head injuries resulting in impairments in one or more areas, such as cognition; language; memory; attention; reasoning; abstract thinking; judgment; problem-solving; sensory, perceptual, and motor abilities; psychosocial behavior; physical functions; information processing; and speech. The term does not include brain injuries that are congenital or degenerative, or brain injuries induced by birth trauma." The characteristics of students with traumatic brain injury will vary depending upon the severity and location of the injury. Some students may experience physical disabilities, difficulties speaking and thinking, and social, emotional and behavioral difficulties. Some students may be partially or completely paralyzed. Students may exhibit only some, or all, of these characteristics.

Classroom Implications: Read and find out as much as you can about the student's educational needs. The student may need extra time for seat work and tests. The student may need to relearn things previously known and have difficulty grasping new concepts. The student may also tire easily. It is important to remain in contact with the parents and note changes that become apparent.

13. Visual Impairment Including Blindness: Visual impairment including blindness is defined as "... an impairment in vision that, even with correction, adversely affects a child's educational performance. The term includes both partial sight and blindness. Children with visual impairments benefit from early intervention programs.

Classroom Implications: Students with visual impairments may need special equipment and modifications in the curriculum. Depending on the severity of the vision loss, students may benefit from technology, low-vision aids, large print materials and books on tape. Some students may also have orientation and mobility concerns.

Accommodations, Adaptations and Modifications

Accommodations, adaptations and modifications are specific, individualized strategies that will help a student to succeed in the classroom. So what are accommodations? And what is the difference between adaptations and modifications? **Accommodations** provide alternate ways for students to learn information and to demonstrate what has been learned. For example, a student who is unable to read the textbook material may listen to the material on tape, or a student who struggles with writing may use a computer to write a report instead of trying to write it freehand. Accommodations also include building accommodations, such as ramps, accessible bathrooms or signs in Braille. The student is learning the same information and has access to the same facilities as everyone else, but changes have been implemented to provide this access. **Adaptations** are ways the delivery is modified to meet the student's individual needs. This may include a change or variation in the method, instruction, evaluation or curriculum. Examples include: allowing the student to use a computer if she or he is unable to write; using a consumable textbook so the student can take notes, highlight and write directly in the book; allowing the student to take tests verbally; or providing class notes to the student. When material is adapted, the student is still expected to have the same outcome. On the other hand, **modifications** actually change the curriculum, and the student may not be expected to complete the same amount of material as his or her peers. Examples of modifications are to: reduce the number of spelling words that a student has to master on a weekly spelling test; allow the student to draw a picture instead of write a response; or provide a parallel curriculum. The strategies in this book have not been divided into separate categories, as it would be very repetitive and cumbersome and would result in an enormous amount of repetition.

Good teachers are continually modifying and adapting the curriculum throughout the day to accommodate students who learn differently. For most teachers, it is simply good teaching practice and occurs without thought. For example, if a student has difficulty reading a textbook, the teacher naturally pairs this student with a peer. If a student is struggling with the completion of an assignment, the teacher may ask the student to orally give their final answers and quickly write them down for the student. These simple accommodations are without even thinking. It's simply a way to help the student complete the assignment quickly and usually is not thought of as an accommodation.

Most classrooms will have students who do not qualify for special education services but still receive service under Section 504 of the Vocational Rehabilitation Act. For example, a student with Attention-Deficit/Hyperactivity Disorder (AD/HD) may not receive services from the special education department, yet the student may be entitled to receive classroom accommodations under Section 504. This 504 Plan details specific accommodations and also lists goals, but it is not as detailed as an Individualized Education Plan, and the classroom teacher is required to carry out these accommodations without additional support.

Students who qualify for special education services under IDEA will have an Individualized Education Plan (IEP). The IEP will include both long- and short-term goals. It will also list the accommodations, adaptations and modifications that the student is to receive. For students with special needs, the accommodations may still be as simple as partnering the student with a peer to accommodate for reading, or they may be very complex and require many modifications to the curriculum. The difference between the 504 Plan and the IEP is that the IEP is a legally binding document, and the accommodations become part of this document. The IEP goals focus on the student's needs and goals. Stated objectives provide guidelines to meet these goals.

In order for the student to be successful in the classroom, often the curriculum is adapted to meet the student's needs. The IEP goals will focus on the student's needs, and the objectives will list the checkpoints to be sure the student is making progress toward the goals. Therefore, the goals and objectives often focus on the student's limitations. In order to successfully make accommodations, it is important to determine the individual strengths of the student. When adapting the curriculum, the following should be addressed:

- What is the goal for the student in the specific academic area?
- What strengths can we capitalize on to meet this goal?
- Will this modification or accommodation assist the student in reaching the final goal?

Accommodations usually fall within one of the following four categories:

The activity or content is reinforced. In this category, supplemental support is provided to the student. This additional support enables the student to complete the classroom assignments and fulfill the class requirements. Previewing, preteaching and reteaching of some assignments may be necessary. Supplemental aids such as study guides, outlines and audiocassettes of the materials may be provided. Direct instruction is usually provided by the general education teacher, with additional support from the special education department.

The activity or content is modified. In this category, the modifications are made to the actual material or content of the curriculum. The number of outcomes in a specific content area may be reduced. The student may be provided with additional time to complete assignments. Assignments may be adjusted in length and content. Grading criteria and assessments may be adapted for the individual student. Instructional groupings may vary, and activities may be presented in large groups, small groups or individually.

A parallel activity is developed. This category includes the use of supplemental materials and activities in which the content is similar or directly related to the curriculum. High interest/low vocabulary texts may be used. At this level, the functional value of the curriculum is determined, and activities created are similar or related to the curricular content. These include "hands-on" or action-based activities. At this level, the use of authentic activities and assessments are appropriate.

The classroom activity is the same, but the final outcome is different. In this category, the student performs the same type of activities as his or her peer group, but the outcome is directly related to the student's goals on the Individualized Education Plan. At this level, the student may listen to a class lecture, but the individual goal may be to "sit quietly" for a predetermined time period without interrupting. The student may copy a sentence from the board, but the individual goal is to develop fine motor skills. In math, the student may add or subtract with the calculator, but the student's actual goal is to learn the functions of the calculator. These are functional goals. Functional goals are based on skills the student needs to acquire to live independently as an adult. This independent setting may be a traditional home setting, a supervised apartment or a group home setting. When adapting material, consider the following areas:

The Student's Goal: The final outcome may be adjusted for the student. The student may be required to learn the location of regional states on a map instead of both location and capitals. The student may practice letter formation instead of learning to spell a specific list of words.

Level of Difficulty: The student may acquire information through a high interest/low vocabulary text or with the use of supplemental materials. Students may work on basic addition facts instead of more complex addition problems.

Length of Assignment: The number of items the student is expected to learn or complete may be adjusted.

Additional time: The time allowed to take a test may be increased, or the student may be allowed an extra day to complete an assignment.

Input/Output of Information: The student may receive information through cooperative groups or small-group instruction, computers or the use of visual aids and manipulative materials. The student may share knowledge in ways that replace the traditional paper and pencil assignments. These may include giving oral presentations or demonstrations, using a tape recorder, communication board or computer, or using gestures.

Participation in Class Activities: The level at which the student participates in classroom activities may be adjusted. The student's goal may be to participate in the group setting without academic expectations.

Support Systems: The student may receive additional support with paraprofessionals, peer teaching, buddy systems or study halls.

Curriculum Accommodations

The easiest way to illustrate the process of adapting material is to use a hypothetical example. Photocopy **Form #30, Curriculum Accommodations,** from the end of this chapter. Read the following hypothetical example, and fill in the worksheet.

John is a seventh grade student with a learning disability. John's ability falls within the average range. He receives special education service in the areas of reading and written language. John's language (both receptive and expressive) is at grade level. John does well in math class and participates in problem-solving activities. He actively participates during group discussions and works well in a cooperative group. John consistently does well on lab experiments in Science class.

Step 1: Note John's strengths:

- Average ability
- Receptive and expressive language commensurate with perceived ability
- Strong aptitude for math
- Participates in class
- Works well in cooperative groups
- Does well with hands-on activities
- Enjoys discussion activities

Since this is a hypothetical situation, the list is short. If John was an actual student, the team would be able to elaborate on these strengths.

Step 2: Determine the goals for the subject area.

- John will complete 80% of the social studies assignments.
- John will complete the classroom assessments with at least 70% accuracy.

After Step 2 is complete, turn to the Table of Contents in this book. This book will save you time, shorten your planning sessions and provide a basis for communication when adapting materials for students with disabilities. First, read through the chapter titles. Determine which chapters are most appropriate for the student. The accommodations have already been compiled for you.

Since John receives support in reading and written language, the following areas were chosen from the Table of Contents:

- Textbook adaptations
- Creating audiocassettes
- Daily assignments
- Written language
- Note taking
- Alternate forms of assessments

Step 3: Brainstorm possible ideas and strategies to help John compensate for his disability. Some ideas may be:

- Provide audiocassettes for the materials that are difficult for John to read independently.

- Use cooperative groups during class. Allow John to work with a partner on written assignments.

- Provide a study guide for each unit. On the study guide, list the objectives for which John will be held accountable.

- Provide a partner when lectures require John to take notes. Provide a copy of the notes to John.

- Written tests should be taken in an individual setting. Allow John to demonstrate knowledge in an alternate form to alleviate long written assignments. Oral presentation for final projects would be appropriate.

Step 4: As a team, discuss the accommodations that are appropriate for John. Determine the person who will be responsible to adapt the material. Tthe audiocassette and typing of the study guide could be completed by a volunteer.) Also decide who will be responsible to implement the accommodations in the classroom setting. **Form #31** and **Form #32, Textbook Accommodations; Form #33, Daily Assignment Accommodations; Form #34, Testing Accommodations;** and **Form #35, Accommodations—Blank Template,** can be used.

When making accommodations, it is important to implement only a few strategies at a time. **Form #36, Log Sheet,** can be used to record and document the results. Be sure to allow ample time for the student to adjust before adding additional strategies or deciding that a specific idea doesn't work. Since all students are unique, a strategy that works for one student will not necessarily work for another.

Differentiating Instruction

The design and development of differentiated instruction as a teaching model began in the general education classroom. The initial application came into practice for students who were gifted and not sufficiently challenged by the content provided in the general classroom setting. As classrooms have become more diverse and inclusive education programs were implemented, differentiated instruction has been applied at all levels for students of all abilities. There are hundreds of books now written on the subject of differentiating instruction. In the Resources section, some of the resources directly related to students with special needs have been listed.

So what is differentiating instruction? A simplified definition for differentiating instruction is: the process of teachers proactively planning to teach students at their current levels of ability, rather than taking a standardized approach to teaching, which has the underlying presumption that all students in the classroom are at the same level. With differentiated instruction, classroom teachers plan what the students need to learn, how they will learn it and how they will demonstrate what they have learned. The intent of differentiating instruction is to maximize each student's growth and individual success by meeting each student where he or she is and assisting in the learning process. One of the most popular terms when referring to differentiating instruction is that "one size does not fit all."

The rationale for differentiated instruction comes from theory, research and common sense. Today's classrooms are more diverse than they have ever been throughout the history of this country. There are students with special needs, students who have come from other countries and only speak a little English, average students, gifted students and students considered at risk for various reasons. All of these students come to school with various backgrounds, abilities and educational readiness for learning and, of course, have different styles of learning.

It's common sense that with the diverse students in today's classrooms, it is next to impossible to teach all students in one way. There are just too many different levels of performance and needs. With differentiated instruction, classroom teachers are encouraged to identify the essential concepts and instructional components for every curriculum unit. During the teaching process, today's teacher continually assesses and reassesses students before, during and following instruction, which allows the teacher to continually group and regroup students. When using differentiated strategies, the students are actively engaged in the learning process and students are offered choices in their learning, as often the activities are based on learning styles, Bloom's taxonomy of cognitive, affective and psychomotor educational objectives and other models that encourage teachers to teach in the way the student learns best.

Differentiating instruction is a wonderful tool for special students. Instead of consistently being placed into one specific group, students with special needs consistently move throughout the various groups, depending upon their strengths. The following chart shows the three main components of differentiating instruction: the content, the process and the evaluation. Depending upon a student's strengths, the student may fall into any one of the three categories. For example, a student may excel in history, as it is an area of great interest to the student. The student may have acquired a wealth of information and background knowledge. Perhaps the student has spent large amounts of time watching programs such as the history channel, has vacationed in historical places and perhaps spends a great deal of time researching history in his spare time. This student may pass a history pretest with flying colors. This student has become an expert on the subject. In the area of content, the student easily falls into the gifted area. On the other hand, a student with cognitive disabilities conceivably will be in the challenged area, as the student takes longer to master the subject, needs lots of reinforcement and may need modifications to meet the minimum content requirements. The student with cognitive delays may not even understand the concept of history, as it is a very abstract concept, and this student is continually working in the "here and now" to master what needs to be learned to live independently. History simply is not a subject this student may need. The student may work on parallel subjects, or the purpose of participation in the group may be to work on the student's social skills. The majority of students with learning disabilities will fall into the average range. Students with learning disabilities usually have average to above average intelligence, so the majority of students will be able to master the unit content but may need some accommodations such as material on tape, a person to help with the writing components, etc. Remember, the accommodations do not change the outcome; accommodations only offer students alternative ways to reach the outcome.

The following chart indicates the three different levels related to the content area. In the differentiated classroom, the majority of special education students will easily fit into one of these categories, and if not, it will be documented in the student's IEP and modifications will be implemented.

General Topic: Civil War

	Challenged	**Average**	**Gifted**
Content	Student is expected to meet three main objectives of the lesson. Students may need many modifications to understand the topic, have low ability or be lacking in the area of language and vocabulary.	Student is expected to master all of the objectives. Students are expected to perform at grade level.	Student is expected to go above and beyond the objectives for the class. Students are gifted, excel in specific areas and/or have a strong knowledge base.

The next step for the teacher is to determine how the unit will be taught. Since students all learn differently, students with special needs will be scattered throughout the three areas. Some students will need additional instruction, others will be able to do the work independently and still others will excel. Accommodations can be implemented in all areas. Students who need modifications (change of outcome) will usually fall into the challenged range.

	Challenged	**Average**	**Gifted**
Process	Student needs direct instruction in each step of the process. Student needs review, practice and reteaching.	Student can learn from modeling. Student can do independent work. Student needs review and practice.	Student learns with minimal instruction. Student conducts independent study. Student learns and grasps basic concepts quickly; may pass pretest.

The final stage on this grid is evaluation. Once again, students will fall within all three categories. In this area of evaluation or assessment, a student may need modifications to meet the evaluation standards (for example, an adult may write the final project for the student), but the outcome is the same.

	Challenged	**Average**	**Gifted**
Evaluation	Student provides a group project for evaluation.	Student is expected to complete a three-page, individual final project.	Student will create a class presentation with models, graphs and discussion points.

Some additional benefits of differentiated instruction for students with special needs is that flexible grouping is consistently used. Strategies for flexible grouping are an essential component of differentiated instruction. Learners are expected to interact and work together as they develop knowledge of new content. Teachers may conduct whole-class introductory discussions of content areas followed by small group or pair work. Student groups may be coached from within or by the teacher to complete assigned tasks. Grouping of students is not fixed. Based on the content, project and on-going evaluations, grouping and regrouping must be a dynamic process as one of the foundations of differentiated instruction.

Differentiated instruction takes the instruction one step further. Often lesson plans are divided into various activities. These activities are often based on Gardner's Multiple Intelligences or Bloom's Taxonomy. By incorporating strategies to address different types of intelligence, students with special needs often have more opportunities to participate.

The strategies in this book will help all students in the classroom. Listed are many accommodation and modification strategies. The games and activities can be adapted to students with varying abilities, ranging from simple tasks to extension activities for the advanced students in the classroom. These strategies have been compiled from educators nationwide, Internet sources and the previous, 2000 edition of *Inclusion: 450 Strategies for Success*. There are hundreds from which to choose! These ideas will contribute to the success of *all* students in the classroom.

Chapter Three Conclusion

This chapter provides a deeper look at special education, with an explanation of how students are evaluated for special services according to the dictates of law as well as common sense. Thirteen different categories of disability are briefly defined, as well as the classroom implications of inclusion.

Today's diverse student population requires an equally diverse approach to teaching in order to meet the students' needs and optimize learning. If a student is determined to have special needs, an Individual Education Plan is devised to set forth the recommended services and accommodations to learning, adaptations to teaching and modifications of curriculum and outcomes, as necessary.

Today's teachers must be flexible and use differentiated instruction, adapting to various learning styles, multiple intelligences and domains of learning (cognitive, affective and psychomotor). Inclusive education is demanding and challenging, but it is also exciting and fulfilling to see students who may have been relegated to the margins of education in years past now be engaged and learning along with their peers—at their own pace and in their own special ways.

Following is a list of the seven forms referenced in this chapter. The reproducible forms are located in the Appendix. You can use these forms to help determine and record the accommodations that will help your students.

Appendix Forms for Chapter Three

#30	Curriculum Accommodations
#31	Textbook Accommodations
#32	Textbook Accommodations - 2
#33	Daily Assignments
#34	Testing Accommodations
#35	Accommodations—Blank Template
#36	Accommodations Log Sheet

"Your goal should be out of reach, but not out of sight."

Anita DeFrantz

"A man who removes a mountain begins by removing small stones."

Chinese Proverb

Chapter Four

Reading

"How can Susan be included when she is unable to read the textbook?" Perhaps this question should be rephrased: "How much of the material is Susan able to learn and understand when the information is presented in another manner?" When rephrasing the question, our focus turns toward the student's strength instead of emphasizing the student's weakness.

The majority of the students who receive special education services encounter difficulty with reading. Although the emphasis in this chapter is on accommodations, formalized reading instruction should continue for the student. As a team, it will need to be determined when this will occur. During the elementary day, it may occur when students are grouped for reading or during a time block predetermined at an IEP meeting. At the middle school and secondary level, it would be appropriate to incorporate reading into a study skills block or during a study hall period.

> **Chapter Note:**
> On page 85, you will find a complete list of the reproducible forms referred to throughout this chapter. The reproducible forms are located in the Appendix.

There are many commercial reading programs available that may be used to supplement the adopted curriculum. If the reading curriculum emphasizes a phonetic approach, consider supplementing the program with a whole language component. This will help the students with auditory processing difficulties and the students who are visual learners. If the program emphasizes whole language, consider incorporating additional phonics-based materials. In reality, some students simply are not ready for a formalized reading program in first grade. For these students, phonemic awareness training may be appropriate. Phonemic awareness is a component of phonics, but it teaches auditory sounds independent of graphic letters. Phonemic awareness training for students can be taught as a prerequisite to reading or used to supplement the reading curriculum. Students who may benefit from phonemic awareness training are student who are unable to hear differences in words such as *pen* and *pin*, who substitute sounds such as *chrain* for *train*, or who have difficulty rhyming words. For students who receive speech and language services, phonemic awareness training could be included with this service.

Although students must continue to receive supplemental reading instruction, textbook accommodations are critical if the student is to experience success throughout the school day. **Forms #31 and #32, Textbook Accommodations,** can be used to document the strategies that you would like to implement.

Textbook Accommodations

The ideas listed below are not limited to the reading textbook. Use the following strategies and ideas for Science, Social Studies, English and supplemental textbooks. Whether the student reads the material alone, with support, or listens to a tape, always make sure the student is aware and is held responsible for the follow-up activities.

1. Determine the reading level of the textbook and compare the level to the student's reading level as documented in the IEP. This will help to determine the students in the class that may encounter difficulty with the textbook.

2. Preview the textbook with the students. Discuss the publisher's organizational strategies. All students in the classroom will benefit from direct instruction on how to use the following: cover, table of contents, index, preface and introduction, conclusion and summary, the images (pictures, graphs, tables, figures), section headings, special formatting (boldface type, italics), chapter and summary questions, captions under photos, vocabulary list, appendices, subject index and glossary. After learning how to use these parts of the book, students should find that reading and understanding the book become easier.

3. Provide an outline of the reading material in advance. Allow the student to take notes on the outline, while the other students read aloud.

4. Give the student a list of the discussion questions for preview. This helps the student to focus on important material. (See section on previewing and pre-teaching for additional strategies.)

5. Give the student a pad of sticky notes. The student may jot down notes, vocabulary words or questions about the material. These notes can then be applied directly to related areas of the textbook for easy reference.

6. Preview and discuss the pictures, diagrams and charts with the student before reading. The student is better able to rely on visual clues and has background information on which to build.

7. Read the text aloud to the class using a guided reading procedure. When reading aloud, frequently provide location clues such as page number and paragraph location.

Students who are unable to read the text may listen and look at the pictures. Guided reading also helps the student who tends to daydream during class.

8. Read the text aloud to a small group of students, while the remainder of the students read silently. The students with disabilities are included in the small group. Vary the groups so students become familiar with small-group procedures and become acquainted with other students in the class.

9. If two adults are available, divide the students into two groups. Each adult can read and discuss the information with separate groups. Be sure both adults have the same list of discussion questions and outcomes for the lesson. This setting allows all students to actively participate in the class activity. Some students may prefer to read silently, so three groups would be another option.

10. While reading textbooks out loud, simultaneously record the material. With textbook material, students can use this tape for chapter review, as it includes both student questions and discussion points. This is also beneficial for students who have been absent, as they will have not only the textbook material but also the class discussion.

11. Group students into small, cooperative groups and allow students to read aloud. The student with special needs may not feel comfortable reading aloud at the beginning. As the student's comfort level increases, more risks will be taken.

>   **Choral reading** allows all students to actively participate. With choral reading, the students read aloud together with the teacher, or a small group of students read aloud together. Choral reading will help students develop read-aloud skills and learn sight words. It's best to keep the passages short.

>   **Cloze reading** is another option when reading in groups. When using a cloze reading procedure, the adult reads aloud and randomly stops, allowing the students to fill in the missing words.

>   **Buddy reading** is an option for two students to read together. Students who use the buddy system can try some of the following options:

>   Buddy #1 reads the sentence. Buddy #2 echoes the sentence, while #1 points to the words.

>   Buddy #1 reads the first sentence, Buddy #2 reads the next sentence and so on.

>   Buddies #1 and #2 read the sentences together.

12. Record the lesson. Allow the student to listen to the tape in a small group or with a peer. (See the section titled Creating Audio files.) Color-code a master textbook to accompany the audiocassette. Highlight the important information that the student is expected to learn: vocabulary words and their definitions; important facts; and

specific material covered on the assessment. Tape a corresponding color key in the front of the textbook, and the text is now individualized for the specific course.

13. Tape record alternate pages of the textbook. Allow the student to listen to one page and then read one either silently or aloud. This helps the student who is struggling to keep the same pace as his or her peers. As with #12, provide a color-coded master textbook that highlights specific "must learn" vocabulary, key facts, etc., and affix the corresponding color key to the inside front cover.

14. Paraphrase textbook material on tape. Include only the most important material. Paraphrasing is difficult. You must be very familiar with the material before attempting to do this, or it is possible for the paraphrased version to become longer than the text version!

15. Provide the student with written chapter summaries. If you have copies of the material in a Microsoft Word document, try the AutoSummarize feature to summarize text.

16. When reading to the class for enjoyment, simultaneously record the novels, chapter books or short stories. The tapes can be placed in a classroom library, and students can check out the book and tape to reread or listen to at a later time.

17. Create Resource Packets to correspond with textbook chapters. The resource packets may include the actual textbook chapter with important information highlighted, additional articles and information related to the topic (which may be teacher created), summary chapters, etc. These items can be placed into a three-ring binder that students may check out for home use.

18. Contact the textbook publisher. Often publishers have adapted materials and supplemental textbooks that correlate to the grade-level textbooks.

Read-Aloud Technology

Technology is continually advancing, and new software is continually becoming less expensive and more readily available. If the school has students who are visually impaired or blind, it already may have software that reads textbooks aloud to students. An abundance of text-to-read software is available, from moderately priced to very expensive. Search online by title for the following software. Many of these also will help students who experience difficulty with written language.

19. The *Cicero Text Reader V. 7.1* effectively takes your computer and scanner and turns them into a reading machine for people with a visual impairment or reading disability. Printed text can be scanned and then translated into speech, Braille or simply a text document, which then can be adjusted, edited, saved and printed.

20. *ClaroRead PLUS* is a software program designed to help struggling readers and writers of all capabilities create, read, view and check text. *ClaroRead PLUS* features powerful reading and writing assistance toolbars, flawless text-to-speech capabilities and easy-to-use features.

21. *Dragon Naturally Speaking* can read highlighted text from the computer.

22. *Kurzweil 3000* offers a combined scanning and reading application that allows easy conversion from printed text to audio feedback. It also helps reading and learning to read by highlighting both the line and word as it is read.

23. *Scan2Text* allows editing and read back from the text on any scanner. Scan2Text is operated from within Microsoft Word, by adding just three extra menu items to the Word File Menu. With *Scan2Text* you scan documents, letters and papers, and the text is dropped straight into Microsoft Word.

24. *Scan N Talk Ultra* accesses the printed word for students with disabilities. This technology allows the "printed" word from documents, books and magazines to be easily accessed. The *Scan N Talk Ultra* includes both software and scanner.

25. The *Ovation Reading Machine* is an easy-to-use solution for reading a wide variety of printed material, including books, mail, newspapers, magazines and much more.

26. *TextAloud* is a software program that uses voice synthesis to convert text into spoken audio.

Strategies for Nonreaders

At times there will be a nonreader in the classroom. Many of the previous strategies, such as reading aloud in a group, allowing the student to listen to tapes and using the software listed will benefit this student. Following are additional strategies that may help.

27. Look for books with similar subjects at a lower readability level. These texts will often have more pictures, which can be discussed with the student. Also look for similar content presented in other media, such as videos, DVDs, etc.

28. Highlight alternating lines in the reading text to help the student keep his place while reading.

29. Rewrite the student's text. Rearrange the material and provide only the information that the student is required to master.

30. Use as may visual aids as possible for curriculum units. Show posters and pictures, create bulletin boards and search online for supplemental visual supports for units.

31. Look for books with larger print size and fewer words per page.

32. *Writing with Symbols 2000* is a word/picture processing software, in which the user has the option to have a picture or symbol appear with each word. It is also a talking word processing program. Search online for "writing with symbols" to find U.S. distributors and find out more. This program has many uses for both spoken and written language, such as learning the differences between homonyms and helping students at various levels gain word comprehension using symbols.

33. **Form #37, The First 50 Instant Words,** includes the first 50 most common words that students will encounter in reading and written language. The 50 word cards can be laminated, cut apart and used as flash cards for drill and practice. The words may be combined into simple sentences and used in spelling lists. By learning these frequently used words, the student will have a basic start with reading. The words on Form #37, The First 50 Instant Words, are taken from Dr. Edward Fry's 1000 Instant Words List. If you have nonreaders (or writers), try using Dr. Fry's wonderful collection of early literacy books for children. (Search *Amazon.com* for Edward Fry.) His publications include word lists, phonics activities, vocabulary builders and more. An alternative to the Fry list is the Dolch word list.

34. Create your own material at the edHelper website *(www.edhelper.com)*. This site provides all the tools you will need to quickly create simple worksheets for students. Registration is required to customize worksheets, but a wealth of information can be printed without registration. The yearly registration fee is minimal, and school site licenses are also available.

Supplemental Reading Activities

35. When reading novels to the class, record the novel simultaneously. If you have a class library – enclose both the audiocassette along with the book in a zip-lock bag. Students may check out the book and tape together to reread or listen to at a later time.

36. It is important for students to read as much as possible. Ask students to donate old books or purchase a selection of used books. As a class activity or an extra credit activity, ask students to read and record these books. Some can be left in the class library, and others can be given to younger students for their library. For nonreaders, these tapes may be used during silent reading time.

    Note: Check with the school library to see if it has books with disability awareness themes. If not, you may want to recommend a list of titles for purchase.

37. Create personal classroom books. Take digital photos of classroom activities such as field trips or special presentations, and take photos of individual students. Write

sentences that correspond with the photos, or ask the students to write autobiographies to go with their photos. Create a classroom library with these books.

38. For nonreaders, ask the paraprofessional, a volunteer or peer to read aloud to the student. Include other students in the group. Elementary students love listening to stories. At the secondary level, select students to read aloud to others.

39. Appoint a student to be the Reader of the Day. This student can practice oral expression, while the nonreader is able to enjoy the story.

40. Choose high interest/low vocabulary level books. Many publishers have chapter books available for purchase in this format.

41. Create individual reading lists. Ask students to maintain lists of books they have read or that have been read to them. Genres may include but are not limited to: poems, autobiographies, historical fiction, biographies, mysteries, fantasy, myths and legends, newspapers, how-to books, comics, science fiction or special interest. **Form #38, My Personal Reading List,** is an easy checklist to keep track of students' reading by genre or subject. **Form #39, My Personal Reading List,** is a reading log for students to keep track of the books they have selected to read. **Form #40, Recommended Reading List,** allows students to recommend their favorite books to other students in the class. Each student's form can be copied and inserted into one three-ring binder for all the students to reference when looking for a particular type of book to read.

42. Popular novels and stories are often available on video. Furnish the student with a video to view before reading. Be sure to preview it first! The video will help the student establish the storyline, develop the characters and build some background before reading. Oftentimes, there are major differences between the video and the author's written work. If this is the case, include a group activity where students compare and contrast the differences between the written and visual presentation of the material. **Form #41, Compare and Contrast,** can be used to compare the two different media versions. The more advanced students can view the video, read the book and complete the Compare and Contrast form on their own.

43. Provide the opportunity for students to read, read, and read some more! Often students who do not like reading books will read short articles in magazines. Ask them to bring in their old magazines, and keep a selection in the reading corner. Many students do not have access to magazines and will enjoy this activity.

Previewing and Pre-teaching Strategies

Many students experience success with the curriculum when allowed to preview the materials before the lesson is actually presented. Previewing and pre-teaching strategies can be completed with the general or special education teacher, with the paraprofessional or at home as a homework assignment. These straightforward techniques produce marvelous results for some students.

44. Allow the student to take home an audiocassette of the material before it is read in class. This will allow the student to become familiar with the main characters, the story and plot.

45. Provide extra time for the student to preview and discuss the photos, illustrations, captions, headings and chapter questions with an adult. This helps to build background information. Relate the new concepts to previously learned concepts.

46. Preview bold-faced print and italicized words, headings and subheadings with the student. Read and define the words in the context presented in the textbook.

47. Provide a list of discussion questions, and ask the student to skim through the text and find the answers. Include page number location clues.

48. Ask students to bring small, recipe card boxes from home. Write the main idea or topic of the various chapter sections on index cards. The students can add details and important facts as they read the chapters.

49. Paraphrasing is helpful for most students. It also helps the teacher know whether or not the student has grasped the concept. To assist with paraphrasing, ask the student to read a section. Then, ask the student to state the main idea in his or her own words and share two or three supporting details. Some students find that paraphrasing the material into a tape recorder is helpful, especially when reviewing for tests.

50. Offer a set of textbooks for home use. Before the student takes the textbooks home, explain how to locate main ideas and key words and how to use the glossary and appendix. If you have color-coded textbooks, these are excellent for home use.

Books on Tape

Audio books not only benefit the nonreader in the classroom but will benefit other students as well. Most students (young and old) enjoy listening to stories. Often the narratives included on the audio cassettes include special sound effects, music and multiple narrative voices, which help to expand the student's imagination. By listening, students hear examples of fluent reading, phrasing and articulation. The students will acquire pronunciation of new words and often will be exposed to new dialects and accents. For students with reading difficulties, audio books level the playing field and allow the students to enjoy the same literary experiences as others, making "reading" more appealing. Experienced readers and struggling readers can listen to stories that are well beyond their independent reading levels. This helps to expand their listening vocabulary, which eventually transfers to written vocabulary.

51. Check with local organizations for learning disabilities and services for the blind. They often have prerecorded materials available. Recording for the Blind and Dyslexic has both student and school memberships available. This organization records almost 4,000 new texts every year, which include the most popular textbooks. The website is *www.rfbd.org*. Another website worth exploring is *www.school.booksontape.com*, which carries a wide selection of audio books that cover a vast array of topics.

52. Check the school library. If books on tape are not available, provide a "Wish List" of books that you would like to use in your classroom. The local public library also will have material available for checkout.

53. Create a listening center in the classroom with headsets for a minimum of four students. With small groups of students all listening to the same tape, follow-up activities can include individual or small-group activities. The follow-up activities can be grouped by level of difficulty—Level 1 (easy), Level 2 (average) or Level 3 (difficult)—for students to complete individually. Activities also can be developed around the "multiple intelligences" conceived by Howard Gardner. Here is a list of seven multiple intelligences with corresponding activities.

Intelligence	Activity
Visual/Spatial Intelligences Students tend to think in pictures and need to create vivid mental images to retain information. These students enjoy looking at maps, charts, pictures, videos and movies. Skills include: reading, writing, understanding charts and graphs, fixing, designing and interpreting visual images.	Play Pictionary! Each student selects several new vocabulary words from the story. One student draws a picture of a chosen word, while other students guess the word.
Verbal/Linguistic Intelligence Students have a strong ability to use words and language. These students have highly developed auditory skills and generally are good speakers. The student tends to think in words instead of pictures. Skills include: listening, speaking, storytelling, explaining, using humor, understanding the syntax of words, remembering information and analyzing language usage.	Create a new ending to the story!
Logical/Mathematical Students have the ability to use reason, logic and numbers. These students think conceptually in logical and numerical patterns, making connections between pieces of information. Always curious about the world around them, these learners ask lots of questions and like to do experiments. Skills include: problem solving, classifying and categorizing information, working with the abstract, questioning and wondering about natural events and working with mathematical shapes.	Select several characters from the story. Compare and contrast the characters in the story. How are they the same? How are they different?

Bodily/Kinesthetic Intelligence These learners have the ability to control body movements and handle objects skillfully. They express themselves through movement. They have a good sense of balance and eye-hand coordination. Through interacting with the space around them, they are able to remember and process information. Skills include: dancing, physical sports, crafts, acting, miming, using their hands to create and build and expressing emotions through the body.	Partner activity. Select several characters from the story. Role-play a major event.
Musical/Rhythmic These students have the ability to produce and appreciate music. These musically inclined learners think in sounds, rhythms and patterns. They immediately respond to music, either by appreciating or criticizing what they hear. Many of these learners are extremely sensitive to environmental sounds. Skills include: singing, whistling, playing musical instruments, recognizing tonal patterns, remembering melodies and understanding the structure and rhythm of music	Create sound effects to correlate with parts of the story. Select several parts of the story to read into a recorder. Add sound effects and a musical background.
Interpersonal Intelligence These students have the ability to relate to and understand others. They try to see things from another person's point of view in order to understand how the person thinks and feels. They often have an uncanny ability to sense feelings, intentions and motivations. They are great organizers, although they sometimes resort to manipulation. Generally, they try to maintain peace in group settings and encourage cooperation. They use both verbal and nonverbal language to open communication channels with others. Skills include: seeing things from other's perspectives, listening, using empathy, counseling, cooperating with groups, building trust and establishing positive relations with other people.	As a group, list the main characters in the story. List the characteristics of each person in the story. What is the person like? How would changing the attributes of one of the characters change the entire story?
Intrapersonal Intelligence This student has the ability to self-reflect and be aware of his or her inner state of being. These learners understand their inner feelings, dreams, relationships with others and strengths and weaknesses. Skills include: recognizing their own strengths and weaknesses, analyzing themselves, being aware of their inner feelings, desires and dreams, and understanding their role in relationship to others.	Imagine that you are a character in the story. What would you do differently? What would you do the same? Explain why.

54. Create book backpacks for students to checkout. The backpacks may include the book and cassette, with activities and ideas for parents to help their children with reading. Backpack ideas are limited only by your imagination. For instance, you

might create holiday backpacks or topical backpacks (dinosaurs, astronomy, particular sports, just for girls/boys, etc.)

55. The Minnesota Humanities Commission provides a PDF titled "Tips for Reading to Your Children." These tips are reproduced on **Form #42, Tips for Reading with Your Children.** On the website *(www.thinkmhc.org/literacy/tips.htm),* the tips are available in 24 different languages, including English. These tip sheets can be included in the book backpacks mentioned in #54.

Creating Audio Files

Audio files are a wonderful tool for many students, whether or not the students have disabilities. The recordings may be used during the day or at home and also provide support to the student who has been absent. If the goal is simply to listen to the material in place of reading, contact the publisher and ask if the book is available in audio format. For students with disabilities, contact Recording for the Blind and Dyslexic (see Resources section). Audio recordings will need to be created if you would like the material paraphrased or partial text (such as every other page) or only material that focuses on specific objectives recorded. Recording materials is time consuming. Once the initial recordings are made, be sure to make additional copies for grade levels or departments. Keep the original in a safe place.

56. Use the many sources of volunteers available: parents, peers, older students, community group members, drama club or honor society members to assist when making audio files. Make additional copies, label and file for future use.

57. When enlisting volunteers to record, carefully examine the reading quality and reading rate of the volunteer before the tapes are made. If the reader speaks too rapidly, students will not be able to follow along. If the reader reads too slowly, students may not grasp the main idea or, worse yet, may fall asleep.

58. When preparing recordings, have the speaker read in a clear voice. Texts should be read at 120-175 words per minute. Eliminate background noise. Doors slamming, telephones ringing, and muffled voices are sound effects that most likely do not correspond with the textbook materials. These sounds often distract the listener.

59. Begin the recordings with a statement of the title, chapter and section or pages recorded on the tape. Use a consistent labeling system for easy filing.

60. Include study guidelines at the beginning to orient the student to the main points of the section.

61. Include comprehension checkpoints on the tape, such as, "Please stop the tape here and list three uses of coal." When the tape resumes, provide the answer(s). This helps the student be actively involved with the lesson.

62. Provide special textbooks that correspond to the audio file. Place a symbol key in the text that relates to specific parts of the recording. For example, an asterisk may indicate a portion of the text that has been paraphrased. A stop sign may indicate that the student should stop and provide the definition for a word in bold type. Devise your own system.

63. For older students, coordinate the audio file with anticipated assessment questions. At strategic points, ask the student to stop and summarize the information, state the main idea of the paragraph or define the bold-faced vocabulary words, which will appear on the assessment. When the audio file restarts, provide the answer to the question, or provide the student ahead of time with a copy of the questions and answers so the student may self-check.

64. Provide students with an outline of important material to use as a guide when listening. The student can add information to the outline.

65. If discussion questions are included at the end of the audio file, provide page number location clues, or include the answers so the student may immediately self-check the response.

66. Paraphrase the entire text with simplified vocabulary for students who are unable to read. Relate the information to the visuals presented in the textbook.

Reading Comprehension

Before a student begins to read, consider the following general reading strategies. First, the student must have a purpose for reading the material. How many times have you heard a student ask, "Why do we have to read this?" It's up to the teacher to provide that rationale! If the student is unable to see a purpose, it may be hard to become or stay engaged in the material. Provide as much background information as possible so the student is able to build on previous knowledge. Secondly, in order for a student to read and comprehend, the textbook or reading material must be at the student's independent or instructional level of reading. It is important to determine this level when providing independent material. If the material is at the student's independent level, the student will be able to read and comprehend the material easily. When the text is at the student's instructional level, the student will be successful given some previewing and pre-teaching. But if the material is at the student's frustration level, the student will need to have the material read aloud, will need to work in small groups or will need supplemental material and accommodations.

67. Check the level of reading difficulty. Ask the student to read several paragraphs and to paraphrase what was read. Determine whether the reading material is at an independent, instructional or frustration level:

Independent Level. The student reads material easily, does not stumble over words and can retell what was read. The student is able to provide correct answers to comprehension questions when asked.

Instructional Level. The student reads the material but stumbles over some of the words. The student is able to answer comprehension questions about the reading.

Frustration Level. The student struggles with many unknown words when reading. The student stops reading and tries to decode the words, often without success. The student is unable to answer comprehension questions about the reading.

68. Some students may stumble when reading aloud but when allowed to read silently will grasp the main idea and concepts. Therefore, allow students to paraphrase some of the material that was read silently to see if there is a difference.

69. Use visual imagery to increase reading comprehension. Practice this technique with the students. Ask the students to close their eyes while you read short, descriptive passages. Stop frequently and ask the students to create a picture in their minds. For example, if you are reading a simple passage about a child playing in the ocean, ask the students: What do you see? Hear? What can you smell? How does the sky look? What does the child look like? What is the child doing? Practice these skills with the students frequently, and encourage the students to do the same with their individual readings. *The Power of Visual Imagery* by Karen P. Kelly (see Resources section) provides simple techniques for teaching visual imagery to students.

70. Talk about reading with your students. Often poor readers do not realize that good readers struggle at times and have to work at the process. Discuss with the students that even good readers (and adults too) often have to:

    - Sound out unfamiliar words
    - Use the content to sometimes make guesses at unfamiliar words
    - Read passages and paragraphs several times to comprehend
    - Take notes to help recall important facts and information
    - Skim through material to find answers
    - Ask for clarification when they do not understand
    - Spend many hours reading lengthy material

71. When comprehension is difficult, reduce the quantity of material the student must read during one sitting.

72. Provide the student with a list of items that the student will be accountable for when the reading is complete. Include areas that will be on assessments so the student pays special attention to these areas.

73. Have students work in small groups. Each student reads several paragraphs and then paraphrases the important information to the group.

74. Allow the student to tape record the passage and listen to it as often as necessary.

75. Learning to read new words and understand their meanings will help students to increase their comprehension. Teach students how to determine root words, and then teach the students the meanings of common suffixes and prefixes to help them understand the meaning of unknown words. See **Form #43, Common Prefixes,** and **Form #44, Common Suffixes,** for a list of common suffixes and prefixes. These may be reproduced for students to keep in a reference folder.

76. Ask the student to create chapter summaries. The student lists the main idea of the chapter in one or two paragraphs and then includes as many supporting detail sentences as possible, without looking back at the reading material. Students may share their detail statements in a small group. At this time, additional supportive details may be added. **Form #45, Chapter Summary,** may be reproduced for students. The students can create chapter summaries easily on their own, if they like. Simply have them fold a piece of paper in half, then list the main ideas on the left side and list the details on the right side.

	Main Idea		Details
1.		1.	
		2.	
		3.	
		4.	
2.		1.	
		2.	
		3.	
		4.	

77. Use graphic organizers to help the students organize what they have read. There are many types of graphic organizers. For example, students can use **Form #46, Chain of Events Organizer**, to document a chain or sequence of events. **Form #47, Compare and Contrast Organizer,** can be used to compare the various attributes of characters or events in a story. **Form #48, Fact and Opinion,** can be used to sort fact from opinion. **Form #49** and **Form #50, Story Map,** are graphic organizers to organize a story. The forms include the main characters, settings and main events of the story and the conclusion. Students can easily create their own organizers once they see how the concept works.

78. Ask the school to purchase additional textbooks specifically for the purpose of highlighting important information. Color code the student textbook. An example would be to use yellow for the vocabulary words, blue for the definitions and green to highlight topic sentences, facts and important information. If it is not possible to purchase additional textbooks, photocopy or scan the relevant information for the student. The student will be able to write on the copy. If you are scanning large amounts of textbook material, call the publisher to request permission before

copying. Often publishers have both hardcover and consumable versions available, and the consumable books are usually less expensive.

79. Disassemble a classroom textbook and place the individual pages into page protectors. The pages may also be laminated, three-hole punched and placed into a three-ring binder. The student can write directly on the page protector or lamination. Be sure to number the pages as you take the book apart so the pages can easily be reassembled.

80. Illustrate the main idea of the story, and write a short sentence describing it.

81. Furnish a weekly list of both vocabulary and boldface words to the student in advance. Use the words in sentences directly related to the context of the reading instead of in isolation to avoid double meanings. The student can preview or study the vocabulary at home.

Reading Decoding

82. Be sure to review basic letter sounds with the student to check for understanding.

83. If a student has difficulty discriminating between subtle sounds, arrange to have the student's hearing tested.

84. If the student experiences difficulty with decoding, start at letter recognition and advance through the levels to determine where the student is experiencing difficulty. The steps are listed below. Stay at each level until the student is confident and secure.

- Review the sounds. When reviewing or re-teaching the sounds, relate all sounds to words. For example, "The letter *t* stands for *table, toy* and *turkey.*" This provides several concrete examples for the student to relate to visually.

- Once the sounds have been mastered, teach simple families, such as *star, car* and *far* or *man, pan* and *can.* Once the student has mastered the word families, change the initial sounds to make new words. When the student is secure with the initial sounds, the final sound can be changed to make new words. Create individual letter groups on index cards, hole-punch the corner and place the cards on rings so the student is able to practice independently. Additional practice options are to use magnetic letters, or purchase or cut one-inch tiles and create your own letter squares.

- Teach blending skills once the student is confident with the word families. Use the families that the student has already learned. For example, instead of sounding out *m-a-n,* the word family now becomes *m-an.*

- Teach the double vowel sounds, such as *oo, ee, ea,* etc. Create and practice reading words with the double vowel sounds.

- Teach suffixes and prefixes independently, and demonstrate how to add these to a base word to make new words. **Forms #43** and **#44** provide a list of common suffixes and prefixes.

85. If you would like to download some great phonics posters for your wall, go to: *http://www.adrianbruce.com/reading/posters/.* The posters are in full color. Print the poster on 8 ½ x 11 size paper, and students will be able to keep these in their study folders!

86. Allow students who read but may not read on grade level to follow along while others read the material aloud.

87. Often students read a word incorrectly over and over again. When this happens, have the student create a word chart with the difficult words. Some common examples are: *where, were, what, here* and *there.* Divide a piece of paper or notebook page into two columns. Label the columns (1) Word I Read (Said) and (2) Correct Word. **Form #51, My Reading Words,** is a ready-made form for use.

88. Emphasize the root words in unknown words. Highlight the root words, and teach the prefixes and suffixes independently. Create Word Analysis charts. Have the student break the words into the individual word parts. **Form #52, Word Analysis Chart,** can be reproduced for student use. Here's a short example:

Prefix	Base Word	Suffix	Compound word
re	make		
			where + ever
	monitor	ed	

89. Provide a vocabulary list. Read and discuss the words before the student reads the material alone.

90. Provide interesting reading materials with a lower readability level. These books should be high interest to encourage the student to read independently. Encourage the student to read silently every day.

91. Allow additional computer time for drill and practice with phonics.

Teaching Vocabulary

Vocabulary is critical to reading success. The ultimate goal of reading is to learn and comprehend the material, but for those with a limited vocabulary or students who have difficulty remembering new words, this is not as easy as it appears. Incorporate new vocabulary as often as possible. As vocabulary increases, comprehension will naturally increase also. A strong vocabulary will help students in all areas of life, not just academically but socially as well.

For many students, the traditional methods of learning vocabulary may not be effective. Some students will learn by simply looking the word up in the dictionary and writing the word in a sentence. But for others, this will not be the case. They need more exposure to the word and more use of the word. So the tried and true methods will be listed here along with new strategies that can be added to your repertoire of material. In addition, websites are provided that have a vast amount of easily accessed information.

92. Most of the new vocabulary that a student is expected to learn in school will be in the context of the daily reading and writing activities. Furnish a weekly list of both vocabulary and boldface words that the student is expected to learn in advance. Define the words in the context of the text, instead of in isolation to avoid double meanings. The student can use this list to preview upcoming chapters and to study the vocabulary at home.

93. Generate chapter vocabulary lists for textbooks. Include only the definitions relevant to the textbook. Place this information into packets. Don't forget to include the chapter title and page numbers as a heading. The students can use this material at home to assist with their homework assignments, unit previews and test reviews.

94. All vocabulary lists that have been created from classroom textbooks should be provided to the speech and language teachers. This will help the specialists coordinate the language services with the curriculum and give the student additional support.

95. Provide an outline of the main ideas and vocabulary words for each unit. After reading the main topic and the related vocabulary words, ask the student to answer the following questions. What do I already know about the topic? How do the words relate to the topic? What would I like to learn about the topic? List additional words that you may find in this reading section.

96. Review and discuss the vocabulary by creating vocabulary review pages. The following three steps will help the student to recall the vocabulary words. **Form #53, Vocabulary,** can be reproduced for students to use with the following:

    1. Write the vocabulary word and definition.
    2. Create a sentence that relates to the story and uses the vocabulary word.
    3. Create a sentence that does not relate to the story using the word.

97. Teach a new word daily by posting a Word of the Day! Post and discuss the new word, its pronunciation and its meaning. After discussing it, ask the students to use the word as many times as possible throughout the day. The daily word may be teacher or student selected. Some websites that offer this service include:

http://www.wordcentral.com
http://www.superkids.com/aweb/tools/words
http://dictionary.reference.com/wordoftheday

98. Students can participate in free vocabulary puzzles plus hundreds of other activities to enhance vocabulary mastery at Vocabulary University, *www.vocabulary.com*. This site states that it is currently used in over 17,000 schools plus home schools and ESL programs. The site is interactive, and material can also be downloaded for classrooms.

Classroom Activities for Vocabulary Development

99. **Create a thesaurus.** Provide a word list to students and ask them to list as many words as possible that have the same meanings as words on the list. To expand the exercise, ask student to list the antonyms also. Students can also add their personal vocabulary list to create their own thesauruses.

100. **Make a Word Wall with synonyms for overused words.** Students frequently use the same words over and over again. Words such as *said, went* and *good* are three examples of common words used frequently in students' writing. Create a word wall in the classroom by placing large pieces of cardboard on a wall, each with an overused word written on it in large letters. Students can write synonyms for these words on index cards and tack them onto the appropriate word boards. It's best to use index cards so the words can be approved before placing them on the word wall and be removed if incorrect. If a student misspells a word, the index card can easily be taken down and rewritten. This wall reference is valuable for all students.

The following example demonstrates a selection of words that can be used to replace the word *said*. Encourage students to extend their vocabulary and use the new words not only in their writing vocabulary but in their speaking vocabulary.

Word Wall Examples for *Said*

cried out	acknowledged	howled	stated	moaned
declared	murmured	hollered	denied	screamed
exclaimed	cried	shrieked	conceded	bawled
shouted	stated	roared	wailed	yelled
whispered	affirmed	squealed	screeched	groaned

101. **Arrange words by degree.** This activity helps students to compare the various synonyms for specific words in terms of a particular quality. In the following example, words that can replace the word said were listed from quiet to loud. By charting the words, the student can use various degrees of the word to be more descriptive. By changing this simple vocabulary word, the student's vocabulary becomes more meaningful in speaking and writing, and reading comprehension increases as well.

For example, instead of writing, "The man said . . . ," the student inserts one of the following synonyms, which are listed in order from quiet to loud expression: *whispered, murmured, moaned, groaned, exclaimed, cried out, yelled* or *screamed.*

This activity can be used for students at all levels by modifying the number of synonyms the student is required to find.

102. **Play Word Detective.** Students frequently encounter new words when reading. Help students become "word detectives" to determine the meaning of these new words. When encountering new words, ask the students to do the following:

> **Look carefully at the word.** Have you seen or heard it before?

> **Read the sentence omitting the word.** Does the surrounding sentence or paragraph provide a clue? Can you insert a word that would make sense?

> **Study the word.** Can you find a base word, prefix or suffix? What do these word parts mean?

103. **Chart word meaning.** Look up the word in a dictionary or thesaurus. Complete the following activity for the word.

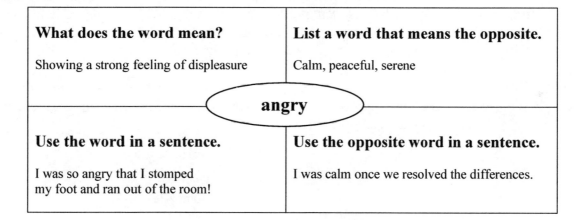

What does the word mean?	**List a word that means the opposite.**
Showing a strong feeling of displeasure	Calm, peaceful, serene

angry

Use the word in a sentence.	**Use the opposite word in a sentence.**
I was so angry that I stomped my foot and ran out of the room!	I was calm once we resolved the differences.

104. **Fill in the Sentence of the Day.** Write a sentence on the board and ask the student to fill in as many responses as possible.

> Today I arrived at school _____. (Responses may include any kind of transportation: on a bus; on a train; in an airplane; in a helicopter; on horseback; on the subway . . .)

> Last month I took a trip to_____ and I _____.
> (Responses may include anywhere and any kind of activity: to Australia

and I went diving in the Great Barrier Reef; to Africa and I went on a safari; to Florida and I swam in the ocean, etc.)

105. **Combine word sets**. Provide the student with specific guidelines, such as "animal plus verb." The student can create any type of sentence (even nonsense ones), as long as the criteria are met. In this example, students are required to write as many verbs as possible showing an action of a dog.

The dog whined.   The dog jumped.   The dog played.

106. **Write descriptors**. Select a picture or an object for the class to view. Have the students write as many words as possible to describe the object. A simple object such as a pen could be described with many different words: long, narrow, pointed, black, white, slim, etc.

107. **Create vocabulary worksheets**. Insert the class vocabulary words, and create individual vocabulary worksheets at *www.edhelper.com/vocabulary.htm*. (Registration is required to fully access this site.)

108. **How many words can you make?** Divide the class into groups. Provide the students with a base word, such as the word *form*. By adding prefixes and suffixes to the word, how many new words can they develop? Does the meaning change? The students may be given copies of **Form #43, Common Prefixes,** and **Form #44, Common Suffixes,** to help generate ideas. For this example, the students may create words such as *formed, reform, inform, formation* and *deform*. Have the groups share their newly created words. Discuss how the prefixes and suffixes can change the meaning of the word.

109. **Create Word Webs.** Have students select a word and create word diagrams, or webs. Word webs can be used not only for vocabulary but for reading, writing and reviewing for tests. Following are examples of Word Webs.

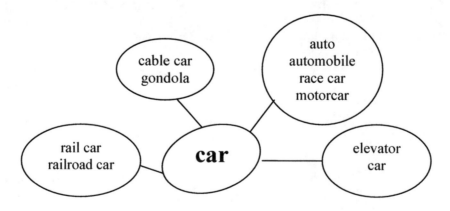

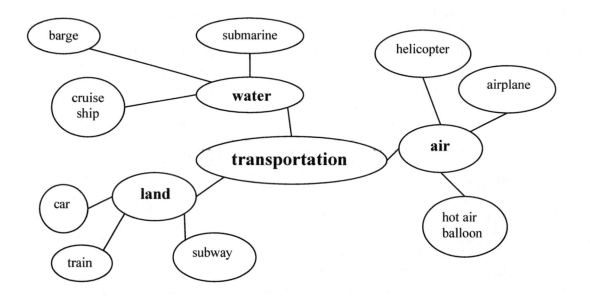

Additional Reading Supports

110. For some students, positioning the textbook at an angle (by using a slant board) will help the student not tire as quickly. A slant board can be created by placing the book on top of a large 3-ring binder (slanted toward the reader) for better viewing (using a non-slip mat to keep the binder in place).

111. For students who are easily distracted, create an index card with a window. The student places the index card over the textbook reading assignment, which will help to block out distracting stimuli. The windows may be created in various sizes, depending on the students' needs. Some students may benefit from viewing only one line of reading text or one math problem at a time, whereas others will benefit from a larger window. The various window card can easily be hole-punched in one corner and stored on a key ring so the student has access to the various sizes at all times.

112. Make photocopies of textbook material that a student must read. The student can use a highlighter to highlight important text. The student will also be able to make notes in the margins, circle key works, note information that is not fully understood, etc.

Tracking Difficulties

Have you ever worked with a student who is continually losing his or her place in the textbook? You may feel as though you are always redirecting the student. If this occurs, the student is probably experiencing difficulty with visual tracking.

113. Partner the student with a peer, and allow the peer to assist the student with visual tracking. Allow students to share a textbook.

114. Give specific instruction as to where the student should begin reading.

115. Highlight alternate lines of the text to help the student keep his or her place.

116. Provide frequent oral location clues (page and paragraph numbers) when reading aloud.

117. Redirect the student by pointing out page and paragraph numbers frequently.

118. Seat the student near the teacher so tracking can be easily monitored. Check frequently to see if the student is in the correct location.

119. Use a bookmark to help the student keep his or her place.

120. Place a horizontal arrow running from the left to the right side of an index card and have the student hold the card so the arrow is pointing to the line he or she is currently reading. Or, have the student hold the card just under the reading line.

121. Cut a window into an index card. This helps the student keep his or her place, because the student can see only a few lines or a small area at a time. Create various sized "windows" in a number of index cards, hole-punch the corner and place the cards on a round key ring. The student will have a collection of window cards to use with various textbooks.

122. Provide a "picture frame" made from construction paper for the student. The student will be able to see several lines of print, yet will be able to block out distracting stimuli.

123. Allow the student to listen to the material and view the pictures, while someone else reads the text aloud.

Hearing Impairments

If there is a student with a mild or severe hearing loss in the classroom, frequently a specialist or consultant for the hearing impaired will provide materials and suggestions to both the general and special educator. If a student has a severe hearing loss, a sign language interpreter is often available to help the student. The specialist provides direct service to the student and supplemental materials to the general and special education teacher. The following suggestions provide additional support for the student with a hearing impairment.

124. Seat the student near the teacher and also positioned so the student is able to see the faces of as many classmates as possible. Desks arranged in a semi-circle are conducive to this. Many students with hearing impairments rely on lip reading. Another option is to provide the student with a swivel chair so the student can see the teacher, classmates and the interpreter.

125. During reading lessons, partner a peer with the student to redirect the student if he loses his place because he is unable to hear what the others are reading aloud. The partner can also redirect the student's attention to the person who is reading aloud.

126. Always use visual signals to secure the student's attention when reading aloud.

127. If the student has stronger hearing in one ear, be sure to seat the student accordingly.

128. Speak and read clearly in a normal tone and at a moderate pace. Ask students in the classroom to also speak clearly and distinctly. There is no need to exaggerate, but it is important to speak a little slower and enunciate words more carefully than usual.

129. Rephrase content areas or questions to make the lesson more easily understood.

130. Provide the student with an outline and vocabulary lists before introducing new material. Encourage the student to preview the information at home before the lesson is presented.

131. Repeat and summarize the information when presented orally.

132. Present vocabulary words in sentences. Many words look similar to lip readers.

133. Use your hands when speaking to help the student better understand the explanation.

Vision Impairments

If a student with a visual impairment is in the classroom, you will consult frequently with a teacher of the visually impaired. This specialist will provide materials and offer suggestions. Oftentimes, enlarged materials are used. If this is the case, additional storage space will be needed, as these materials often will not fit on a traditional bookshelf.

It is important to note that if the student with visual impairments appears to be inattentive or looking around in the classroom, the student may be relying on auditory skills to gain information. Students with visual impairments often experience visual fatigue during classroom assignments.

134. Be sure the classroom is well lit, allowing the student to see more clearly.

135. Keep in mind that the student may become fatigued more quickly that peers.

136. Partner the student with a peer for support, clarification and redirection, if needed.

137. Arrange for a personal reader, if necessary. This person may be a peer, parent volunteer or classroom assistant.

138. Make or obtain age-appropriate magazines and books for the student. Many books and magazines are available on audiotape and in Braille. Contact the National Library Service for the Blind and Physically Handicapped.

139. Order specialized materials, such as enlarged textbooks, magnifiers and closed circuit television and computer software with enlarged fonts and pictures. Another option is to scan and enlarge the material for the student.

140. Provide audiocassettes for the student's textbooks. Create audiocassettes on cassette players that have variable speeds. This will allow the student to increase the speed as the auditory skills become more refined. Contact the local Society for the Blind and become aware of the services they have to offer.

141. Allow extra time for assignment completion. Be aware of the visual fatigue that often occurs during activities requiring continuous use of visual skills. Some possible signs of visual fatigue are red eyes, rubbing of the eyes, laying the head on the desk and squinting.

142. Minimize fatigue by modifying the number and length of the activities when visual concentration is required. Always remember the objective of the lesson. If a student is able to listen to the information or demonstrate knowledge in an alternate format, allow the student to do so.

143. When addressing the student, be sure to verbally call the student by name. Often the student will not see the visual clues.

144. Tape record assignments so the student can replay them as often as needed.

145. When using Braille or new supplemental devices in the classroom, provide training for the entire class, when appropriate. Allow the student to demonstrate to others how to write their names or label various objects in the classroom with Braille. Allow students to try the magnifiers and experiment with the computer programs. They will be excited by the newly acquired knowledge, and the situation becomes a learning experience for all the students.

146. Touch is important for visually impaired students. Provide hands-on experiences whenever possible.

147. Combine visual activities with auditory and motor activities whenever possible. For example, small groups of students can act out stories that have been read in class.

Chapter Four Conclusion

Reading is an important life skill worth supporting in every way possible. This chapter has provided a wide range of ideas for helping students who have difficulties learning to read for one reason or another. Support can take the form of textbook accommodations, reading buddies or groups, color coding, tape recordings, books on tape, outlines, discussion questions, charts, games, forms for organizing, activities based on the multiple intelligences and teacher-created materials such as window cards. Don't forget "high/low" books, phonemic awareness and vocabulary building. The ideas presented here may spark your own creativity and result in even more activities and approaches. Remember to capitalize on your students' strengths and make it as easy and fun as possible for them to learn reading!

Following is a list of 18 reproducible forms that you will find in the Appendix to support your teaching of this skill.

Appendix Forms for Chapter Four

#31	Textbook Accommodations
#32	Textbook Accommodations – 2
#37	The First 50 Instant Words
#38	My Personal Reading List – Genre and Topics
#39	My Personal Reading List
#40	Recommended Reading List
#41	Compare and Contrast – Book / Video
#42	Tips for Reading with Your Children
#43	Common Prefixes
#44	Common Suffixes
#45	Chapter Summary
#46	Chain of Events Organizer
#47	Compare and Contrast Organizer
#48	Fact or Opinion
#49	Story Map
#50	Story Map #2
#51	My Reading Words
#52	Word Analysis Chart
#53	Vocabulary

"Your goal should be out of reach, but not out of sight."

Anita DeFrantz

Notes:

"Limitations live only in our minds. But if we use our imaginations, our possibilities become limitless."

Jamie Paolinetti

Chapter Five

Daily Assignments

Daily assignments often present a problem not only for students with special needs but for many others as well. Students may have difficulty with daily assignments simply because they are unorganized. Some students habitually arrive late to class and miss the instruction. Others tend to "forget" what is needed for class and must return to their lockers and often get sidetracked on the return route. There are students who are unable to prioritize their assignments and may not complete the assignment that is due the next day but may have completed an assignment for the upcoming week. Of course there is always the student who completes the assignment but forgets to bring it back to school. Many of these students are putting forth the effort but are horribly disorganized. It is often assumed students naturally know how to organize, but actually, many students need to be taught these skills and provided with tools. The organizational strategies that work for one student will not necessarily work for another.

> **Chapter Note:**
> On page 95, you will find a complete list of the reproducible forms referred to throughout this chapter. The reproducible forms are located in the Appendix.

Daily assignments should be meaningful. Whenever a daily assignment is given, the purpose of the assignment should be determined. Usually daily assignments are given to verify a student's understanding of a concept presented during class. Some schools require daily homework, and these assignments should be given with care. The student who experiences difficulty in school often has so much homework that careful consideration should be given to the purpose of the assignment.

Although it is customary to ask the student to respond in a written format, this is not always possible for students with disabilities. Some students are overwhelmed, which results in frustration and acting out on the part of the student. If this is the case, the assignment may need to be adapted. Therefore, it is important to always determine the objective of the assignment and adapt the assignment according to the student's needs.

An important question that arises when discussing inclusive education is, "How will the student receive remedial support when the student is included in the classroom the entire day?" When students are working on daily assignments, it is an optimum time for the special needs student to receive direct instruction from the special education teacher or reteaching from the paraprofessional. As mentioned previously, often daily seatwork activities (and homework) are designed to reinforce previously taught skills or to check for understanding of a specific skill. Determine the appropriateness of the activity. Ask, "Is this beneficial to the student?" and "Is it important for the student to complete the entire assignment?" "Can the student complete the assignment orally so he or she can move on to an area where additional support is needed?" This may be an optimum time to provide supplemental materials or to reinforce areas where the student experiences difficulty. If other students in the classroom would also benefit from reteaching or reinforcement, consider including these students in the group.

This section includes ideas for adaptations of daily assignments and some ways to help organize the student. Additional adaptations can be found under specific subject areas. **Form #33, Daily Assignments,** can be reproduced to document accommodations for specific students.

Classroom Supports

148. Assign a Study Buddy to help students organize material and turn in assignments or to gather material at the end of the class period and help in any area that is appropriate. Study Buddies can be assigned to students daily, weekly or monthly. **Form #54, Study Buddies**, includes some templates that can be printed for use. These forms may also be used for students who need a Buddy assigned to help with transitions, recess, lunch, etc.

149. Help students be prepared. Students frequently lose valuable class time and miss important information because the student is unprepared and must return to the locker to retrieve material. Provide the list of materials that a student must have in class. **Form #55, Required Class Material,** in the Appendix can be reproduced and given to students.

150. Modify the length of the assignment. Allow the student to complete the even or odd problems. If the student is able to demonstrate mastery by completing only a portion of the assignment, allow the student to work on other assignments where additional time is needed or the student struggles. Break the assignment into segments, and allow the student to complete the assignment over a period of several days.

151. Provide a cover sheet for long assignments. Oftentimes a long assignment seems so overwhelming the student feels frustrated before beginning. Sometimes if the assignment is divided into sections, the student does not feel so overwhelmed.

152. Pair students so one student can read aloud while another student writes the response. If a student has difficulty with both reading and writing, the student can listen and contribute responses orally, as a student will be appointed to write the group answers.

153. Use cooperative groups. The groups and roles can be changed frequently. When using cooperative groups, each member is responsible for an assigned role and a fair share of the group activity. Team members learn to rely on one another and work together for a positive outcome, while practicing leadership, communication and decision-making skills. Students can be grouped so all students can participate. For a student with severe difficulties, participation may be limited to being the timekeeper, passing out materials to the group and putting away supplies. **Form #56, Cooperative Groups,** is a checklist that can be used to define the student's role in a group. It contains multiple items that may or may not be part of each cooperative group.

154. Allow the student to answer verbally into a tape recorder. The material can be transcribed at a later time. This works especially well for the student who has difficulty with fine motor coordination but is able to read and understand the material.

155. If the assignment permits, provide the student with a photocopy. Allow the student to highlight, underline or fill in the blank on the copy instead of copying the entire paragraph, list of sentences or page of math problems.

156. Rewrite materials at an appropriate reading level, or provide a parallel activity for the same skill.

157. Permit a partner to write the student's response. The partner responsible for recording the student's response must be aware that he or she is to transcribe the student's exact words and not elaborate or interject any personal answers or views.

158. Allow the student to respond orally. Oftentimes, material can be summarized and related questions answered within several minutes. By permitting the student to complete some assignments orally, the student has more time to produce quality results with the remainder of the daily assignments. This is appropriate for the student who is continually behind the class with daily assignments.

159. Provide additional drill and practice sessions for the student. Work towards mastery of the skill. Monitor and adjust the final outcome, if necessary.

160. Allow additional time for completion of assignments. The student may not be able to complete the entire assignment during one class period.

161. When appropriate, allow the student to illustrate the answer instead of responding in a written format.

162. Create supplementary materials that coincide with the text at an easier readability level. Many teachers' guides include blackline masters for various levels. Often supplemental materials developed for students with English as a second language are appropriate for the student with special needs.

163. Supply the student with a pad of sticky notes. The student can write incomplete assignments on separate notes. When an assignment is completed, the student throws the note away. If the assignment is not completed during the school day, the student places the note in the assignment book at the end of the class.

164. Provide parallel activities at an appropriate level. For example, if the objective is to locate nouns, use the student's reading text and ask the student to write the nouns from the story. If the student is unable to read, have the student locate objects in the classroom that are nouns.

165. Develop written contracts for curriculum units. These contracts can be used year after year, as projects on the contract can include very simple to complex activities that will meet all the students' needs. Those who are more advanced can choose to complete as many of the projects as they wish. The same contract can be used to provide projects for students who need additional time and less complexity. See **Form #57, World War II Supplemental Project Sheet**, for a sample contract with instructions.

166. Allow the student to use a computer, word processor or calculator to complete required work.

167. Maintain a Student Helper Directory in the classroom. This is a general log with one sheet per subject area. For example, the student who loves to read can sign up to be a reading helper, a student who is good with numbers can sign up to be a math helper and so forth. Include subject areas such as art, physical education, media and music. Staple the sheets together and ask students to sign up to be Student Helpers. All students in the class can access the list if they need additional support in a specific area.

Organizational Supports

Student organization is very important, and it is often overlooked. Some students need to be taught to organize. This section provides some organizational worksheets for students to use with daily assignments. For additional information, see Chapter 9, Organizational Skills, which covers student, teacher and classroom organization.

168. Provide students with a list of required materials. **Form #55, Required Class Materials**, is a blank form for students to list the materials. If the student still forgets and needs to borrow items such as markers, pencils, rulers, etc., require the

student to provide an ID card, driver's license, cell phone or something else of value in exchange for the item's safe return.

169. It is important to hold the student accountable for all assignments, including those that have been modified. **Form #58, Incomplete Class Assignments,** includes three different forms that can be filled out if the student does not complete the daily assignments.

170. Provide an assignment sheet to help students organize and prioritize daily assignments. Include due dates! Be sure the student understands the difference between *do* and *due!* If parents are participating with a home/school assignment book, it is important that the student also have the correct spelling of these two words. **Form #59, Assignment Sheet,** and **Form #60, Daily Assignments,** are two that can be used daily or weekly, depending upon the student and the amount of homework assigned. The student can easily check off the assignment as it is completed. **Form #61, Daily Homework Log,** is another organizer, which may work better for some students. If all work is completed at the end of the day, the student may throw away the Daily Homework Log. If the assignments are not complete, it can be three-hole punched and placed into a binder or a homework folder.

171. Discuss with the class how to prioritize daily assignments. Incomplete daily assignments may be transferred to **Form #62, Priority Checklist,** in order of priority to help the student budget time and complete assignments on time.

172. Have all students in the classroom document their after-school time! **Form #63, Weekly Planner,** can be used for all students to help better organize their personal time. Instruct students to fill in required after-school activities first, such as after-school sports, music classes, religion classes, dinner, etc. Once these items are entered, ask students to block out a specified amount of time (depending upon the grade level) for a Study Block. Once this block is scheduled, the student may include time for favorite television programs, telephone chat time, computer time, etc. Have students try the schedule for one week. Discuss the results with them. Most students will find they have ample time to complete homework if they follow the schedule.

Strategies for Students with Significant Delays

Some students need additional materials to help with daily assignments. Some may need to improve fine or large motor skills, others may need practice with visual motor skills or simply help staying in their seats. Listed here are some strategies and items available that may provide help for these students. The majority of the commercial items can be purchased from Pocket Full of Therapy at *www.pfot.com.*

173. Provide alternative activities to pencil and paper tasks to help maintain the student's motivation. Allow the student to work with play dough, clay, Wikki-Stix, paints, dry erase boards, etc.

174. Provide commercial templates and tracers to practice letter and number formation.

175. For fine motor practice, use simple drawings from younger children's coloring books or online by placing the picture in a page protector so the student can trace it.

176. Create individual worksheets on the computer and increase the font size.

177. Create simple activity boxes that the student can be responsible to retrieve and work on alone. Activity boxes can easily be made from items found in the home. For example, during a written language class, the student could work from a "Learn the Alphabet" Activity Box. The box would include items that correspond to the student's IEP. For example, if the student's goal is to practice the alphabet, the activity box might include letter tiles for the student to arrange in alphabetical order and connect-the-dots letters for the student to complete and color. If the student's goal is to recognize letters, the student may be required to match upper- and lowercase letters or complete A, B, C puzzles. The book *Hands-On Activities for Exceptional Children* by Beverly Thorne, listed in the Resources section, includes many simple suggestions for activity boxes. **Form #64, Curriculum Modifications,** can be used to keep track of modified supplemental activities for students. Following is an example of this modification form used with an ABC Activity Box.

Date of Implementation: January 10, 2010
IEP Goal: The student will recognize the letters of the alphabet.

Time Block	Date and Activity	Student Expectations	Additional Information and Notes
2:00 – 3:00 daily	01/10/2010 **ABC Activity Box.** Student will match upper- and lowercase letters by completing various activities such as matching, puzzles and tracing.	To complete the daily activity and raise a hand for teacher or peer to check assignment	**ABC Activity Box** provided by Special Education Teacher or peer to monitor and document results 01/10 Student correctly matched upper- and lowercase vowels.
	01/11 **ABC Activity Box.** Continue with activity. Add ABC puzzle.	Same	01/11 Student was off task; did not complete puzzle. Student colored picture for ABC book.
	01/12 Continue with ABC order of letter tiles and puzzle.	Same	1/12 A peer helper worked with the student and helped student to verbally state the names of the letters of the alphabet. Peer helped the student arrange the letter tiles in ABC order and provided encouragement with the puzzle.

Adaptive Materials

178. Be sure that the student is positioned correctly, with feet flat on the floor and elbows able to rest on the table.

179. Classroom seat cushions are available for the "antsy" student. These cushions help to center the student's hips by providing a small, padded, physical well. This is appropriate for students who always sit on the edge of their seats or on the corner with their feet extended into the aisle.

180. Use a slant board for the student's books, or create one with a large, three-ring binder. A non-slip mat under the binder will keep the binder from moving.

181. Some students benefit from the use of a bookstand. Some of the new bookstands are collapsible for easy storage. If purchasing bookstands, be sure to look for the ones that adapt to all sizes of books, from novels to textbooks.

182. Provide pencil grips, or place masking tape on writing utensils for the student who has difficulty grasping the pen or pencil correctly. Many different types of grips are available for purchase. Here is a list of some items that may be useful. The occupational therapist will have a list of materials for students who receive service, but these items may benefit other students as well.

> **Fits Write Pen** – This pen cradles the index finger like a hammock, providing support to the whole hand.

> **Flex Grip** – This is often referred to as the porcupine grip, as it has hundreds of soft, tiny massaging bristles. It can also be rubbed between the palms for students who need sensory stimulation.

> **Jumbo Triangle Crayons** – The triangular shape fosters a correct, three-point writing grasp for students.

> **Spongy Pencil Grips** – These fit standard pencils and pens. They are perfect for the student who squeezes too hard or needs a visual or tactile cue as to where to place fingers.

> **Thick and Thin Pencil Grips** – These are thickly padded grips with thicker ridges to help with grasping.

Chapter Five Conclusion

For some students, just getting through daily assignments can be a trial. With various types of support, these students can succeed and thus be encouraged to learn more. This chapter points out the importance of making sure that assignments are meaningful to the student. It also provides suggestions for support from other students, such as using Study Buddies, Student Helpers and a group format when appropriate. It points out ways to modify or adapt assignments so they aren't overwhelming and ways to help students organize themselves with lists, assignment sheets, planners, priority checklists and homework logs. For students with significant delays, ideas are presented to support fine motor coordination and enhance learning by using manipulative materials. Suggestions are also provided for physical support, such as special pillows, writing grips and bookstands. Any one or a combination of these tips and adaptations may give a student the extra help that makes a significant difference.

Following is a list of 12 Appendix forms that are valuable assets in supporting students with daily assignments and organization.

Appendix Forms for Chapter Five

#33	Daily Assignments
#54	Study Buddies
#55	Required Class Materials
#56	Cooperative Groups
#57	World War II Supplemental Project Sheet (Example)
#58	Incomplete Assignments
#59	Assignment Sheet
#60	Daily Assignments
#61	Daily Homework Log
#62	Priority Checklist
#63	Weekly Planner
#64	Curriculum Modifications

"The impossible is often the untried."

Jim Goodman

Notes:

_____

_____

_____

_____

_____

_____

_____

_____

_____

_____

_____

_____

_____

"Rough diamonds may sometimes be mistaken for worthless pebbles."

Sir Thomas Browne

Chapter Six

Written Language

Written language incorporates a wide range of skills. Students may experience difficulty for a variety of reasons. Some students are unable to transfer their ideas into a written format. Others have trouble with grammar, syntax or mechanics. A third group may experience difficulty due to language limitations or the ability to process language.

For some students, writing is so laborious, you may need to bypass the writing process altogether. For this student, the mode of output often will be different than the other students in the class. In this situation, the student may need a "buddy" to take notes and transcribe answers, projects may need to be presented orally, recorded or perhaps videotaped, and written exams may need to be followed up with a short oral exam or interview.

> **Chapter Note:**
> On page 114, you will find a complete list of the reproducible forms referred to throughout this chapter. The reproducible forms are located in the Appendix.

Encouraging Students to Write

"I have a student who simply refuses to write," or "I have a student who sits and just stares at the paper. The student refuses to even attempt to write." These concerns are heard frequently among educators. There may be times when a student is so frustrated with writing because language processing is so difficult that he or she simply refuses to write. However, all students must be given the opportunity to write and encouraged to do so.

Written language is dependent on the student having adequate ability to produce and process oral language. For some students it is important increase the student's oral language skill before expecting the student to write. The book *Let's Learn About Language* listed in the Resource Section is a resource that includes an abundance of oral language activities that can be used with students basis. The book covers a wide range of activities including word meanings, words in groups, opposites, synonyms, analogies, same and different, riddles, analogies and more. There are three levels of difficulty therefore the activities can easily be differentiated to meet the needs of all students. The flexibility of the book allows for the activities to be completed orally but easily can be expanded for written activity also.

Generating Ideas

Encourage all forms of writing, including using the computer. Students should be given opportunities to write on a daily basis.

183. Journaling is a form of writing that can be completed daily and provides some structure for students who have difficulty generating ideas. Students who are unable to write may draw pictures or copy sentences. The teacher writes the assignment on the board, and students start right in as soon as they arrive.

   Question of the day! (descriptions): I have recently arrived to the United States, and I see that today is Groundhog Day. What is that?

   Topic (vocabulary builder): Tell me as much as you can about the ocean. Use your five senses! How does it look, smell, taste, feel and sound?

   Curriculum based (recall): Yesterday we learned the parts of an insect. Write as much as you can recall about the topic, and make a drawing in your journal.

   Question and Answer (sentence structure): Yesterday after school I went to the grocery store to buy milk and bread, to the dry cleaners to pick up some clothes and to the bakery to buy a birthday cake for my son's birthday. By the time I arrived home, it was 7:00! What did you do after school yesterday? List at least three things.

   Directions (sequencing): Explain to me how to make a peanut butter and jelly sandwich. Write the directions as a narrative, or create a list of the steps.

   Pictures: Here is a picture of some cloud formations. As you look at the picture, what do you see? Tell me!

   Major Event: Often students arrive to school after a weather event such as a snowstorm, tornado, hurricane, etc., and they want to share their experiences right away. Instead of talking about them, have the students write them down and then share.

184. Keep a box of old photographs, pictures from magazines and animal or nature pictures in the classroom. Ask the student to select a picture and spend several minutes listing words that describe the picture.

185. Ask the student to bring a favorite photograph. It may be a picture of a vacation, a party, an important event or an important person in the student's life. Since the student has background information about the photo, brainstorm with the student to

create a list of corresponding words. This "word bank" can be used by the student while writing. The word bank will often include vocabulary words which the student normally does not use due to the fact the student does not know how to write the word correctly.

186. Topical writing can be used for all students at all levels. Following are charts of three different levels of topical writing. Chart #1 is appropriate for students just beginning to write. Students in the emerging stage may be required to write only one sentence per day. The student can add an additional sentence each following day for a week. For example, Chart #1 illustrates the topic of "My Dog."

My Dog

Chart #1

Monday	I have a dog.
Tuesday	My dog is a black lab.
Wednesday	Her name is Bean.
Thursday	She loves to run and eat!
Friday	She sleeps with me at night.

The next two charts can be used for more advanced students. In Chart #2, the student is asked to select a topic and write descriptors relating to the topic. An alternative is for the student to write only the topic on the chart and to create a small booklet to write the descriptors.

Food

Chart #2

A apple	B banana	C corn	D donuts	E eggs	F fish
round	long	kernels			
red	yellow	sweet			
green	firm	yellow			
juicy	peeling	cob			

For more advanced students, provide a Topic Grid. In Chart #3 is a topical science chart. The student fills in the grid with words related to science and writes several sentences related to each word.

Science

Chart #3

A amphibians	B blood cells	C clouds	D dinosaurs	E environment	F fossils

Form #65, Alphabetical Grid Chart, can be reproduced for students and used with the activities shown on Charts 2 and 3.

187. **Free Choice Writing Grid.** Provide students with a writing grid. Distribute the grid to all students. Students may fill in the grid with various subjects they would like to write about. This allows the students choices for writing and can be easily created to meet the needs of all students. In the following grid, small pictures are inserted, so the student was required to include an activity related to music, a book from class and some sort of letter or communication. The teacher can easily incorporate several writing activities to meet curriculum goals, if desired.

Free Choice Writing

	Write a letter to a relative or friend who lives far away.	
Write a song and put it to music!		
		Write a book review about a book you have read.

Pre-writing Stage

With some students, there is a large discrepancy between the student's ability to write and the writing ability of his or her peers. Some students may be in a pre-writing stage. If the student is in a pre-writing stage, parallel or supplemental activities can be provided according to the student's Individualized Education Plan.

188. Allow the student to dictate the story to you, while an adult writes. The student can practice reading the story aloud and tracing the letters of individual words.

189. Use the student's personal vocabulary to learn to read new words.

   1. Ask the student to dictate a simple sentence.

   2. Provide a sentence strip, and have the student write the words (or trace them) onto the sentence strip.

3. Read the sentence aloud with the student until all words have been mastered.

4. Cut the sentence apart into individual words.

5. Mix the words up and ask the student to reconstruct the sentence.

190. Use the student's personal vocabulary to combine reading, written language and spelling. Follow these simple steps:Ask the student to dictate a simple story to an adult.

    1. Divide the story into individual sentences.

    2. Ask the student to copy one sentence onto each individual sentence strip.

    3. Organize the sentence strips into the final story.

    4. Once complete, the student can practice reading the story aloud. If you feel the student simply has memorized the story, rearrange the sentence strips and ask the student to read the story again.

    5. Once the student has mastered the story, have the student record the story on tape so he or she can read along.

    6. The individual story words can also be incorporated into a spelling list.

191. Purchase specialized paper for students to practice writing. Various types of specialized paper are available: paper with raised lines, paper with multicolored lines and paper in many different widths. A good online source for these materials is Therapro at *www.theraproducts.com*. **Form #66, Skip-a-Line Paper,** is appropriate for many students. If you have only one student who needs this type of paper, it may be easier and less expensive to reproduce it instead of purchasing the paper.

192. Write a question to the student, and ask the student to respond verbally. Write the question and the student's response in pencil. Ask the student to trace the response with a felt tip pen and illustrate it. If the student needs additional practice with letter formation, ask the student to trace the words with colored pencils. If you would like the student to trace each word twice, provide two different-colored pencils and so forth.

193. Provide the student with a labyrinth design, and ask the student to trace the labyrinth pathway from the outer edge into the center and back again with a colored pencil or marker. The student may draw a picture in the middle, if desired. This activity helps improve concentration and fine motor coordination, which are necessary for writing.

194. Provide the student with a watercolor brush, paint and paper, and give the student a picture of a simple, traditional Japanese character that was created with a brush. Tell the student what the character means, and perhaps give a little background on Japanese characters and brush painting. You may want to have the student begin by using water instead of paint to get used to the brush. Painting characters can be fun and offers practice in using a utensil that is held like a pencil or pen. If copying the character is too difficult, tell the student to make one up—or try painting a few letters of our alphabet. This activity and the previous one were adapted from the book *Creating Balance in Children: Activities to Optimize Learning and Behavior*, listed in the Resources section.

195. Have the student practice copying material from the board, the overhead or a model onto paper. For students with a large discrepancy in academics, the final outcome is often different than that of peers. In this situation, the outcome may be a handwriting goal instead of the curriculum goal set for the other students in the classroom.

196. In place of writing the response, ask the student to illustrate it.

197. When working on writing numbers, letters and shapes, provide multiple models for the student to trace before asking the student to create them freehand.

198. Use multi-sensory materials to develop fine motor coordination. Use clay, sand trays, pudding, shaving cream, tracers and templates to create letters and numbers. Some students will need assistance and will need an adult to provide prompts. If a paraprofessional or an adult volunteer is available, he or she may need to give verbal prompts or gently guide the student's hand during the initial stages.

199. Allow the student to work on dot-to-dot pictures. Use both A, B, C and 1, 2, 3 pictures. The following websites have free coloring materials plus much more that you will be able to use as supplemental student material. Some sites require membership, but they also have material that can be downloaded without a membership.

   Resources for Christian Teachers has an excellent website that includes a large amount of free materials and links to hundreds of sites. This site can be used for all subject/curriculum areas: *www.teacherhelp.org/color3.htm.*

   Another great site for material is *www.abcteach.com.* The site offers 5,000 free printable pages and worksheets and 12,000 worksheets for an annual membership fee of $35 (as of this printing).

   The site *www.edHelper.com* has curriculum materials, theme units, puzzles and other classroom helpers for a basic subscription of $19.99 per year and an "everything" subscription of $39.98 (as of this printing).

Disney offers online games and activities at:
http://disney.go.com/disneychannel/playhouse/bop/bop_letters.html

200. Use the written language block to develop fine motor skills. Incorporate activities that are not paper/pencil tasks, such as:

Play dough or Plastaline modeling clay activities

- Roll the modeling material into balls in the palms of the hands.
- Use a pincher and create tiny play dough "beads."
- Make sculptures by placing the play dough beads onto toothpicks.
- Pick up small pieces of the modeling material with tweezers.

Additional fine motor activities

- Provide pages of stickers, where the student needs to peel the sticker from the background paper and affix them to another page.
- Create pegboard designs.
- Practice with sewing cards.
- Use scissors to cut pictures from old magazines.
- Water classroom plants with a spray bottle.
- String beads, pasta, life savers or Cheerios.

201. For those who are unable to write, keep a selection of old magazines and catalogs in the classroom. Provide the student with a specific topic related to the curriculum. Topics can be varied depending upon the ability level of the student. Simple topics may include food, clothing, colors or plants. The student looks for pictures in magazines related to the topic, creates a collage and turns it into a topical list of new vocabulary words. More complex topics might include the weather, products made of wood, items that require electricity to run or mammals. Have the student work on the following activity:

1. Select a topic. (plants)
2. Cut out pictures pertaining to the topic. (house plant, tree, flowers)
3. Paste the cutout pictures onto a large sheet of construction paper.
4. Label the pictures.
5. Use the topic for a header and create a word list.
6. This list of words may also be used for vocabulary activities and to generate sentences.

202. If the student is unable to write, the paraprofessional or another adult can write the student's responses. The student may trace the response with multicolored pencils, crayons or fine tip markers. For motivation, add variety to the student assignment. Vary the size, shape, texture and color of the paper, or use a small chalkboard.

Emerging Writers

203. If the student is unable to write a sentence, ask the student to write descriptive words or illustrate the idea. The words can be combined into simple sentences at a later time.

204. Language Sequence Cards are available in three- and six-step sequences. These can be purchased, or you can create your own. In the following "Build a Snowman" drawing, verbally discuss the three pictures with the student. Next, ask the student to place the words in correct order. Once complete, ask the student to dictate a sentence for each picture. The adult or student can write the sentences on separate sentence strips to create a simple story.

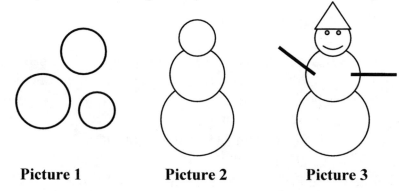

| **Picture 1** | **Picture 2** | **Picture 3** |

If this process is too difficult, ask the student to dictate only one sentence, beginning with Picture #3 and working backwards. This will help the student move from a concrete picture (the finished snowman) to the more abstract. More advanced students will be able to complete this on their own.

205. Provide specific directions for the student when writing. Write a sentence or two to help the student get started. Gradually decrease the structure as the student becomes more confident in his or her ability to write. Some students may require a Story Frame, which allows them to fill in the blanks. See **Form #67, Story Frame,** for an example.

206. Provide Story Starters for students. Discuss various types of sentences that could be used as story starters. Ask each student to provide one. Write each sentence on an individual Popsicle stick or tongue depressor, and place the sticks in a decorated Story Starter Can. If a student is unable to generate an idea, the student may select a stick from the Story Starter Can to get started. To add variety, create three different story cans. Label the containers: #1 Story Starters, #2 Detail Sentences and #3 Ending Sentences. More advanced students can select 1, 2, or 3 sticks to create a story. **Form #68, Story Starters,** includes some samples of story starters that can be used.

207. Create word banks. Ask the student to select a familiar topic. Generate a specific word bank, and allow the student to write about the same topic for several days. Another option is to assemble a small group of students to work together. The group can brainstorm for three to five minutes. The word bank can be provided to all students in the group. The students may help each other with the structure, grammar and spelling. Vary the group of students.

208. When the student is able to generate ideas, help the student develop an outline of the story or topic. The student can follow the outline to sequence thoughts and organize the ideas.

209. Have the students write short poems, such as Haiku, to encourage writing. Haiku poems are easy to write and no rhyming is required, so most students find them enjoyable. (Haiku is three lines of five, seven and five syllables, respectively.) If the syllable concept is too difficult for the student, have the student write three lines, counting words instead of syllables.

210. Provide a picture or photo, and ask the student to write descriptive words about the object. Ask the student to look up the words in a thesaurus and add additional descriptors.

211. Partner with another classroom and send Pal Notes between the classes. Instead of the students signing their names, each student can be assigned a number and remain anonymous.

212. Allow peers to work together to write a story. It allows students to share ideas, and students who have difficulty writing can share the process with another.

213. Create Chain Stories. The first student writes the introductory sentence and passes it to the next student. The second student adds a sentence and passes it on.

214. Look for opportunities to encourage students to write. Older students can practice preparing job applications, write book reviews and create vacation and travel brochures. Students may also enjoy writing letters and jokes and designing comic books.

215. Create a class newspaper. Students can write articles, create cartoons and write book reviews. Include an "ask the student" section, where students ask questions and students in the class provide the answers. Sections on trivia or "advice" columns are also ways that encourage students to write.

The Writing Process

Written language is difficult for many students in the classroom, but especially for those with special needs. Spelling, grammar, mechanics, organization, punctuation, sentence structure, sequence and subject-verb agreement are only a few of the complexities involved in a sentence, paragraph and short story. Students need direct instruction and a great deal of guided practice to become proficient writers.

216. Post reference charts and various lists throughout the classroom as reminders. Some examples of helpful charts and lists include: manuscript and cursive alphabets, commonly misspelled words, steps in the writing process (pre-writing, composition, response, revision, editing and final product), transition words, capitalized words, abbreviations, contractions and a model of the expected standards for written daily assignments. Most of these posters can be purchased, or create your own!

217. Adrian Bruce has a beautiful set of posters that can be downloaded and printed free. (Donations are accepted). The phonetic posters are perfect for students who experience difficulty remembering the double vowel sounds and blends. Posters are available for the following sounds: *ight, ck, oa, ea, ou, ow, all, ch, wh, ear, sh* and *th.* All posters are in full color. Print these posters in 8 ½ x 11 size and students can have their own sets! Small samples are on the next page. The website to obtain these posters and other materials such as reading games is *www.adrianbruce.com.*

218. Determine the outcome of the lesson. If students are working on vocabulary and idea development, avoid excessive corrections in the mechanical aspects of writing so the student does not become discouraged with the process. When the emphasis is placed on mechanics and spelling, many students will play safe. Some will not experiment with new words, others will write far less for fear of making mistakes, and still other students will not write anything.

219. Help students organize their ideas before writing. Provide students with a selection of reference organizers to choose from. Several types of graphic organizers and their uses are listed in the following strategies.

220. Venn diagrams are frequently used to compare and contrast two or more characters, people or events. To create a simple Venn diagram, the student draws two or three overlapping circles in the center of the paper. The similarities between the topics are placed in the space where the circles overlap. The student uses the outside portion of each circle to list the contrasting information. To compare three stories or events, three circles may be used. Use 11" x 17" paper when comparing more than two, so students have ample room to write.

221. Demonstrate how to use mapping skills. A "map" should include the key ideas and words for the main topic. Mapping helps the student to visualize the relationship between the topic and the paragraphs of the story. A topic map is simple to create. To illustrate, the topic of Dogs will be used. In the center of an 8 ½" x 11" paper, write the word DOG. Now fold the paper into quarter sections. In each of the four sections, a word is written that pertains to some aspect of the DOG. Subtopics may include: feeding, exercising, grooming and training. In each of the four sections, list words and phrases that pertain to the individual subtopic. When the mapping exercise is complete, the student creates an introduction, uses the four individual subtopics to write the paragraphs and adds a closing paragraph. The story is completely organized for the student.

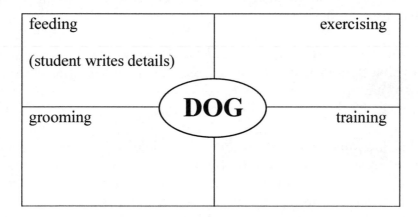

222. Charts are also used to compare and contrast ideas. To compare only one characteristic, students can simply fold a piece of paper and use one column to list the similarities and another to list the differences. Students may create Venn diagrams to compare and contrast two or more items. **Form #68, Compare and Contrast,** in the Appendix can be used to list an attribute and compare it to three items.

223. Timelines are appropriate for students to organize ideas in chronological order. Have students create timelines of their own lives. At the website Our Time Lines *(www.ourtimelines.com/create_tl_2c.html),* students can create custom timelines for historical events. This site is appropriate for middle school and high school students.

My Personal Timeline

2000	2001	2002	2003	2005	2006
I was born on Feb 6.	Sister was born Nov. 19.	We got a puppy!	We moved to Florida.	We went to Disney World.	I started kindergarten.

Historic Natural Events

2001	2002	2003	2004	2005	2006
Earthquake Gujarat, India 20,000 deaths		Earthquake Iran 28,000 deaths	Earthquake/Tsunami Indian Ocean 290,000 deaths	Hurricanes Katrina & Rita devastate New Orleans.	

224. Create storylines before beginning to write. Ask students to think about the following questions to create an organized storyline:

> Who is the main character?
> Who are the secondary characters in the story?
> What does the main character want to do in the story?
> What happens when the main character does this?
> How does the story end?

These simple questions help students to organize their thoughts and develop the basic outline for the story.

225. Story maps are located in the Appendix. These story maps may be used to prepare for writing a story and also can be used after reading a story to help the student organize information. **Forms #69** and **#70, Story Maps,** may be reproduced to help students generate ideas before writing.

226. Explain the importance of a beginning, middle and end in each paragraph. Teach students how to incorporate transition words when writing paragraphs. For the younger students, begin with simple transition words, such as *first, next, then, last* or *finally,* when writing paragraphs. It will help the students sequence their thoughts. **Form #72, Transition Words and Phrases,** is a list of the most common transition words and phrases. Use these words to create a wall poster with the words and phrases that are most appropriate for your grade level, or reproduce it for students to include in their study folders. Space is provided for students to include additional words.

227. Practice the use of transition words by asking students to teach a peer or small group how to do something. At the elementary level, it may be as simple as how to make a sandwich, lace a pair of tennis shoes or introduce an adult. At the secondary level, the student may want to share an area of expertise, such as how to shoot a basket, apply makeup, set a table correctly or use a video camera.

228. Provide plenty of practice editing. Some teachers do this effectively by placing a "Sentence of the Day" on the board. Students immediately copy the sentence upon entering the classroom (either in the morning or after lunch) and edit the sentence. The results are discussed as a group. This simple activity takes less than five minutes a day and provides good practice.

    Example: susan and john quickly ran into the white house

    Correction: <u>S</u>usan and <u>J</u>ohn quickly ran into the (<u>W</u>hite <u>H</u>ouse) or (white house).

    In this situation, "white house" may be lowercase or uppercase, depending upon whether the student interprets it as a house that is white in color or the home of the president of the United States. Each example can be discussed.

229. Periodically, edit a story with the class. Create a transparency of a student's story (name omitted), or create your own story. Work as a group to edit the story, discussing the corresponding rules.

230. Teach students to proofread and edit their own work. Provide a simple proofreading checklist for individual assignments, or post a proofreading checklist on a wall chart. Individual checklists are appropriate for students with IEPs, as they can be adapted to the students' goals. Depending upon a student's grade level, some or all of the following may be included: capitalization, punctuation, misspelled words, margins, paragraph indentation, sentence sense and descriptive words. Whether using an individual chart or a classroom chart, students should be taught to look through the entire story, checking for one item at a time for final edits. For example, at the final edit, the student should read the entire paper and edit the paper for capital letters. When complete, the student may cross capitalization off the form. Next, the student reads the entire paper and edits for punctuation, etc. The student continues until all aspects of the entire paper are corrected. **Form #73, Proofreading Checklist,** is a simple version, and **Form #74, Proofreading Checklist-2**, is for the more advanced student.

231. The SPACE strategy may be used as an error monitoring strategy when writing. Post this strategy in your classroom. The acronym SPACE stands for the following:

    <u>S</u>pelling
    <u>P</u>unctuation
    <u>A</u>ppearance
    <u>C</u>apitalization
    <u>E</u>xtra Areas to Analyze

    Form #74, Proofreading Checklist-2, is a form students can use to implement the SPACE strategy.

232. To enhance neatness and legibility, incorporate real-life situations into the writing experience. Writing pen pal letters, thank you notes, job applications and checks are all examples of real-life situations where neatness and legibility are very important.

233. Ask students to read their stories aloud or record them when complete. Ask the students to pause after each sentence. Many students will be able to detect run-on sentences and grammatical errors when reading aloud. Allow the students ample time to make the corrections to their papers.

234. Since written language is a form of communication, provide the opportunity for the students to share their stories and reports often. It is important for all students to see and hear good models. Do not require students to read in front of the class if they are struggling readers, without allowing time to practice.

235. Allow students to use a word processing program for final edit copies. Students can conduct a final grammar and spell check.

236. For some students, you may need to look at the quality of the assignment instead of the quantity. When working on topic sentences, details and a closing sentence, allow the student to produce one quality paragraph instead of a series of paragraphs.

237. When working on class reports, allow the student to use a fill-in-the-blank form. An example for the topic Birds might be:

My bird is a _____. He lives in the _____ part of the United States. He is _____ in color.

The student can add as many details as necessary. This procedure can be adapted for those with minimal writing skills at all grade levels.

238. When writing research papers, assist the student with the formulation of the topic sentence. Encourage the student to look for details. For elementary students, begin with one topic sentence and several supporting detail sentences. At the secondary level, you may have five to ten topic sentences, depending upon the subject and the class requirements. For some students, modify the number of sources required in the bibliography, especially if the student has difficulty reading.

239. Some students may need alternatives to long research papers and written reports. Alternatives may include writing several short reports in place of one long one or giving an oral report instead of a written research paper. The student still needs to do research and compile information from several sources.

240. Allow the student to present the final projects in another format. A videotape, demonstration, display or oral presentation may capitalize on the student's strengths.

Spelling Difficulties

Spelling is difficult for many adults. Imagine the difficulties many students encounter! Set a positive example for students by frequently looking up unknown words in the dictionary. Also demonstrate the use of a thesaurus. A collection of resources and reference aids should be available in the classroom. If possible, include several levels of both a dictionary and a thesaurus. Provide students with a list of commonly misspelled words. Teach students how to use both the grammar and spell check on the computer.

241. At first glance, a paper with numerous spelling errors appears to lack creativity or solid ideas. Allow the student to spell phonetically. Have the student read the paper to you, if necessary. Revise the paper with the student. Give encouragement for all attempts.

242. Ask students to keep a personal list of commonly misspelled words. Each time a student asks how to spell a word or looks it up in a reference book, have the student list it in his or her individual dictionary. Most students continually misspell the same words over and over. The following website includes a list of the most common misspelled words: *www.yourdictionary.com/library/mispron.html*.

243. Allow the student to tape record the response and transcribe it at a later time. Encourage the student to use a dictionary and a thesaurus.

Handwriting and Fine Motor Difficulties

Most students have wonderful ideas and are very creative. But for some, producing a good quality paper is very laborious. This may be due to poor handwriting or a delay in the development of fine motor skills, which often causes difficulty and frustration for the student when transferring ideas to paper. Instead of allowing the creativity to flow, the student may write in short, choppy sentences to compensate for the difficulty. Interestingly, when the obstacle of writing is removed, these students may become some of the most creative students in the classroom.

Developing Handwriting Skills

244. Clearly explain to the student what is acceptable. Levels of acceptability may vary depending upon the type of assignment. For example, when taking notes, the quality of penmanship is not as important as it is in the final copy of a written report.

245. Demonstrate correct pencil grip and proper writing position.

246. Check the student's pencil grip. Place adhesive tape or a pencil grip on the pencil. If the paper frequently moves on the desk, tape the paper in place. For older students,

a clipboard can be used to keep the paper in place. The Resources section lists websites where adaptive materials can be purchased.

247. Try different sizes of pencils.

248. Use tape to keep the paper positioned in the correct location.

249. Allow the student to use paper with their choice of line width at upper grade levels.

250. For younger students, begin with the large-ruled paper and slowly decrease the line size until the student is able to use grade-appropriate lined paper. If the desired line size is unavailable commercially, create the appropriate size either manually or on the computer, and photocopy it.

251. Write the student's answer or story in pencil and allow the student to trace it with a fine tip marker or colored pencils. For final copies, encourage students to use erasable pens.

252. Provide a close-up model for the student to copy instead of a distant model such as the board or an overhead. If an older student struggles with cursive writing, allow the student to print or use a laptop computer.

253. Offer alphabet cards so the student can see the correct formation of the letters. Allow either manuscript or cursive, depending on the student's preference. Search online printable versions. This website link provides a full-color, printable manuscript alphabet strip: *www.abcteach.com/ABC/alphaline3.htm.*

254. If appropriate, write some or all of the assignment for the student. The parents should be made aware of the expectations regarding homework assignments. Indicate under which circumstances the homework assignment may be handwritten or typed for the student.

255. Modify the length of the assignment. If the assignment is long, break it into sections and allow the student to complete one section at a time. A long assignment may take several days for completion.

256. Look at the quality instead of the quantity produced. When looking for a quality assignment, make sure the student has ample time to complete the final product.

257. Provide the student with a word processor or a laptop computer to use with long assignments.

258. Reinforce efforts to produce a good-quality paper, and reward quality.

259. Shorten written tasks, and allow extra time to complete them.

260. Allow a parent, guardian or sibling to write the answers for the student, if appropriate. Answers should be written verbatim and initialed by the parent.

Chapter Six Conclusion

This chapter has provided a wealth of ideas on nurturing the skill of writing for students who have difficulties with written language. For some of these students, fine motor coordination needs to be developed first. Activities to accomplish this are suggested, as well as activities to support these students on their path to self-expression through writing. This support may involve having the student dictate and trace words or use a computer. It may mean using sentence strips and learning spelling words. For those who have mastered the physical aspect of writing but don't know where to start, this chapter presents ideas for using charts, pictures, diagrams, story maps, timelines and other sources of inspiration to help students get past writer's block. Also offered are ways to deal with some of the mechanics of writing and editing and lots of websites with wonderful resources for all levels of learning. You should now have what it takes to get your students writing. Remember to provide opportunities every day!

Also, be sure to take advantage of the 10 Appendix forms that support activities suggested in this chapter. The list is on the following page.

Appendix Forms for Chapter Six

#65	Alphabetical Chart
#66	Skip-a-Line Paper
#67	Story Frame
#68	Story Starters
#69	Story Map
#70	Story Map – 2
#71	Compare and Contrast - Attributes
#72	Transition Words and Phrases
#73	Proofreading Checklist
#74	Proofreading Checklist – 2

"Educational progress depends on the ability of the teacher to perceive the untapped resources of the student and to develop techniques of using these resources to the best advantage."

Rudolf Dreikurs

What I hear, I forget; what I see, I remember; what I do, I understand.

Chinese Proverb

Chapter Seven

Spelling

For many students, spelling can be difficult and frustrating. In order to spell, the student must have the ability to break the spoken word into a sequence of sounds (phonological skills), remember the sounds that are represented by the letters, be able to recall visual sequences, have knowledge of spelling rules and be able to retain spelling patterns that have been learned. This chapter discusses the many aspects of spelling. Chapter 6, Written Language, has additional strategies to apply when spelling impacts the student's daily writing.

To support the student's ability to spell, use words that are compatible with the student's independent reading level. Accommodations for spelling programs may be as simple as adapting the length of the word list or as complex as creating an appropriate spelling program "from scratch."

> **Chapter Note:**
> On page 131, you will find a complete list of the reproducible forms referred to throughout this chapter. The reproducible forms are located in the Appendix.

For the student who is not yet ready for a formalized spelling program, structured classroom spelling time can be used to develop fine motor skills and letter/sound association. For some students, phonemic awareness training may be appropriate to help develop sensitivity to the sound structures of the spoken word. When students understand the sound structure and are able to manipulate the sound segments, they will then be able to make a gradual transition into a spelling program.

In the Study Methods section of this chapter, three different study methods for spelling are provided.

Spelling Practice Strategies

Often students with disabilities can succeed in the regular spelling curriculum with minimal adaptations. Many students can do well on spelling lists if they have time to prepare, but some students frequently forget the words immediately after the spelling test.

261. More of the same is not always the best teaching strategy. If a student is unable to learn and retain the spelling words, examine the current study method and perhaps try one of the other methods listed in this chapter.

262. Practice makes perfect, but only if you are practicing the correct spelling. Be sure to monitor students' practice sessions! Once a student has learned the words, encourage the student to use them in daily writing so the spelling is retained.

263. Set individual spelling goals. For students who continually fail spelling tests, the goal may have to be changed to master two or three words per week instead of the required number on the class list. The goal can be increased slowly, after the student has experienced some success. If a student continually experiences failure, it is unrealistic to expect the student to increase the number of words on the list.

264. Increase the number of words when the student reaches mastery level on three consecutive tests. Continually recycle the words in the list. Keep track by using one of the following options:

   Option 1: Make two separate index cards. Title one card *Spelling Words* and the second *Words I Know.* Write the student's spelling words on the individual index cards. Ask the student to orally spell the words. If the student spells the word correctly, place a tally mark on the back of the index card. When the student spells the word correctly three times sequentially, the word is moved to the *Words I Know* pile. The index cards in the *Words I Know* pile should be periodically reviewed to be sure the student has retained the information. If the student does not retain the spelling, place the index card back into the *Spelling Words* pile for additional practice. For some students, the goal may need to be increased to four or five correct, consecutive tally marks before the word is moved to the *Words I Know* pile.

   Option 2: Create a Word List Chart. In place of index cards, oral spelling can be documented on the following chart. In the example provided, the student's beginning goal is to learn four new spelling words. The student is tested orally on a daily basis. If the student spells the word correctly, a mark is placed in the box. If the student is unable to spell the word, the box is left blank. Once the student has mastered the word on three consecutive tries, the word is removed from the list. If the student does not master the word, it is added to the list for the following week along with any new words. **Form #75, Word List Chart,** is a blank copy that can be reproduced to use with students. During the week, the student can practice and review the words alongside peers.

Word List Chart

Word	Date	#1	#2	#3	#4	#5	Mastery
when	10/2	☺	☺	☺			Yes
this	10/2	☺		☺	☺		No
make	10/2		☺	☺	☺		Yes
seen	10/2		☺	☺		☺	No
this	10/2		☺	☺	☺		Yes
seen	10/9		☺	☺	☺		Yes
could	10/9			☺	☺	☺	Yes
below	10/9		☺	☺	☺		Yes
play	10/16	☺	☺	☺			Yes
would	10/16		☺	☺		☺	No
because	10/16	☺	☺		☺		No
house	10/16	☺	☺	☺			Yes

265. Group spelling words into word families, allowing phonetic learners to focus on the individual word patterns. When the student understands the simple word families, such as *at, hat, pat, rat* and is able to apply this skill, change the vowel. *Hat, pat* and *rat* now become *hot, pot* and *rot.*

Make flashcards for individual letters. Use one color for consonants and one for vowels. The students can create their own words. **Form #77, Alphabet Chart,** includes the vowels and consonants on separate pages and may be reproduced, if needed.

266. Teach difficult word patterns together, such as "ie" words: *believe, relieve* and *achieve.* Have students make flash cards, with the irregular or "hard part" in another color.

bel**ie**ve   rel**ie**ve   ach**ie**ve

267. If the student is unable to read a large number of the words on the list, delete the unfamiliar words. Insert commonly used sight words or words that follow the current word patterns.

268. Spelling mnemonics are intended to help students remember the spelling of difficult words. Students with memory problems will have difficulty with this, but for most of the students in the classroom, mnemonics will be an effective teaching tool. Students will enjoy creating their own mnemonic strategies. Here are some of the most common examples found in online searches.

> **arithmetic:** A Rat In The House May Eat The Ice Cream
> **because:** Big Elephants Can Always Understand Small Elephants
> **geography:** George's Elderly Old Grandfather Rode A Pig Home Yesterday.
> **necessary:** Not Every Cat Eats Sardines (Some Are Really Yummy)
> **ocean:** Only Cats' Eyes Are Narrow
> **rhythm:** Rhythm Helps Your Two Hips Move

269. Ask students to create mnemonics to remember the most commonly misspelled words. Find a list of the 100 Most Commonly Misspelled Words by searching online. The site *http://yourdictionary.com/library/misspelled.html* provides some mnemonics and other information to help students spell the words correctly.

    The alphaDictionary website is another site that provides commonly misspelled words, and it has memory aids titled "Memory Medicine" to help remember them. (See *http://www.alphadictionary.com/articles/misspelled_words.html.*) Check *http://www.alphadictionary.com/articles/confused_words.html* for a list of 250 commonly confused words, such as *a lot* and *allot, accept* and *except, advice* and *advise*, etc. These tips will definitely help students end the confusion.

270. Encourage students to create their own charts to help them remember how to avoid these common blunders. It doesn't matter if their tips make sense to others, as long as they help trigger the students' own memories. Here are some examples:

> **a lot:** Two words! Hopefully, you won't have to allot a lot of time to fix this problem.
>
> **argument:** I lost an *e* in the argument.
>
> **believe:** It's hard to believe that the word *believe* has a "lie"!

bookkeeper: This word has a triple compound: *oo kk ee.*

desert / dessert: *Dessert* has two *s*'s, like *s*trawberry *s*hortcake.

grateful: *Grateful* is G - rated!

here / hear: You hear with your ear.

no / know: No, I do not know the correct answer.

misspell: What is more embarrassing than to misspell the name of this word? Just remember that it is mis + spell.

mosquito: Tell that mosquito to quit biting me!

principal: The principal person is our school is the principal. He is a pal to all!

potassium: Remember, one tea, two sugars.

there / here: There is a place that is just like here. Add a *t* to here to get there.

together: If you go "get her," you will be together.

weather: You have no choice, whether you like the weather or not.

Creating Spelling Lists

271. When creating supplemental spelling lists, a list should be consistent with the student's reading level. Incorporate words from the student's basal reader when creating a supplemental spelling program.

272. Choose spelling words that are relevant to the curriculum and consistent with the student's vocabulary. For students that have difficulty mastering the regular spelling list, expectations for learning supplemental or challenging spelling words will need to be altered. An appropriate goal may be for the student to learn to just read the words.

273. Select a word bank from the student's basal reader. Group the words according to word families. Include several sight words. You also may want to select several bonus words from the reading.

274. Create three separate spelling lists on the computer. The three lists should include: a list of phonetic words, a list of sight words and a list of both phonetic and sight words. All students can do the same practice exercises as their peers, even though the individual lists may contain words that meet each student's style of learning. This should help meet the needs of all students in the classroom.

275. Use the previous year's spelling list, and adapt it to the format of the current grade-level list.

Parallel Spelling Activities

Not all students are ready for a formalized spelling program. Some students may need parallel activities. These activities may be completed alone, with a peer or with the paraprofessional. A recommended book is *Phonemic Awareness: Ready-to-Use Lessons, Activities and Games,* listed in the Resources section. The lessons are scripted, and the book contains everything needed to teach phonemic awareness skills. The companion video, titled *Phonemic Awareness: The Sounds of Reading,* is a staff development video showing how to incorporate phonemic awareness training into the classroom. Since lessons are scripted, it can easily be used by a support person who works with students. To get started, here is a simple introduction to work on sound skills with students who are not yet able to read or spell.

276. If a volunteer or paraprofessional is available to work with the student, have that person spend 15 to 20 minutes teaching sound association (phonemic awareness). Begin with familiar words that have three different sounds, such as: *cat, man, car, pig, mop,* or use any simple pictures available. Emphasize the sounds at the beginning, middle and end of the word. A simple example follows:

Words with Three Sounds

Step 1: Show the student a picture of a cat.

Step 2: Demonstrate how to say the sounds in the word C A T. (C – A – T)

Step 3: Ask the student: "How many sounds do you hear?" (Three)

Step 4: Practice saying the three individual sounds: C – A – T.

Step 5: Provide the student with a simple chart (see example below), and practice placing a token into the box where each sound is heard. For example, the student may be asked to place a token into the box where they hear the sound of "c" (initial sound). **Form #76, Sound Chart,** can be laminated and provided to the student.

Initial Sound	Medial Sound	Ending Sound
☻		

Step 6: Continue the procedure until the student is able to place the token into the correct space for the sound (initial, medial, ending).

Step 7: Continue with words that have three phonetic sounds until the student demonstrates mastery.

Once the student has mastered the technique of determining initial, medial and ending sounds with the word *cat,* provide additional words and follow Steps 1–7.

Change the Initial Sound:

Using the same words from the previous exercise, change the initial sounds to make rhyming words. In the demonstration word *cat,* the word can be changed to *mat, hat* or *fat.* Explain to the student that they are creating word families.

When the student is able to apply these skills at the sound level, the student is ready to move to the next level—the relationship between the sound and graphic letter of the alphabet.

An option for students at this level (since the student does not have an actual spelling list) is to write the letter corresponding to the initial sound or ending sound of words in the class spelling list. In the following example, the spelling list included the following words: *door, boat, keep, went, how* and *seed.*

The student's IEP goal was to be able to write the initial consonant sounds of words. Therefore, the student filled in the following chart. The student was able to fill in some of the ending sounds also.

	Initial Sound	Medial Sound	Ending Sound
1.	d		
2.	b		t
3.	k	e	p
4.	w		
5.	h		
6.	s		

277. For students working on mastering the sound relationship in words (and not ready for a formal spelling program), provide alphabet cards or picture cards that correspond to the spelling list. For example, if the class spelling word is *manage,*

the student may select a corresponding picture card (man or mat) that begins with the "m" sound (or the letter *m).*

278. Provide the student with a selection of consonant sounds on index cards. As a spelling word is dictated to the class, the student can select the appropriate initial consonant flash card and hold it up. For students working on both initial and ending sounds, the student may demonstrate knowledge by holding up both the initial consonant and the ending consonant.

279. Begin teaching the basic sight words and simple phonetic words, such as *a, at, am* and *an,* as soon as the student knows several letters and sounds.

280. Associate familiar words with spelling. The student's proper name and the names of family members, friends, peers or pets may be appropriate. Use the spelling list to create simple sentences. Practice the sentence until mastery has been reached. The words from the lesson may be incorporated into spelling, handwriting or written language activities. For example:

Word List: Meg, am, is, name
Sentences: I am Meg. My name is Meg. Meg is my name.

281. Teach only one spelling rule at a time. Post spelling rules in the classroom.

Drill and Practice Activities

Drill and practice activities take place daily in the classroom. Vary the assignments. Make sure the student is held accountable for meeting the daily goals.

282. Provide students with word analysis charts to divide their words into parts. Advanced students can create new words by adding prefixes and suffixes to their lists to make new words. **Form # 52, Word Analysis Chart,** in the Appendix can be reproduced and given to students.

Prefix	Base Word	Suffix	Compound Word
	study	ing	
un	**known**		
	aware	ness	
	repeat	ed	
	homework		home + work

283. Teach the meaning of the suffixes and prefixes in isolation. This especially helps middle and secondary students, who no longer have formalized spelling programs.

Form #43, Common Prefixes, and **Form #44, Common Suffixes,** include the common prefixes and suffixes and can be reproduced and placed in the students' spelling folders.

284. Provide highlighters so students can highlight base words, suffixes and prefixes to aid with visual discrimination. Another option is to ask the students to write each syllable with a different color of marker.

285. Provide the student with a close-up model from which to work. Many students experience difficulty when copying unknown words. A close-up model helps students, as they do not have to continually look up, remember the symbol and then transfer it to the paper.

286. Combine spelling and handwriting goals to allow time for additional drill and practice.

287. When assigning drill and practice activities for spelling, allow a minimum of ten minutes. Students who experience difficulty with organizational skills will need at least ten minutes to find and organize their materials and then practice the activity.

288. Do not require students to practice all of the words on a daily basis. It may be too overwhelming. Allow the student to practice two or three words per day, if the student is frustrated by a long list.

289. Vary the daily drill and practice exercises. Along with paper and pencil tasks, allow the student to practice on the chalkboard, in small groups or orally on tape.

290. Provide the student with an audiocassette of the word list. The student can practice alone during extra class time or take the tape home. This audiocassette may also be used if a student needs to retest or was absent during the test. If a pretest is given to students at the beginning of the week, turn on the tape recorder. The list is then recorded for students who would like to practice with the tape, those who were absent or those who need it for a final test.

291. Encourage the student to verbalize the sounds and syllables while writing the words.

292. Configuration clues often help students to recall the correct spelling. For example, the configuration of the word *because* would include one tall box at the beginning, followed by six small boxes. A common mistake when spelling the word *because* is the insertion of the letter *k*. As there is only one tall letter, configuration clues help students to remember it is a *c* rather than a *k*. The five small boxes for the *cause* part of the word will help the student to remember *cause* instead of the many variations *(cuz, cuse* and *cuze)* often mistakenly given.

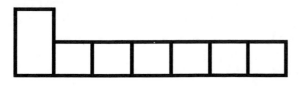

Provide a list of drill and practice exercises. Each of the following activities can *be lis*ted on a handout, and the student may select several activities per week. As an alternative, divide the class into *small g*roups, and assign each group a *di*fferent activity.

293. **3-D Words.** Select a word from your list and create the letters with cla*y*. Mold the clay *l*etters together to create a "w*ord o*f art."

294. **Alphabet Words.** Divide the students into gr*oups*. Provide each group with a cup o*f alph*abet cere*al. S*et a timer, and see how many spelling words the students can make.

295. **Alphabetical Order.** Students list their words in alphabetical order.

296. **Crack the Code.** Have small groups of students translate their spelling words into code. The students may create codes by assigning numbers to each letter (such as on a telephone keyboard), numbering each letter of the alphabet or drawing a simple picture to correspond to each letter. Students may exchange spelling lists and see if they are able to crack the codes of the other groups.

297. **Crossword Puzzles.** Students create crossword puzzles on graph paper. The puzzles can be distributed as drill and practice activities.

298. **Computer Games.** Students use commercial software for drill and practice. If the school does not have commercial software that can be programmed, search online, as there are many free games specifically designed for use on a classroom computer.

299. **Get Up and Move!** Create sets of alphabet letters on 8½" x 11" construction paper. Each set should include four cards for each vowel (four of letter *a,* four of letter *e* and so forth) and two cards for each consonant. Each group should have a complete set of cards. Call out a spelling word, and each team works together to assemble their letters in the correct order. The alphabet letters may also be placed on index cards, if you prefer that students play at their desks.

300. **Hangman.** The student must guess the word without more than six mistakes (head, body, two arms and two legs).

301. **Human Bingo.** Draw two large bingo "boards" on shower curtains. The drawing should look like a regular bingo board. Divide the class into two groups, and provide each student with an index card that includes a spelling word from the spelling list. The teacher calls out a Bingo number such as B6. The team must determine whether they have a B6 on their curtain Bingo Board. If the group has B6, the teacher provides a spelling word (e.g. house). The student with the index card with the spelling word ***house*** stands on the B6 block and spells the word aloud (with or without viewing the card). If the student spells the word correctly the student remains in position on the Bingo Card. The team that makes the first Bingo

wins the round. If is the board is too confined of a space for students to physically stand provide the students with pieces of construction paper that can be placed on the respective numbers. This game can be adapted for many subject areas.

302. **Jewelry Designs.** Older students will enjoy using letter beads from the local craft store. The student may use the beads to create a spelling bracelet or necklace with the individual spelling words. The student may wear the beads and simply unstring them when it is time to learn new words.

303. **Letter Mix-Up!** Students write their spelling words onto graph paper with one-inch squares. Students may elect to color in the vowels or the consonants. Each word is cut into individual letters. For beginning **spellers,** the letters for individual words may be clipped together, and the student may recreate the words one by one. More advanced spellers may receive an envelope with all the le*tters* for the entire spelling list, which can then be used to recreate the words.

304. **Make a Mess!** Younger students can practice writing the words in shaving cream, in finger paint on an easel or in instant pudding. "Writing" in a tray full of multicolored rice or flour is also fun for younger students.

305. **Manual Typewriters.** Have the student use an old, manual typewriter, if you can find one! If the student makes a mistake, the word must be retyped, and there's no spell check to help out. This will make the student think twice before typing a word!

306. **Memory Match.** Make two sets of each spelling word on index cards. Spread the cards face down on the table, and see who can find the most pairs of matching cards. Begin with one card face up. Players take turns turning over a card. If it matches the one face up, the player gets to keep the two, turn up another one and try for a second match. If not successful, the cards must be turned over again—and players must try to remember where those cards are for future tries. As an alternative to two matching spelling words, students can write a spelling word on one card and an illustration of the word on a second card. Then, they must match the word with its corresponding picture.

307. **Multiple Meanings – Guess the Word!** Students look up spelling words in a thesaurus and make a secret list of synonyms for each word on the list. Students work in small groups to try and guess the team members' synonyms. For example:

Target word: *practice*

Possible synonyms used in sentences to show the different aspects of meaning:
In our house we have special *traditions* for birthdays.
I must *rehearse* for the play.

308. **Picture Art.** Students draw silly pictures and include illustrations of spelling words (that are nouns and can be pictured).

309. **Poems, Stories, Riddles and Jokes.** Students create short stories, poems, riddles and jokes with their words to share with others in the class.

310. **Puzzles.** Students create pictures or designs with their spelling words on construction paper. When finished, have them cut the construction paper into puzzle pieces for others to put back together.

311. **Rainbow Words.** Provide the student with blank sentence strips. The student writes the spelling words in sentences and traces the words with multiple colors of crayons, felt tip pens or colored pencils to create rainbow words.

312. **Scrambled Letters.** Purchase one-inch tiles (or make your own from tag board), and write the letters from the spelling words on tiles. Write the consonants in one color and vowels in another. The student can create words with the tiles. Have peers drill the student and monitor the student's progress. **Form #77, Alphabet Chart,** includes one master for vowels and one for consonants. Photocopy the vowels on one color of paper and the consonants on a second color.

313. **Silly Rhymes.** Students group the word lists into word families. For example: *make, bake* and *take*. Then, they create short, silly rhymes with the spelling words and their word families. For example: "I take what I bake to old Uncle Jake!"

314. **Silly Sentences.** Students write silly sentences with their spelling lists. The student receives one point for each spelling word used. If a sentence includes one spelling word, the sentence is worth one point. If the sentence includes two spelling words, it is worth two points and so on.

315. **Spelling Group Games.** If using spelling games, such as Spelling Baseball or Spell Downs, be sure students are allowed to use their own learning styles. Not all students can spell the words aloud immediately. Allow students to use paper and pencil to write the word before demonstrating their responses.

316. **Student-Created Activities.** Brainstorm with the class various ways to provide additional spelling practice.

317. **Synonyms, Antonyms and Homonyms.** Students select synonyms, antonyms or homonyms corresponding to the spelling list, and a peer tries to guess the related spelling word.

318. **Spelling Usage Cards.** Students create a spelling chart with their weekly words. Each time the student uses one of the words (speaking or in an assignment), the student places a check on his or her individual chart. Students earn a small reward

when the chart is filled. **Form #78, Spelling Usage Card,** includes an example that you can reproduce.

319. **Story Time!** Have students write stories using the spelling words and share their stories with the class.

320. **Train Words.** Students select one spelling word from their list. They use the last letter of the word to start the next word. See who can make the longest train of words. For example: train – next – time – elephant – table – egg . . .

For a more difficult version, the student must use the last two letters to create new words. For example: train – inside – develop – open – envelope – penny . . .

321. **Tongue Twisters.** Students select a word from their spelling list and create tongue twisters with the word.

322. **Thesaurus.** Students look up the spelling words in a thesaurus and list several additional words with the same meaning. The student writes sentences with the new words. Students may also look up the word and create sentences that have the opposite meaning.

323. **Wet Words!** Write words on a black or green board with paint brushes and water!

324. **Word Finds.** Students write their spelling words onto graph paper and fill in the additional spaces with random letters. The individual Word Find can be shared with others.

325. **Words without Consonants.** Students each make a list of the spelling words in random order without the consonants. For example, for the word *consonant,* the student would write _ o _ _ o _ a _ _. The lists are exchanged, and the students fill in the blanks to correctly spell the weekly spelling words.

326. **Words without Vowels.** Students each make a list of the spelling words in random order without the vowels. For example, for the word *consonant*, the student would write c _ n s _ n _ n t. The lists are exchanged, and the students fill in the blanks to correctly spell the weekly spelling words.

327. **Word Puzzles.** Write spelling words onto index cards and cut the words apart. The student can put the parts together to recreate the spelling word.

Study Methods for Spelling

For students with disabilities, the most effective method is one that capitalizes on the student's strengths. Three guidelines for studying spelling are listed here. Allow students to experiment with the various methods to determine which best meets their personal learning styles. **Form #79, Study Methods for Spelling,** includes these three methods and may be reproduced for students to keep in their spelling folders.

Study Method #1 for Visual Learners

328. This method focuses on the student's visual strength. It may be appropriate for students with a hearing impairment, students who rely on visual patterning and students who have difficulty with auditory processing.

> The student looks at the word while the teacher reads the word aloud.

> The student studies the word by reading it, spelling it and reading it again.

> With eyes closed, the student attempts to spell the word orally two times without the model.

> Finally, the student attempts to write the word without the model.

Study Method #2 for Auditory Learners

329. If the student relies heavily on auditory skills to learn new words, the following steps may be implemented into the spelling program. This method may be appropriate for some students with visual impairments and students with fine motor difficulties.

> The student observes the teacher reading, spelling and writing the word.

> The student reads the word and repeats the letters verbally after the teacher.

> Once again, the student listens to the teacher spell the word, then the student repeats it after the teacher.

> The student spells the word without assistance.

Study Method #3 for Multi-Sensory Learners

330. A cover and write method is appropriate for the student who prefers a multi-sensory approach.

> The student looks at the word and pronounces it.

> The student spells the word aloud.

> The student covers the model and writes the word down.

> The student compares the written word to the model.

If the student has written the word correctly, the student practices the word three times. (If the word is incorrect, the student repeats the entire process.)

A final check is made. If all the words are correct, the student moves to the next word.

331. Allow the student to experiment with various programs. The student will be able to choose a study method that best meets the individual's needs. If the student continues to do poorly on final assessments, encourage the student to try a different study method.

332. Periodically have the student practice with a peer, teacher or paraprofessional to ensure the student is practicing the words correctly. When the student is practicing alone, frequently check to make sure the student is practicing correctly.

333. Provide the student with a spelling contract for the week. The contract can include a wide variety of activities and accommodate a wide variety of needs. Simply check or highlight the activities that the student must complete during the week. If the student has extra time, the student may select additional activities. The requirements can be expanded for more advanced students. See **Form #80, Spelling Contract Example.**

Spelling Assessments

For some students, spelling tests produce a great deal of anxiety. Not only must the students learn to spell the words, but they may also need to learn to *read* the words. For those who experience difficulty with fine motor coordination, so much effort is put into creating a legible product that the actual spelling of the word escapes the student. Some students just cannot keep pace with others during a group test.

334. Test early and test often! Give the spelling test earlier in the week—for example, on Wednesday or Thursday. Students who pass the test can work on extension activities, and others may retest the following day. Allow the student to retest only on the words that were missed.

335. Test the student orally instead of in writing. Give the student an index card or paper with the score to turn in to the general education teacher.

336. Write the response for the student, if necessary—especially for students with severe fine motor difficulties.

337. Cue the student as to the number of letters in each word when working with silent letters. This will help the phonetic speller remember the silent letters.

338. Test students over several words daily instead of one final test.

339. Allow the student to take the test with the special education teacher or paraprofessional at a separate time. Use the group test as a practice test.

340. If the student needs long periods of time to process information, give the student a prerecorded version of the test. The student is able to stop the tape and think about the word for as long as needed.

341. If the student reverses letters frequently, ask the student to spell the word orally. Allow credit for the correct oral response.

342. With the lower functioning student, allow the student to select the correct spelling flashcard (word recognition goal).

343. Provide a word recognition spelling test, where the student is given four choices per line and is asked to circle the correct word.

    Target word: **cat**   1. **car   mat   cat   sat**
    Target word: **man**   2. **mat   make   man   mom**

344. Provide the students with a word list, and ask the student to match the words to pictures.

Grading

Record pretest and final test scores. Consider giving two grades: one based on the improvement between the pretest and final test score and a percentage score.

345. Encourage students to self-monitor their spelling progress by charting pretest and final test scores. Many students are motivated by self-monitoring techniques.

346. Have the student set a weekly spelling goal. Reward the student if the individual goal is met, even if the student does not obtain the required class percentage.

347. Be sure to adhere to changes in grading or criteria noted on the Individualized Education Plan.

Chapter Seven Conclusion

This chapter is full of ideas for helping students learn how to spell and remember their spelling words—from flashcards and mnemonics to configuration clues, alphabet cereal, letter bead jewelry, poems and puzzles. You will find plenty of activities to vary drill and practice! Consideration is given to phonemic awareness, word families, suffixes and prefixes and other means of instruction. Also presented are three study methods for different learning styles and various strategies for spelling assessments and grading to accommodate students with difficulties. Armed with the activities, approaches and strategies offered in this chapter and the Appendix forms listed below, you will be well prepared to help your students learn how to spell.

Appendix Forms for Chapter Seven

#43	Common Prefixes
#44	Common Suffixes
#52	Word Analysis Chart
#75	Word List Chart
#76	Sound Chart
#77	Alphabet Chart – Vowels / Consonants
#78	Spelling Usage Card
#79	Study Methods for Spelling
#80	Spelling Contract Example

"Enlarge the opportunity and the person will expand to fill it"

Eli Ginzberg

Notes:

_____

_____

_____

_____

_____

_____

_____

_____

_____

_____

_____

_____

_____

"In the end, we retain from our studies only that which we practically apply."
                                                        Johan Wolfgang Von Goethe

Chapter Eight

Mathematics

Difficulties in mathematics manifest themselves in many ways. A student who has difficulty in math often exhibits totally different learning characteristics than a peer who also receives service. Some students may experience difficulty with processing the information. The student often is unable to hold information in short-term memory (working memory) long enough to complete the second step of a problem. On the other hand, a student may have difficulty with long-term memory retrieval and therefore be unable to remember previously learned skills or previously memorized math facts. Since math skills are built upon previously learned skills, students who lack the basic skills (perhaps due to memory problems) experience difficulty with advanced mathematics. For many students, complex word problems are difficult, as the student is unable to complete multiple steps and understand specific vocabulary, and often is unable to perform the multiple types of calculations required to complete the problem. Often students have difficulty with fine motor skills, and the effort involved in copying math problems is extremely laborious. For many, it is difficult to line up the columns or copy the numbers from a model, as the numbers are unrelated to one another. Auditory processing, visual processing, difficulty sequencing, and transferring information from short- into long-term memory are only a few of the factors that impact learning math.

> **Chapter Note:**
> On page 153, you will find a complete list of the reproducible forms referred to throughout this chapter. The reproducible forms are located in the Appendix.

When learning basic math skills, some students need to use concrete manipulative materials to demonstrate the operation. Once the answer is obtained, the student is required to hold the information in short-term memory and then transfer the answer to paper. For the many students who have memory problems, this is no simple task! For some students, the use of manipulative materials causes confusion, as they do not see the relationship between the concrete materials and the actual problem. For others, manipulative materials are crucial to help visualize and understand the concept. Awareness of these issues can help educators understand and determine why some students are having difficulty and determine possible strategies to help them succeed.

It is also important to analyze the classroom curriculum. At the elementary level, some mathematics programs present new concepts daily and allow minimal time for drill and practice for students who experience difficulties. Although the mathematical concepts continue to be recycled throughout the upcoming lessons, often the student with a disability does not get enough drill and practice to actually internalize the concept. When the skill appears several days later, some students may feel as though it is a new concept and have little recollection of learning the skill previously. For some students, the concepts may need to be regrouped, allowing for daily drill and practice.

In the upper grades, many students experience difficulty because they have not mastered the basic skills that are the prerequisites for more advanced learning. For example, the student who has not learned the basic skills of addition and subtraction certainly will have difficulty with multiplication and division. As the student advances through the grades, the prerequisite skills required increase, and the student tends to fall further behind.

When providing service to the student with disabilities in the math setting, refer to the chapters titled Daily Assignments and Classroom Assessments. Both of these chapters have many practical ideas that can be adapted to the area of mathematics.

General Teaching Strategies

348. Many students with disabilities experience difficulty with abstract concepts. How many times has a student asked, "Why do we have to learn this?" Introduce new math concepts in "real life" situations. Brainstorm and create a class list of ways math is used daily. Continually refer to the original list, and add to it as students discover more ways that math is used in daily life. Following are some examples to which students will be able to relate.

Addition, subtraction and decimals: checking and savings accounts

Averages: weather reports with weekly, monthly and yearly temperature averages; batting averages; and report card final grades

Geometry: shapes in nature; in the classroom; in architecture

Graphs: test scores; weather conditions for a month; individual eating habits by kinds of food consumed during a week. The book *Creating Balance in Children: Activities to Optimize Learning and Behavior,* listed in the Resources section, includes an activity for creating a bar graph of food colors. How many green foods can the students think of? How many red foods? How many yellow? This type activity can be adapted for many types of graphing activity.

Measurement: decreasing or increasing the ingredients for a recipe; measuring for new furniture or new room arrangements; creating woodworking projects

Percentages: Calculate clothing discounts; interest on savings accounts; statistics from the local sports teams

Time: public transportation schedules; television schedules; work time cards

349. Provide the student with graph paper when copying from the board and to use with daily assignments to aid in problem alignment. If graph paper is not available, students can turn their notebooks horizontally to create columns. This is especially important for students who have difficulty with spatial relationships and visual processing. Graph paper squares range in size from one inch to one centimeter square, so the paper can be used with students at all levels.

350. When asking students to copy from the board, separate the number of the problem from the actual problem. For example:

$$(1)\ 6 \times 3 = 18 \qquad (2)\ 9 \times 7 = 63$$

351. Colored pens for overhead transparencies and colored chalk or markers for the board will help to separate important parts of the math problem. Problems can also be color coded. For example, green can indicate the place to begin the problem.

352. Color coding is also important when demonstrating new skills. It will help to direct the student's attention to the important points. For example, color code the groups of ones, tens or hundreds when teaching regrouping of numbers.

353. Provide verbal as well as written instructions for students with auditory and visual difficulties. Write the assignments on the board, post them on the class website, and send home weekly assignment sheets.

354. When teaching abstract concepts, use drawings, diagrams and visual demonstrations to help the student establish the relationship.

355. Identify the specific problem for which the student experiences difficulty. For example, is the student experiencing difficulty with division due to the multiple steps, or is the student experiencing difficulty with addition, subtraction or multiplication? Remediate the specific skill. **Form #81, Error Analysis Chart – Math,** is a general checklist that can be used for basic skills.

356. When teaching new mathematical concepts, do not worry about perfect calculations. First teach the concept, and be sure the student understands the process. The use of manipulative materials and diagrams will aid many students. Concrete aids, such as a number line, shapes, rulers, yardsticks, clocks, actual money, etc., will help many students to visualize the problems.

357. Many commercial math practice pages include mixed problems on a page, such as addition and subtraction or multiplication and division. Ask the student to highlight all problems with the same operations. Students should complete all similar problems (for example, addition) before proceeding to the next type of problem.

358. Teach only one skill at a time. If the assignment includes several types of math calculations in one lesson, provide ample drill and practice on one skill before moving on to the next skill. Many of the websites in the Resources section allow you to customize worksheets.

359. Demonstrate and teach the relationship between math fact families. Help students look for patterns. This will help to establish the relationship between numbers. Allow students who are unable to memorize the basic facts to use a calculator without penalty. **Form #82, Addition and Subtraction Charts,** and **Form # 83, Multiplication Chart,** located in the Appendix can be reproduced for these students, if needed.

360. Whenever possible, model math problems for students using manipulative materials. When modeling, explain each step verbally to the student. During student practice sessions, also ask the student to verbalize each step. Listen to the student. You will be able to understand the student's thought process and easily analyze why the student is experiencing difficulty.

361. Analyze the student's homework assignment. Can you see consistent errors? Following are two common errors with addition. What did the student do in each of the following?

    $14 + 2 = 34$ (Problem was misaligned when adding in a column.)
    $11 + 9 = 19$ (The student may be counting—in this case, counting on from
                 11—but the student begins counting at 11 instead of 12.)

    To be certain, ask the student to explain the process.

362. Provide ample workspace on worksheets so that students do not need to transfer information. For students who have fine motor difficulties, providing four problems per page allows for sufficient space to show their work. Assign fewer problems to the student. Require the student to complete only enough to demonstrate that the process is mastered.

363. When lecturing (and students are required to take notes), provide the student with photocopies of the notes. Copies can be made of your teaching notes, or if you have a student who is able to take concise and clear notes, ask the student to use carbon paper so that an additional copy is available if needed.

364. With classroom assignments, allow the student additional class time to complete the assignment if needed. If the student understands the process and can demonstrate

mastery of the material, after a few problems, allow the student to move on to some additional class work.

365. Allow the student to begin all homework assignments in class, and check for understanding before the student leaves the classroom.

366. If consumable texts are unavailable, enlarge the text so the student may write on the photocopied page.

367. Allow the student to use charts, tables and calculators when the processes of addition, subtraction, multiplication and division are understood.

368. When using addition or multiplication charts, provide the student with a cut out L. This will help the student to find the intersection box of columns and rows.

369. Frequently review and reinforce previously taught skills. Begin each math class with a daily review of the concept taught the previous day. As a teacher, you will be able to check to see whether or not the students retained the information from the previous lesson. If not, review or re-teach the lesson. In math, this is especially important, as many of the new skills are built upon previously learned skills.

370. Many students with disabilities need immediate feedback on their assignments. Math centers are an excellent way to review and reinforce previously taught concepts. The following math centers can be set up with minimal effort. Multiple-level activities may be included in the centers so students of all ability levels can easily participate. Self - correction sheets may be included, or students may be assigned to cooperative groups. Here are some suggestions to get you started.

The Restaurant – Collect take-out menus from various establishments. The student selects a menu, chooses several individual items, and determines the total cost of the items, including the tax and tip. On **Form #84, Menu Card,** is an example of a teacher-created card. The student uses the menu and follows the directions on the back of the card. Students may use calculators to check their calculations. Laminate the cards.

The Store – Create a grocery store, toy store, video store or clothing store. Provide a collection of various catalogs and newspaper or grocery store ads. For older students, you may want to include special sales and provide check blanks and a check register to record purchases. For advanced students, a store credit card could also be available, allowing the student to calculate the monthly payment with interest. Once again, the student may purchase items, or specific directions with self-check cards may be provided.

Furnish-a-Home Center – Provide collections of catalogs with home furnishings. The student can create a dream room or furnish a home with an allotted budget. Older students can actually measure their rooms and purchase only items that would fit. With catalog specifications for the lengths and widths of the furniture, students can use graph paper and create layouts of their rooms.

The Manipulative Center – In this center, you may want to include geoboards, tangrams and pattern blocks. (Search online for interesting sites on geoboards and tangrams. Begin by checking the Resources section.)

The Computer Center – In this center, include math programs for student review and programs related to current math objectives. You may want to include a signup sheet and a clock or timer so all students have an opportunity to participate.

The Counting Center – Include numbers, tracers and templates. Small objects can be used for one-to-one correspondence. Add puzzles, coloring sheets, connect-the-dots pages, etc. Card games and place value activities would also be appropriate.

371. The Teacher File Box website *(www.teacherfilebox.com/index.aspx)* includes over 30,000 searchable PreK–6 activities, organized so you can find what you need quickly. The site has math centers, if you would prefer to have ready-made centers. Although the site is for students PreK–6, activities can be used for older students with cognitive disabilities. The current price for membership is $9.99 per month.

372. When teaching the concept of money, use real money in place of paper or cardboard money. For a student with visual processing problems, it is very difficult to tell the difference between coins on worksheets. For students who have difficulty changing their thinking process when counting various coin denominations, here is a little trick. With fingernail polish, paint one red dot on the nickels, two dots on the dimes and five on the quarters. The student can simply count by fives. Eventually the process will transfer. For example, the student would count the following:

Quarter + dime + penny
5, 10, 15, 20 25   30, 35   36

373. Provide practice using money by setting up a class store. Keep the classroom store stocked with school supplies, such as paper, pencils, folders, rulers, protractors, compasses or other items that are required during the school day. Students can take turns being the storekeeper, and the class can purchase the items needed for the school day. Often parents appreciate this, as when a student needs a special item such as colored pencils, the parent sends the money, and the student is able to purchase the item in class.

374. Develop task analysis sheets for the basic areas of mathematics. Use these checklists to determine the specific areas of difficulty. Look for error patterns in daily assignments. If a student has extreme difficulty with a problem or process, ask the student to verbalize the steps. Some students experience difficulties because a step has been eliminated, or they are performing a step incorrectly. Patterns of errors usually emerge in the following areas: inadequate knowledge of facts, incorrect operations or the use

of ineffective strategies. **Form #81, Error Analysis Chart for Math,** provides a checklist to use for addition, subtraction, multiplication, division and decimals.

Problem Solving and Word Problems

375. When working with problem-solving activities, emphasize the problem-solving steps, not the final answer. Many students do not participate for fear their final computations will be incorrect.

376. Number the steps in word problems. If using teacher-made worksheets, include one sentence per line. Highlight the important words.

377. When teaching and solving word problems, simplify the vocabulary and take out all irrelevant information. Teach the key words that are associated with word problems.

378. Create a class chart with steps to solving a word problem. The steps might include:

   1. Read the entire problem from beginning to end one time.

   2. Reread the problem to determine what needs to be solved.

   3. Look for key words. Some of the key words are: *altogether, together, in all, are left, spent* or *remain.* Try to determine the operation that will be needed to solve the problem.

   4. Draw a diagram or picture of the problem.

   5. Write the mathematical equation.

   6. Estimate the answer before solving it. If the estimated answer seems reasonable, solve the problem.

379. The following strategies are appropriate for solving word problems. Demonstrate how to use these skills, and create a classroom poster. Encourage students to use these strategies when solving word problems.

Estimate the answer.	Break the problem into parts.
Guess and check the answer.	Create a chart or table.
Draw a picture.	Look for a pattern.
Work the problem backwards.	Make a list.

Pre-Teaching Vocabulary

Math has a special language of its own. It is quite different from reading, as math vocabulary usually corresponds to an entire set of separate symbols that are unfamiliar to the student. With reading vocabulary, students are often able to get the meaning of a sentence even if they cannot understand all of the vocabulary. With math, if a symbol is misunderstood, the student may not be able to complete the exercise. Try to incorporate math vocabulary as much as possible into the school day.

380. Incorporate math vocabulary into daily activities. Some examples may include:

> "There are 28 students in the classroom, and three are absent. How can we create a math problem to determine the number of students in the class?"

> "It's time to divide into cooperative groups. Today I would like to divide the class into four groups. There are 28 students, so how many students would be in each group? Can we divide the class into equal groups? Yes, we can divide the students into four equal groups of seven. What percentage of the class is in each group?"

> "In 15 minutes, it's time to get ready for lunch. What time is it now? Can you think of other ways that we can state the time for lunch?"

> "Half of the class has returned the permission slips for the field trip on Friday. Half is the same as 50% of the class—which is 14 students."

381. Keep a math journal. List a question on the board for the student to respond to. The questions may include items such as using math words in sentences, creating math diagrams or solving a problem.

382. Students may enjoy drawing or creating their own memory tricks in their math journals also. Here are some examples. See how many other examples students can come up with by either creating them or searching online.

   • **Gallons, quarts, pints and cups.** Create a drawing to help you remember.

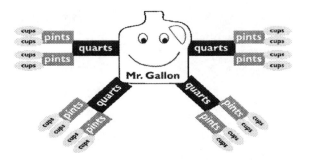

- **Long Division.** This family list will help students remember the steps to long division.

Dad – Divide	Sister – Subtract
Mom – Multiply	Brother – Bring Down

- **Fractions: Division.** Remember the steps for dividing fractions!
  Kids **C**an **R**un (Keep, Change and Reverse)

  Keep the first fraction.
  Change the sign from divide to multiply.
  Reverse the last fraction.

- **Median.** The road has a median in the center. (It splits the road in half!)

- **Money.** The following math rhymes were submitted by a classroom teacher online. The original source is unknown.

  Penny, penny, so easily spent. Copper brown and worth one cent.

  Nickel, nickel, silver and fat! You are worth five cents! I know that.

  Dime, dime, tiny and thin! I can remember that you are worth ten.

  Quarter, quarter, the biggest to hold! You are worth 25 I am told.

- **Numerator and Denominator Confusion?**
  Think "**N**aughty **D**ogs jump up and down!"
  n**U**merator **U**p / **D**enominator **D**own

383. Teach key math terms separately. Have students create their own math terminology dictionaries. Include simple drawings and examples to illustrate the terms and the various steps of the problems. Students can add memory aids to this book, if they do not have math journals. This is a handy reference tool for students. Here are some simple ideas that can be used for demonstration.

- **addend:** Any numbers that are added together are called addends. The answer is the sum.

  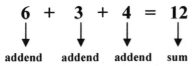

- **alike:** These shapes are alike because they are the same color and they both have four sides.

- **discount:** An amount that is taken away from the regular price of an item.

| Full Price: $10.00 |
| Discount: $ 3.00 |
| Price: $ 7.00 |

Sale Price $7.00	Discount $3.00 (30%)
FULL PRICE $10.00	

384. The Resources section includes websites with interactive math dictionaries. Students can access these sites to look up math vocabulary words, view interactive demonstrations and look for ideas for their own math dictionaries.

385. **Math Words.** The following website lists thousands of math terms in an alphabetical list. Teachers can use this site for ways to easily explain math vocabulary to students, and students can use the site to look up words when needed. Go to: *www.mathwords.com/a_to_z.htm*

   Here is an example for *acute angle.*

   Acute Angle. An angle that has measure less than 90°. See also: obtuse angle, degrees. (All of the underlined words [on the site] may be clicked on for additional explanation.)

Additional Math Activities

386. Help students to correct number reversals by verbalizing the problem out loud. For example, when a student is learning to write the number 7, the student would say, "I start at the left and make a short line to the right, and then I make a slanted line to the bottom." For the number 3, the student might say, "I start at the left and make a half circle to the right, and then I do it again."

387. Help students to over-learn math facts and consistently drill, drill and drill some more. Math games and computer games can add variety.

388. When teaching strategies for a number line, create a long line on the floor with masking tape for the student to walk on. This will also assist the student with directionality. A number line can also be placed on the student's desk or in the student's math folder to be referred to as needed.

389. Demonstrate how to use the number line for addition, subtraction and counting by up or down. For students who reverse numbers, it can be used as a close-up reference tool to help with number formation. For the older student, who may be embarrassed to use one, demonstrate how the face clock in the classroom, a watch or a ruler can serve the same purpose and is not quite as obvious.

390. Place colored arrows on the student's worksheet to assist with directionality. Often students try to perform math calculations from left to right (as with reading), instead of right to left.

391. Draw lines between the columns of math problems so the student is able to record the information in the correct column.

392. Box in or highlight the "ones" column so the student knows where to begin the math calculation.

393. To help students line up columns, turn lined notebook paper so the lines run vertically instead of horizontally, or use graph paper for instant organization.

394. Purchase consumable texts from the publisher. Students with fine motor difficulty will not have to copy problems and will be able to spend more time with the actual calculations.

395. Use good judgment. Some students are able to memorize basic facts, so allow ample time before providing a calculator. For others, memorization may be extremely difficult, and you may want to use a calculator from the beginning.

Parallel Math Activities

Some students are unable and will never be able to complete the same curriculum as the rest of the class. For these students, it is important to be aware of the goals and objectives on the Individualized Educational Plan. When support is available, often the supplementary materials can be made to correspond with the current class activity. Listed below are just a few ideas for activities that can be completed with a paraprofessional or peer tutor.

396. Decide whether or not the skill is a "functional" life skill. Functional skills are those that will support the student in independent living. An excellent resource, *Teaching Math to People with Down Syndrome and Other Hands-On-Learners* by Dr. DeAnna Horstmeier, includes an abundance of supplemental games and activities. This book is a must-have resource if there are students in the class with cognitive delays. See the Resources section for more details.

Be sure the student not only recognizes the numbers but understands one-to-one correspondence. **Form #85, Numerals and Math Symbols,** includes the numerals and beginning math symbols, and **Form #86, One-to-One Correspondence,** includes simple pictures that can be used to check a student's understanding of one-to-one correspondence.

397. Keep an assortment of materials in the classroom that the student can use independently. These materials may be stored in a basket. Be sure the student knows where the special basket is located. The basket may include dice, a calculator with self-correctors, flashcards, clock activities, puzzles, classifying activities and color sheets. All of the activities should be activities the student can work on independently, but the teacher or peer can monitor the activity.

398. Create Math Activity Boxes for students to work with individually in the classroom. **Form #64 Curriculum Modifications,** can be used to document math activities for Activity Boxes. Following is an example of such a documentation form.

Date of Implementation: January 10, 2010
IEP Goal: The student will recognize numbers 0-9.
The student will match numerals to correct number of items (one-to-one correspondence).

Time Block	Date and Activity	Student Expectations	Additional Information and Notes
9:00 – 10:00 daily	01/10/2010 – **Number Recognition Activity Box.** Student will correctly identify the numbers 0-9 with various activities in box.	To complete the daily activity and raise hand for teacher or peer to check assignment.	**1, 2, 3 Activity Box** provided by Special Education Teacher or peer to monitor and document results
	Number puzzle	1. Student will complete puzzle without assistance.	Student completed puzzle with peer coaching – continue.
	One-to-one correspondence	2. Student will place two items in each section of an egg carton.	Student filled 8 of the 12 containers correctly – continue.
	Number cards Student will match number cards (1 with 1, 2 with 2, etc.)	3. Student will match cards, raise hand and wait for teacher to check.	Student matched numbers 0 , 1 , 2 and 3 correctly. Goal met. Tomorrow add numbers 4 and 5.
	01/11 – Continue with activities 1, 2 and 3.	Same	

400. Provide supplemental materials in the same content area as the curriculum for the rest of the class. For example, if the class is learning addition with regrouping, the student may work on basic addition facts. It is possible the student can still be involved in the discussion and demonstration and use the same manipulative materials, if the general education teacher varies the questions and directs specific questions towards the student.

401. Correlate the objectives from the Individualized Education Plan with the instruction. If the student's goal is number recognition, use the daily assignment or the classroom textbook to practice. If the objective is to be able to correctly write the numbers, the student could copy problems from the general education textbook.

402. Order a supplemental text for the student's direct instruction. Direct instruction can be provided for the student when the class is receiving instruction. During independent work time, the student will be able to complete the assignment in the supplementary text.

403. Purchase inexpensive dot-to-dot books at local stores. The dot-to-dot activities help with number sequencing and recognition. These are also available online. See the Resources section for websites with printable PDFs.

404. Work on number formation with the use of tracers or templates.

405. Make a set of number cards. Use the cards to work on the chronological sequencing of numbers. Use the same cards for one-to-one correspondence, ordering from least to greatest and number recognition. **Form #85, Numerals and Operations for Math**, can be reproduced if needed.

406. Provide the student with mathematical symbol cards. The student can use the cards to make mathematical equations. The student may copy the equation onto paper. **Form # 85, Numerals and Operations for Math,** can also be used for this activity.

407. Collect shells, beads, seeds, pasta in various shapes and buttons. Put them into boxes or bags. Use these collections to sort and classify objects. The materials may also be used to assist with one-to-one correspondence.

408. Use egg cartons to sort various materials and establish the concept of group. Use this concept of group to introduce addition and subtraction.

409. Teach the student to use a calculator. Allow the student to do some of the textbook problems with a calculator.

410. Have the student collate papers in chronological order.

411. Coordinate the student's assessments, daily assignments and rewards with the general math class.

412. Create games the student may play with other students in the classroom. Activities can easily be included into math centers (Strategy #370). Vary the peer group.

Student Aids

413. When teaching multiple-step calculations, write the steps of the process for students to use as a guide. Provide a visual model next to the written steps so the student can see the correlation between the model and the written problem.

414. Create a small booklet for the student to keep as a math reference book. The booklet should include the basic math concepts covered in the class. The student can then refer to the guide if confused about a mathematical operation. Include the math vocabulary and a visual diagram for each step.

415. Attach a number line to the student's desk or in the math book. This will assist the student with addition, subtraction and the correct formation of the numbers. This will also assist students who experience difficulties with number reversals.

416. Teach the student to use the face clock in the classroom as a number line for facts to 12. This will support the student who is opposed to having a number line placed on the desk.

417. Create a chart with two number lines. Label one for addition, with arrows to the right, and label the other chart for subtraction, with arrows to the left. This will help the student internalize the concepts.

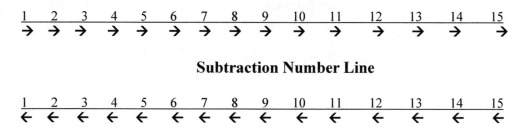

Addition Number Line

1 2 3 4 5 6 7 8 9 10 11 12 13 14 15
→ → → → → → → → → → → → → → →

Subtraction Number Line

1 2 3 4 5 6 7 8 9 10 11 12 13 14 15
← ← ← ← ← ← ← ← ← ← ← ← ← ← ←

418. Allow the student to use rubber number stamps or a computer, if number formation is extremely difficult.

419. Allow the student to use a calculator for all math calculations, once the processes and the concepts are mastered.

420. Use self-stick notes to help the student keep his/her place in the text.

421. *Touch Math* is an excellent program for students who struggle with computation. Touch points or black dots are placed strategically on numbers 1-9, and the students touch the points and count either forward for addition or backwards for subtraction. Touch Math can be used in addition, subtraction, multiplication and division. This program is available from Innovative Learning Concepts, Inc., in Colorado Springs, CO: *www.touchmath.com*.

Drill and Practice Games

422. Math games that can be played in class or at home provide a simple way to review basic math facts—without mundane drill and practice. Listed here are some games that classroom teachers have recommended. These games can be adapted in many ways.

Take Two Card Game. This simple game can be used for review of addition, subtraction and multiplication math facts.

Materials needed: Form # 87, Take Two Playing Cards
Photocopy the cards onto colored paper. Cut apart and laminate. Each set of cards becomes a playing hand for one student. By using various-colored card groups, the cards are simple to sort.

Directions: Take Two Addition for two students
- Each student receives a set of colored cards.
- Students shuffle their cards.
- The first student draws two cards from the second player and lays them face down.
- The second student does the same.
- Students add the two numbers on the cards they drew, and the student with the largest sum earns the game point.

Variations:
- Addition Three Card Draw: Each player draws three cards. Largest sum earns game point.
- Subtraction: Student with the smallest difference earns the point.
- Multiplication: Student with the largest product earns the game point.
- Counting: Students who are unable to add can play by counting all the stars for addition; counting backwards for subtraction; or using the cards for number recognition and simply saying the numeral aloud.

423. **Beach Ball Toss.** This game can be used for review of addition, subtraction and multiplication facts.

Materials needed: Beach ball with numbers 0-9 written on the ball.

Directions:
- Students throw the ball to each other.
- The student who catches the ball looks at the numbers positioned closest to the student's thumbs.
- The student states the problem and the answer out loud, for example, "3 x 6 = 18," and passes the ball. If the student does not know the answer, the student can say "Help" and pass the ball to another player.
- All students can play. Students continue to play until the predetermined time has been met.

Variations:
- Math: Students can add, subtract or multiply the two numbers on the ball.
- Students who are unable to add, subtract or multiply may catch the ball and say the numbers out loud.
- Vocabulary: Write letters on the ball instead of numbers. Select a topic. The student must say a word beginning with one of the letters positioned closest to the thumbs.

424. **Place Value Roll.** This game is used to practice place value by making either the largest or smallest number by inserting random numbers.

Materials needed: A die with 10 sides (numbers 0-9). If you do not have a 10-sided die, use a 6-sided die. A place value chart for each student.

Directions: Hand out place value charts to each student.
- Explain the objective to the students.
- Roll the die and say the number out loud.
- The students write the number in one of the spaces on the place value chart.
- The die is rolled again, and a second number is called. Students once again write the number into the place value chart.
- When all of the spaces have been filled, students share their answers.
- The students who meet the criteria win. (Largest number, smallest number)

Variations:
- Place value charts may be created in any size. Younger students may have three-column place value charts, whereas older students may use as many columns as the teacher determines.
- Number practice: Some students may use the charts to practice writing numerals only.

425. **Math Fact Relay.** This game is used to practice addition, subtraction or multiplication facts. Decide before you start, and let the students know which they will be doing.

Materials needed: Two sheets of chart paper large enough to create a 3″ x 3″ grid that students will be able to see from their seats. Grids also may be drawn on the board.

Directions:

- Divide the students into two or more teams.
- Create a 3″ x 3″ grid for each group. Number the squares on the grid horizontally.
- Explain to the students that only one person can be at the board from each team. The next student cannot get up until his or her team member is seated.
- Student #1 goes to the board and writes a number in the grid.
- Student #2 goes to the board and writes a second number in one of the adjacent boxes in the grid.
- Student #3 must provide the answer to the problem.
- If a student writes an incorrect answer, the next student in line must correct the student's mistake.
- The first group to complete its grid correctly wins.

1 **6** student #1	2 **4** student #2	3 **10** student #3
4	5 **3** student #4	6
7	8 **7** student #5	9

Variations:

- Teams can be divided into groups depending upon skill level. For example, students working on math facts may be required always to begin in column #1 and work the grid ONLY horizontally or vertically.
- More advanced students may be required to complete problems that can be read both horizontally and vertically.
- Students with a large discrepancy in math can be paired with another student and work as a team. One student provides the answer, and the second student fills in the chart with the number.

424. **Fraction Frenzy!** This game is used to practice fractions.

     Materials needed: Teacher-created word list for students.

     Directions:
     • Provide direction sheets for students.

     One fraction at a time! (for beginning levels)
     Divide the following two words in half: GRID and DEFEAT.
     Write the first 1/2 of the word <u>GR</u>ID and add the second half of the word DEF<u>EAT</u>.
     What is the new word? (GREAT)

     Divide the following words in half: GAME and FELT.
     Write the second 1/2 of the word GA<u>ME</u> and add the second half of the word FE<u>LT</u>.
     What is the new word? (MELT)

     Mix and Match Fractions! (for more advanced)
     Divide the following word into fourths: PRACTICE. Divide the following word into fifths: RAISE.
     Write the first 1/4 of the word <u>PR</u>ACTICE and add the last 4/5 of the word R<u>AISE</u>.
     What is the new word? (PRAISE)

     Divide the following word in half: TREK. Divide the following word into thirds: STAIRS. Divide the following into sixths: ACTION.
     Write the first half of the word <u>TR</u>EK, add the second 1/3 of the word ST<u>AI</u>RS and add the final 1/6 of the word ACTIO<u>N</u>. What is the new word? (TRAIN)

     Variations:
     • Students may create their own Fraction Frenzy Words to share with the class.

425. **Springtime Math.** This activity allows students to create math word problems and enjoy the outside at the same time!

     Materials needed: One clipboard, paper and pencil per student. (Add colored pencils or crayons, if students would like to illustrate their math problems.)

     Directions: Ask the students to create their own word problems related to what they see. The students share their math problems and provide other students the opportunity to figure out the answer.

     I saw one white butterfly and two yellow ones flutter by. How many butterflies did I see?

There were three classrooms outside for recess. One class had 24 students, another class had 28 students and the third class was still playing, so I couldn't count them. I will guess the class had 26 students. How many students were on the playground?

I saw 10 cars parked in the teachers' parking lot. How many tires are in the parking lot?

Variations:

- Provide specific guidelines, such as students must write one multiplication problem and rewrite it to reflect a division problem.

- Students may illustrate the math problems.

Homework Assignments

It is important when assigning math homework to check for understanding. Therefore, always allow students to begin their homework assignments during class, and check for understanding before the students leave the classroom. The purpose of the homework is to reinforce what the student has learned in class. If the student has not mastered the concept, the student will be unable to do the homework. If this is the case, either excuse the student from the homework assignment or provide an alternative review assignment. Several of the Forms from Chapter Five can be used for math homework as well. **Forms #58 to #64** include various Assignment Sheets, a Homework Log, a Priority Checklist and Curriculum Modifications.

426. Allow the student to begin the homework assignment in class, and check for understanding of the concept before the student leaves class.

427. Post assignments on a classroom website, if available, so the student can cross-reference the assignment from home, if needed. Parents can also stay current on class assignments with a website.

428. Provide clear guidelines and expectations for the student regarding homework. Perhaps the student is able to use a calculator on homework assignments or is expected to complete only parts of the assignment. Be sure parents are aware of any expectations that may be different than those posted on the website.

429. Pre-teach all new vocabulary so the student understands the assignment.

430. Highlight key words on homework assignments. Present the directions clearly to the student, and ask the student to paraphrase each assignment.

431. Be sure the student has the supplies at home that are needed to complete the assignment. These may include number lines, rulers, clocks, multiplication grids, graph paper, calculator, projector, compass, etc. Supply lists should be provided to parents at the beginning of the semester.

432. Modify the length of the assignment, if needed, to accommodate the student's level.

433. Allow a student to use a calculator.

434. If the student uses an assignment book, double check to see that the homework is noted correctly.

Assessment Strategies

Assessment procedures will be documented in the student's IEP. Listed here are some specific assessment strategies for mathematics. Additional appropriate strategies will be listed in Chapter 11, Classroom Assessments.

435. Use computer programs in place of timed tests. If the class is given a timed three-minute multiplication quiz, allow the student six minutes on the computer and divide his results by two. This will provide a fairly accurate timed result. It also allows the student a little additional time to get organized and adjust to the computer.

436. When scoring timed tests, look for improvement. Instead of signing a letter grade, ask students to graph their results from the timed tests. For the majority of students with disabilities, timed tests often cause a great amount frustration, and the student will do poorly. By graphing the results, the student is able to look for improvement.

437. Test the student orally by asking probing questions, such as:

> Can you explain how you solved the problem?
> Can you demonstrate how the problem was solved?

438. Create a math portfolio. Have the student keep samples of his best work to be graded as a final assignment.

439. Allow the student to use a calculator during testing, if the student has difficulty with math facts.

440. Avoid timed tests.

441. If creating your own assessments, provide ample work space, group similar problems together and provide clear and concise directions.

442. Refer to Chapter 11, Classroom Assessments, and the student's IEP for additional strategies.

Chapter Eight Conclusion

Chapter Eight is about the language of numbers—and the new vocabulary that students must learn, not to mention new concepts, calculations and methods of problem solving. All this learning can be fun—and made easier with the multiple strategies presented here. The creative use of manipulatives, visuals and math games make abstract math concepts come alive for students and also make the concepts more concrete and understandable. Mathematics is an important life tool, and students will pick it up more readily if they can see its functionality and meaning in their lives. This chapter provides strategies for relating math to real-life situations and for helping students remember what they need to know to do what they need to do with numbers and the language of mathematics.

The Appendix forms for this chapter include several handy number charts, math symbols, playing cards for a math card game and more. The 14 forms listed include not only those specifically related to math, but forms from previous chapters that are helpful in any subject area.

Appendix Forms for Chapter Eight

#58	Incomplete Assignments
#59	Assignment Sheet
#60	Daily Assignments
#61	Daily Homework Log
#62	Priority Checklist
#63	Weekly Planner
#64	Curriculum Modifications
#81	Error Analysis Chart – Math
#82	Addition and Subtraction Charts
#83	Multiplication Charts
#84	Menu Card
#85	Numerals and Math Symbols
#86	One-to-One Correspondence
#87	Take Two Card Game

"One person's constant is another person's variable."

Susan Gerhart

Notes:

_____

_____

_____

_____

_____

_____

_____

_____

_____

_____

_____

_____

_____

_____

Chapter Nine

Organizational Skills

"I can't find my homework. I know I turned it in! I know I did it!" Does this sound familiar?

Students can complete assignments when adapted to their specific needs, but frequently the assignment is lost or misplaced. Some students experience difficulty with organization of time and others of their physical space. Some appear to be unorganized because they are unable to follow oral and written directions.

This section focuses on organization of the physical environment of the student.

> **Chapter Note:**
> On page 163, you will find a complete list of the reproducible forms referred to throughout this chapter. The reproducible forms are located in the Appendix.

Classroom Organization

As an educator, consider your personal organizational skills. Think about how you organize your time and space. Now step back and look at the classroom environment. Is the classroom organized? Is there a specific location for supplies, materials and books? Is there a designated location to turn in assignments? Is the seating arrangement conducive to learning? Is there a space for paraprofessionals and volunteers to organize and keep their supplies? It is important to evaluate the classroom environment. It is difficult to expect a student to be organized if the classroom is not organized and the expectations for the student are inconsistent.

444.   Introduce specific routines to students on the first day.

> **Entering the Classroom in the Morning**. Provide a specific activity for students to begin as soon as they are seated. This may include writing in a daily journal, copying something from the board, etc. This activity will help students settle into their seats and be prepared for learning.

Transition between Subjects. Some students need to be aware of transition times. Play music, turn the lights on or off, sing a song, ring a bell or the like. This indicates to students that it is time to put away materials and prepare for the next subject or activity.

Moving about the Classroom. Do you have a pass? Where is it located? When can a student get up and walk around and when must the student remain seated?

Breaks. Is there a daily break? What may students do during this break time?

445. Organize the classroom environment. Provide a specific location for students to hand in their daily assignments and late assignments, and also a place to retrieve take-home materials.

446. Enlist student support by assigning some of the routine classroom organization jobs to students. Create job descriptions, and discuss the duties with the students before assigning the jobs. Some jobs will be more desirable than others, so it is important to rotate the jobs on a weekly basis. The following jobs are included on **Form #88, Classroom Managers.** List the students' names, and place a check as students are assigned jobs so the Manager positions are rotated. If there are jobs specific to your classroom, add them to the list.

Assignment Book Manager: This student is responsible to check and see if students have written the assignment into their assignment books. Set a designated time at the end of the day to check assignment books. The Assignment Book Manager can quickly glance at the assignment book to be sure the homework is listed correctly. Students who need special help should see the teacher. If the assignments are posted on a website, the note may simply say, "See class website for Reading." If students do not have assignment books, **Form #59, Assignment Sheet; Form #60, Daily Assignments; or Form #61, Daily Homework Log,** can be provided to the student.

Board Manager: This manager cleans the boards after a class session so they are ready for the next lesson. The student should also check to see that there are markers for white boards and chalk and clean erasers for blackboards. If transparencies are used, the student may also clean these. Be sure to keep a folder for the transparencies that need to be cleaned, and separately store the ones that you want to keep.

Classroom Manager: The classroom manager oversees the general tidiness of the classroom. The student can be in charge of picking up "stuff" left on the floor and on tables in common areas such as listening centers, reading centers and study centers. The classroom manager can also water plants and feed the fish and pets.

Computer Manager: This student is assigned the job of making sure that all computers are booted up before the class uses them and are turned off at the end of the day.

First- and Last-in-Line Leaders: Younger students tend to enjoy being first in line. The purpose of this job is really just to eliminate fights over who gets to be first! The last person in line can be responsible for turning off the light and closing the door.

Homework Manager: This person passes out and collects homework assignments, checks off assignments as students turn them in and inserts homework into students' cubbies or folders, if necessary. **Form #89, Class Homework Log,** can be used to document the return of assignments. Assign each student a number ID. It will be easier for students to find the number on the list and will also help with confidentiality. The Homework Manager places a check in the appropriate dated box. This also may be used to check off required material, such as field trip forms.

Paper Manager: Assign a student to collect daily assignments and pass out papers.

Substitute Helper: The role of this student is to fill in for any student who is absent and cannot complete an assigned job. This student also can run errands, deliver messages and help with any other jobs that the teacher may need doing.

Additional Jobs: Often there are jobs specific to a classroom. Create a title, write the job description and add it to the list!

447. Provide the student with a simplified map of the school. Number and highlight classroom locations. Include the most direct route for the student.

448. Write the daily schedule on the board, and try to follow it as closely as possible. Some students cannot function without a schedule, and many need to anticipate what will happen next. Also check to be sure the student is able to tell time. Often students have only digital clocks at home and may not know how to read a face clock. Make sure students know how to tell time—don't just assume.

449. Picture schedules are appropriate for the student who is unable to read. The pictures may be posted alongside the class schedule, or take digital photos of classroom activities and place the picture alongside the written schedule. **Form #90, Picture Schedule,** includes some simple icons that can be used to create individual charts for students.

450. Build transition time into the schedule. Allow the student a little extra time to organize materials during transition time.

451. Keep all student supplies in a central area. Clearly state which materials the students may use during the day. If there are specific materials that should not be used by students, put them away or establish an area of Adult Supplies Only!

452. Create seating arrangements that allow the students to see the board easily without turning their bodies. Also consider special seating arrangements for students who receive daily support. These students should be seated in a location where they can easily receive support without interrupting the entire class. For obvious reasons, seats around the perimeter of the class work better than seating the student in the center aisles.

453. Provide students with proper subject headings for all papers. This will help students to put papers into the appropriate folders. A report for a Social Studies class will not end up in the Language Arts folder.

454. Develop a color code chart and post it. Each color should refer to a specific subject. For example, Reading – red, Math – blue, etc. Ask students to place a small colored dot in the right-hand corner of the paper to help with filing. This especially helps with written language assignments, as it is easy to confuse a social studies rough draft report with an English rough draft report on a similar topic—especially at the secondary level.

455. Weekly folders for parents also help with organization. If you send home a folder on the same day each week, parents will begin to look for the weekly calendar, weekly reminders, the spelling list, etc. Parents can be notified that this will occur on a weekly basis, so they know when to check their children's backpacks.

456. Parents should also be encouraged to work on organization with students at home.

457. Encourage parents to insist that their children pack homework into their school bags when assignments are complete. Many snacks can also be packed the night before.

458. Often teachers will post weekly information, assignments, etc. on a classroom website. Although most parents do have access to a computer, some may not, so it is important to have additional means of communication with parents.

Student Organization

Organization feels good. As organized adults, we know what we need, where it is and how to find it quickly—most of the time. When our lives become disorganized, life naturally becomes more stressful. Most adults know how to organize. Often when we feel we have too much to do, a simple 'To do' list is created. Once the priority items are checked off, immediately some of the stress is relieved. Students also become more stressed when they are disorganized. They often become frustrated when they have completed the assignment but forget it at home. After numerous times of forgetting, often the adult simply doesn't believe that the student is actually doing the work—until, of course, the student finally produces all of the assignments, folded, crumpled and in disarray. Following are some strategies to help students. What works for one student will not necessarily work for another. By providing various ideas to students, they will be able to determine what works best for them.

459.   Many students need to be taught how to organize. Allow students time to discuss and share their individual organizational strategies. List some ideas, and encourage the students to experiment with various methods of organization. Some systems will make no sense to those not using it. But if it works for a student, allow it. Often adults will have piles of papers on their desks, and to an outsider, it makes no sense—yet the adult is able to find what is needed quickly. It is the same with students. What works for one may make no sense to another!

460.   Color code folders for each subject. Consider purchasing a box of folders at an office supply store, and provide (or have the students purchase) identical folders. The folders can be color-coded with the textbooks. If the math textbook is predominately blue, assign a blue folder for math also. If the entire class has exactly the same color, it will help the student visually by observing the other students in the class.

461.   Create individual subject folders. Use color-coded folders for the various academic areas. Keep a pencil, pen, paper and other necessary items in each folder. Two-pocket folders may also be stapled together to create a four-pocket folder. Four-pocket folders are good for subject areas that have many steps to assignments. Written language or creative writing is a perfect example of a subject that can utilize a four-pocket system. Simply label the pockets as follows: Pocket #1: writing ideas; #2: rough drafts; #3: final copies; and #4: graded and completed projects to take home.

462.   If folders are confusing for the student, use a three-ring notebook with a plastic supply pouch. This will help the student to keep all folders and papers in one place. Instruct the student to keep ALL assignments in the notebook until it is time to hand them in. Loose papers can be three-hole punched. Pocket folders can be inserted to keep final papers neat. The student's assignment sheet can also be inserted. Forms #59, 60 and 61 may be reproduced, if the student does not use an assignment book.

463.   Use an accordion file. These files may have anywhere from three to 12 or more pockets. Each file should be labeled. Besides academics, the student may also include a file for Home/School Correspondence, After-School Activities, etc. With this system, the student will file every science paper in the Science section, every math paper in the Math section, etc. If the student is unsure whether to keep the paper, instruct the student to file it. An adult can help to sort through the papers at a later time. This will take care of many of the loose papers that tend to get lost or misplaced.

464.   Ask students to clean and organize their desks and/or lockers at least once a week. Have them organize papers into three piles: file into folders; take home; and toss. Also ask them to sharpen pencils and throw away unusable pencils and pens, and toss any clutter that accumulates on the floor of the locker and bottom of the desk.

465. Students often have trouble finding items in their lockers. It is a good idea to encourage students with organizational difficulties to use their locker less frequently during the day. Encourage the student to keep two piles of materials—one for the morning and one for the afternoon. All books and folders for the morning are grouped (perhaps in a bag or box in the locker), and the items for the afternoon classes are also grouped. Some students use red folders in the morning and blue in the afternoon. As homework is assigned, the book and folder are placed on the top shelf.

466. When cleaning desks and lockers, the student should use the One Touch Rule. In other words, try to handle material as little as possible to avoid losing it. For example, if the student receives a syllabus for class, the student should put it directly into the proper place (folder, three-ring notebook). If the student places it in the desk and later looks for the syllabus to file it, the student has increased the touch to two times. Papers are less apt to become lost, if the student uses the One Touch Rule.

467. Some students start over multiple times on an assignment, and the crumpled paper ends up in their desks, or they continually walk to the trash to dispose of it. Simply place a paper bag under their seats so they can dispose of their trash immediately, without leaving their desks and getting distracted.

468. Use a homework book or an assignment sheet. Explain the difference between the words "due" and "do." Teach the student to prioritize assignments by estimating the amount of time the assignment will take in relation to the due date. Some students need a daily, weekly and monthly calendar to understand the concept of time.

469. When assigning projects, list the approximate length of time needed to complete each assignment. With complex assignments, provide specific dates for the various steps. Check the assignments on the specified due dates to make sure the student is keeping pace. **Form#59, Assignment Sheet,** in the Appendix may be reproduced for this purpose.

470. Supply the student with a pad of notepaper for "Assignments to Do Today." Help the student to write reminder notes. **Form #62, Priority Checklist,** may be used to prioritize what needs to be done.

471. Use a peer to help monitor assignments. The peer can assist the student in placing assignments in correct folders or turning in assignments. **Form #54, Study Buddies,** may be used.

472. Permit students who have difficulty remembering to do homework to call home and leave a message, send a text message, leave a cell phone message or send a reminder e-mail. Make sure students note the subject and page number of assignments. Teenagers may forget homework assignments, but they always seem to check the telephone or computer for messages! Students often have electronic organizers where

they keep messages, friends' telephone numbers, etc. Homework assignments can also be programmed in.

473. Ask students to think about and develop their own organizational strategies. **Form #91, How Organized Are You?** is a simple checklist that students can use to evaluate their personal lives. After using this simple checklist, students may use **Form #92, My Personal Goals,** to select several personal goals to work on. The students can self-monitor their progress, and within several weeks, they hopefully will see some improvements in their personal organization.

474. Many schools now provide laptop computers for students. If this is the case, be sure to teach students how to save their work into file folders and to back up the folders on a disk—in fact several disks, in case one is corrupt.

475. Allow the student to check out an extra set of textbooks for home use.

476. Provide the student with a packet of self-stick notes. The student can write down each assignment as given. The note can be placed on the student's desk. The student may throw the note when the assignment is complete or stick it into an assignment book.

477. Create a simple daily checklist with assignments and reminders. The student can tape it onto the top of the desk or into a notebook. When the assignment is complete, the student crosses it off the list. If daily assignments remain, the student can staple or tape the checklist into his or her assignment book.

478. If an assignment is completed during the class period, encourage the student to turn it in immediately instead of waiting until the next day. If the student uses the three-ring notebook and has a folder for complete assignments, it may be inserted into the folder.

479. Plastic zip-lock bags can be used to store pencils, crayons, markers and supplies in the students' desks. Students who have difficulty with organization will want to keep several bags in their desks or lockers. The students will need to periodically reorganize and restock their bags.

480. Provide extra time for students with organizational difficulties to locate materials and organize them before beginning a new lesson. Let students know a transition is about to occur by using a visual or auditory signal. Turn the lights off/on, ring a bell, play some music or clap your hands. Once the signal is given, allow students two or three minutes to put away supplies and prepare for the next activity.

481. If a student works with someone (such as a school psychologist or social worker) for daily monitoring of behavior or daily check-ins or check-outs, ask the adult to stop by the classroom. This way, the student will not miss valuable class time or important beginning-of-the-day or end-of-the-day instructions.

482. Allow 10 minutes at the end of the day for students to copy assignments from the board and to double-check their assignment books. This also allows the teacher to spot-check the assignment books for students who have difficulty.

483. Teach the student to monitor self-talk. Often disorganized students feel frustrated and begin to think negative thoughts, such as, "I can't do this," "I just don't understand" or "I'll never get it!" Have the student practice taking several deep breaths and repeating positive statements, such as "I can do this," "I *can* understand it" or "Slow down and focus." When directions are complex, ask the student to verbalize the steps.

484. Assign a hanging folder, a numbered file folder or mailbox to each student. Students who continually lose assignments may place their assignments immediately upon completion into the folder for safekeeping. Often these assignments get lost in transit between home and school.

485. Many classrooms maintain a website. Home assignments and other pertinent information can be posted on this website, allowing access for both students and parents.

486. Enlist parents' cooperation with setting a specific daily time for homework. Send a supply list home so parents know what is needed. Be specific. Not all homes have calculators, protractors and rulers on hand.

487. At parent meetings, open houses, etc, encourage parents to have consistent, daily study times in the home. If the student does not have homework, this time can be spent reading or cleaning and organizing folders and backpack.

Homework Accommodations

When you assign homework to students, be sure it is meaningful and that the student understands the homework assignment. Also, students are more likely to be accountable for assignments when they know the homework will count and be graded.

488. Allow students who are consistently unprepared for class to have two sets of books—one for school and one for home use. This way, if the student forgets the homework, the books are at home, and all the student will need to do is to check his or her assignment book or the class website for a list of the assignments. This will eliminate the excuse, "I forgot to bring my science book home!"

489. Use an assignment book, or have an assignment sheet available to the student. See the Appendix for assignment sheet forms.

490. Provide self-stick notes that the student may affix to the textbook with important reminders.

491.   Create Homework Folders. In the left pocket the student may store the assignment log where the daily homework assignments are recorded. Assignments "in progress" remain in the left pocket until they are complete. When the assignment is complete, it can be checked off the assignment sheet and moved to the right pocket. Separate folders for each subject area should be used at the secondary level, whereas elementary students should be able to use only one folder.

492.   Remind students of the importance of "backing up" assignments when completing them on the computer. Most word processing programs can be set to automatically back up work. If the student is required to return a disk to school, a copy should be kept at home also.

Chapter Nine Conclusion

This chapter has presented strategies to help students who have difficulties organizing themselves. Such strategies are beneficial for a number of reasons, but one of the most important is that better organization relieves students of considerable stress and thus may significantly improve the students' work overall. The judicious use of folders, color coding, reminder notes, lists, time management and technology, for example, can help ensure that students complete the right assignments, on time, and get them handed in without losing them somewhere along the way. Better organization also ensures that students have the right materials on hand, so time isn't lost and assignments can be completed properly. Assigning students to help as classroom managers gives them pride and a stake in the organization of the classroom. When teachers enlist the help of parents at home, even more benefit accrues. Take advantage of the strategies presented here to give your students the comforting feeling that everything is in its place and all's right with the classroom (never mind the world!). Remember to use the reproducible forms in the Appendix to help you in this endeavor.

Appendix Forms for Chapter Nine

#54	Study Buddy
#59	Assignment Sheet
#60	Daily Assignments
#61	Daily Homework Log
#62	Priority Checklist
#88	Classroom Managers
#89	Class Homework Log
#90	Schedule Pictures
#91	How Organized Are You?
#92	My Personal Goals!

"To get what you want, STOP doing what isn't working."

Dennis Weaver

Notes:

_____

_____

_____

_____

_____

_____

_____

_____

_____

_____

_____

_____

_____

"Children are apt to live up to what you believe of them."

Lady Bird Johnson

Chapter Ten

Giving and Receiving Instruction

For students, a large portion of the school day is spent listening to material presented orally. At the secondary level, the majority of the day is spent in class lecture sessions. This can be a frustrating experience for students who have difficulties with auditory processing, taking notes or sustaining attention for large periods of time.

This chapter encourages you to analyze your own teaching style and provides some options to help meet the needs of these students. It discusses oral and written directions and presents ideas to help students develop listening and note-taking skills.

Self-Check of Oral Presentation

As a teacher, self-evaluation of your oral presentation style is important, and it can be accomplished in a number of ways. Some schools incorporate a peer mentor program, which allows teachers time to observe their peers and offer suggestions to one another. Other schools have a formal evaluation system. Some teachers choose to videotape their lessons and evaluate their own teaching styles. No matter what option you select, evaluating your teaching style is highly recommended. You can note areas for improvement and set goals to increase your skills as a presenter so students will learn more easily. **Form #93, Self-Evaluation Worksheet,** is a simple self-evaluation option. Take a few moments to read through the checklist, and check off what usually occurs in your classroom during large-group instruction. If you feel you could improve in certain areas, set personal goals and challenge yourself!

> **Chapter Note:**
> On page 178, you will find a complete list of the reproducible forms referred to throughout this chapter. The reproducible forms are located in the Appendix.

493. Is the classroom arrangement conducive to the lesson? Think about the classroom arrangement. Can the students see you without turning their chairs? If students need to move their chairs to see you, be sure to provide clipboards for note-taking. Some students may need to sit closer to see better or hear better. Those who are easily distracted should be seated away from doors and windows and should put away all distracting objects. Close the door so hallway noise is reduced.

494. Do the students see a purpose for learning the new information? If students do not understand the purpose or see a connection between the lesson and the reason for learning it, retention will be lower. It's up to the presenter to provide the purpose.

495. Do you state the goals and objectives at the beginning of each lesson? Writing the goals and objectives on the blackboard or providing a syllabus to students will help them focus on the most important material.

496. Do you begin each new lecture with a review of the previous lesson, the important points presented, and the vocabulary? This will help students refresh their memories and will build new knowledge on prior information. Some students have very short memories. Simply taking a few minutes to review the previous lesson will increase retention.

497. Does the lesson have a definite starting and ending point? Do you provide an anticipatory set to draw the students into the lesson? Do you summarize main points at the end of the lesson? All of these strategies help students maintain their interest and retain information.

498. Do you incorporate humor into your lectures? It has been found that humor, when relevant, increases retention.

499. What is your rate of speaking? Is it too slow, too fast or appropriate for the lesson? Depending upon the material presented, your rate of speaking will vary. When expecting students to take notes, slow down and allow students time to write.

500. Is your pronunciation clear? As you speak, do you use natural phrasing and sentence structure? Is the information presented in a logical, understandable sequence?

501. When lecturing and presenting to a group, do you teach for understanding? By providing background information and building on previously learned concepts, the students' retention will be enhanced.

502. Do you organize your thoughts before the lesson and stay on track when teaching? Stay on topic, and redirect student questions that tend to steer away from the objective of the lesson. Once off topic, some students are lost forever!

503. Do you stop frequently and ask questions to check for understanding? It is important to check continually so you will know if the students are tracking or lost. Ask relevant questions, and ask students to paraphrase material in their own words. Adopt the classroom attitude that "no question is a dumb question." When students seem confused, be ready to repeat information and summarize what you have said.

504. Do you support your lectures by providing supplemental materials, such as visual aids, diagrams and demonstrations? These supplemental materials will aid students who learn visually.

505. Do you allow sufficient time for the student to process the information presented? When asking a question, wait a minimum of 10 seconds to allow students to think and formulate an answer. When asking a question, do not allow students to raise their hands with their answers until you provide a signal. This allows students a little extra thinking time and allows those who process information slowly to formulate their answers.

506. Do you allow time for students to take notes and copy material from the board? If students are required to take notes, allow additional time after main points for students to write. For students who are unable to take notes, provide an outline of the key points or lecture notes for the student to follow.

507. Do you present as many examples as possible related to the lesson? Have the students close their eyes and visualize what is said. By creating visual images, the student will better retain the information.

508. Do you present only relevant information during lectures? Do you use nouns in place of pronouns whenever possible? The consistent use of pronouns may cause confusion to some students, especially if they did not understand or pay attention at the beginning, or if you move rapidly from one topic to another.

509. When students are required to take notes, do you simplify the vocabulary? Important information can be highlighted on overhead transparencies, or use colored chalk on the chalkboard or various colors of markers on white boards.

510. Do you highlight key words, phrases and steps to the lessons when presenting the items visually?

511. Do you pause frequently during presentations and ask the student to summarize information? Do you ask probing questions to check for understanding and relate the information to previously learned concepts when appropriate?

512. Do you consistently use cueing? For example: "Remember this, as it will be on a test." "This is important, so please write it in your notes."

These techniques should also be used when reviewing for a test. Specifically tell the students for which information they will be accountable. Use cuing techniques such as, "Remember this point," "This will be on the test," and "Please write this down, as you will be tested on this material."

513. Do you vary the level of questioning during the classroom discussions so all students can participate? This is especially important if you have students who may be working on social skills, listening skills, etc. Even though a student's goal may be different, the level of questioning can be adjusted so the student is able to participate.

514. Do you make special arrangements for students who are perceived by others as "never having the correct answer"? This image can often be changed by providing the student with the questions beforehand. Make an arrangement with the student prior to the lesson so the student knows exactly what will be expected of him or her.

515. Pass or play! Place all students' names on craft sticks. When it is time to answer a question, draw a student's name. Allow students one "Pass" opportunity per class session. Student participation increases, as students never know when they will be called upon.

516. Encourage active participation by using whole-group response. There are several ways to incorporate a whole-group response to lessons:

- **Individual chalkboards.** Provide each student with a small chalkboard, an old sock and a piece of chalk. Students work alone or in partners to formulate short responses. Allow ample time for students to write their responses.

- **Index cards.** Provide each student with two index cards. These cards can be used during group activities to answer questions. Once the question is asked, students show their responses by holding up their cards.

TRUE	FALSE
I AGREE	I DISAGREE

- **Thumbs up/thumbs down!** This is a simple way to encourage active group participation during presentations. Once again, be sure to allow ample time for slow students to process the question before asking for the response.

Providing Oral Directions

Students are bombarded with hundreds of directions daily. Many students experience difficulty in school because they are not able to process the directions. Inattention, difficulty with auditory processing, memory deficits, poor listening skills, limited receptive language or the inability to sequence information are only a few of the reasons. No matter what the root of the problem is, it is often a very frustrating experience for the student.

517. Be sure you have the student's attention before giving directions. Pause and wait if you do not. Eye contact is important.

518. Change the format of oral directions. Provide the directions in written format so the student can refer to the information frequently.

519. Do not interject irrelevant information when giving oral directions. Keep directions concise and simple.

520. Simplify the vocabulary.

521. When giving verbal explanations, also use visuals if possible.

522. Divide lengthy and complex directions into one- and two-step segments. If the directions are complex, allow students to complete the first step before adding more directions.

523. Appoint a peer tutor to coach the student through multiple-step directions.

524. Be sure the student understands the direction before starting the assignment. Ask the student to repeat the direction back to you or a peer to check for understanding.

525. Use a combination of visual and auditory directions for the student. Use the blackboard, a white board, the overhead or a flip chart.

526. Include rebus pictures with written directions for students who are unable to read the directions.

527. Photograph the steps of experiments, demonstrations and activities that have multiple steps. Glue the photographs in chronological order inside a file folder. The student may use this folder if a visual aid is needed. File directions with the unit for future use.

528. Record daily assignments on tape. The student may listen to the directions as many times as needed. Include the due dates.

529. If the student has a hearing impairment, appoint a peer to cue the student when oral directions are given. Be sure the student is also cued into intercom messages. Always check for understanding.

Providing Written Directions

530. Write the directions in sequential order. If multiple steps are involved, number the steps.

531. Allow sufficient time for students to copy the assignment into their notebooks or assignment books. If a student is unable to copy from a distant model, allow the student to copy another student's paper, or appoint a peer to write the directions for the student.

532. Accompany written directions with a visual demonstration or model whenever possible.

533. Ask the student to read the written directions from start to finish at least two times before asking for help. Allow the student extra time to underline or highlight key words and phrases.

534. When a string of directions is presented at the beginning of the assignment, have the student place a colored dot between each segment of the instruction.

535. Always check for understanding before the student begins the assignment.

536. If you have visually impaired students, always give test directions, assignments and important directions orally along with the written.

537. Place a piece of yellow acetate over the page of print to enhance the contrast and darken the print for the visually impaired.

538. Use black, fine tip pens to trace over directions and darken the print for students with low vision.

539. For visually impaired students, use a white board with erasable black marker for greater contrast.

Note-Taking Skills for Students

Note taking is a difficult process. Think about the last time you attended a class or a workshop and were required to take notes. Did you write on the syllabus provided? Perhaps you brought a tape player and recorded the information so you could listen to it in your car or during a quiet time at home. Did you jot down key words and phrases? Or did you write entire phrases verbatim? Perhaps you were able to generalize the information and fill in a chart or a graph. When the presenter stated, "This is important!" did you furiously try to write every word? Taking notes is not a simple skill. It requires the student to process information both auditorily and visually and then output the information in written format—another skill altogether. Students must be taught various strategies to take notes successfully, beginning with listening.

540. Make sure the student removes all unnecessary materials from the desktop during lectures and oral presentations. The student should have two sharpened pencils, paper and a highlighter on top of the desk. All other objects should be put away.

Listening

541. Listening is a skill that must be developed. Most students have selective listening patterns. The following strategies should be discussed with students.

542. Discuss that listening is difficult. It is important that students focus on what the presenter is saying and try not to let their minds wander. Good listeners listen even when they know the subject. They listen to see if they can learn anything new! Good listening takes practice!

543. Ask students to analyze their personal listening skills. Do they have difficulty listening to music or concentrating when listening to the radio or watching television? Probably not! It is important to emphasize that students should apply the same strategy to school subjects. It's not that students cannot listen; it's that they often have selective listening.

544. Discuss classroom distractions. Students must learn to avoid the distractions. Sometimes it's hard to ignore the passing of notes, the people whispering and the shuffling of papers, but good listeners learn to ignore these distractions and focus on the presenter.

545. Discuss the importance of knowing the reason for the presentation. If students do not see a purpose, it will be hard to concentrate and listen.

546. Tell students that learning is up to the individual. It is up to the student to learn the material, and it is not up to the teacher to continually amuse and entertain. Some subjects can be entertaining, but not all. The message is important, or the teacher would not be presenting it. Explain to students that they need to take charge of themselves, and they should not be passive listeners.

547. Stress the importance of not tuning out the presenter—even if the student does not like the subject (or the person doing the talking).

548. Explain the importance of listening to pick up the main idea. The facts will back up the main idea. If the student has difficulty construing the main idea, it is important to ask the teacher to provide an outline. Students need to learn to be assertive and not be afraid to ask for help when needed.

Taking Notes

549. Encourage students to take notes while listening. Explain that often they may think they will remember what the speaker is saying, but usually if information is not written down, it will be forgotten.

550. Encourage students to write notes using their own words, with the exceptions of formulas, definitions and specific facts.

551. Spend class time teaching students how to take notes. This is a life-long skill that students will use into adulthood.

552. Teach common abbreviations used during note taking. The trick with using abbreviations is that students must be consistent. As a class, develop a list of common abbreviations, and practice using them. Post the list in the classroom.

553. Help students to understand that they needn't write a sentence when taking notes, if the same thing can be captured in a phrase. Likewise, skip the phrase, if the same meaning can be portrayed with a word.

554. Teach students that if they miss a main idea or topic, they shouldn't stop writing. Information can be filled in later. Often, worrying about one point and asking another student during the lecture means you will miss the *next* key point.

555. Explain that sometimes it's okay to just listen. Students do not have to be furiously writing at all times. Not all material requires note taking. Be sure to let them know when they should record important points.

556. White space is okay! This extra space can be used to add details later.

557. Class notes should have a date. This will help to organize the notes later. Use a notebook to take notes, as loose papers often get lost.

558. Explain to students that reviewing their notes frequently will help them retain the information. They actually will retain more by reading through notes daily than by trying to study all the information the night before a test.

559. Students often benefit from a list of discussion questions provided before the lecture. This will help them focus on the general idea instead of many small details. They can take notes right on the same page.

560. Cue the student to the major points with key phrases during the presentation, such as "Please remember this," "This point is very important" or "Write this down."

561. Stop and draw! Some students are very visual. At appropriate times during the lessons, ask students to stop and illustrate what they have just heard. In the process of illustrating, they will need to think about the details of the presentation.

562. Provide the student with an outline of the main topics on the board. Students can copy the main ideas then list the details during the lecture.

563. List major points on the blackboard or overhead before or during the presentation. When the presentation is complete, use the following technique to immediately reinforce the key concepts of the lesson.

564. Ask students to fold a piece of notebook paper in half to create two columns. Have them list the major points from the blackboard in the left column. Leave three blank lines between each major point. When the presentation is finished, ask the students to recall and write as much as they can remember about each specific point on the blank lines. Allow extra time for the students to compare their responses and add information. This page can be used as a study guide.

565. **Form # 94, Outline,** is a simple outline that can be used for four main topics and four supporting details. Partial outlines can also be created with this form. With a partial outline, the teacher fills in some of the information for the student. For example, the outline form may have the main ideas and some of the details filled in for the student. The student is required to fill in the missing information. In other words, the student is still required to take notes, but some of the information is already provided.

566. The Cornell Method, developed by Walter Pauk of Cornell University, is a widely used method that students can use not only to take notes during class but to review as well. This method works best for lessons that are well organized and presented in a sequential manner. With this method, the student divides a single page into three sections: Main Idea, Details and Summary. During the lecture, the student takes notes in the Detail Section. After the lecture, the student reviews the notes and writes memory joggers in the Main Idea section. These memory joggers may include questions, main ideas, diagrams, etc. The final section on the page is the Summary section. In this section, the student summarizes the lesson in a few simple sentences. For additional information, search for Cornell Method online.

Following is the typical page layout for the Cornell Method of note taking.

Step #2 – Main Ideas	Step #1 – Details
Memory joggers Main ideas Diagrams	**(Student takes class notes here.)**
Step #3 – Summary The student summarizes the lecture and notes in several sentences.	

567. When comparing and contrasting information, provide a chart or a Venn diagram for the student to complete. **Form #47, Compare and Contrast Organizer,** can be used. Additional forms from the Appendix that may help with note-taking skills include **Form #46, Chain of Events Organizer,** and **Form #48, Fact or Opinion.** These forms can be adapted for use.

568. For some students, mapping instead of standard note-taking skills may be used. Simple mind maps allow the students to write down just the facts. This is a good strategy for students who are unable to write quickly, as only key words are used. The following examples can easily be recreated by students.

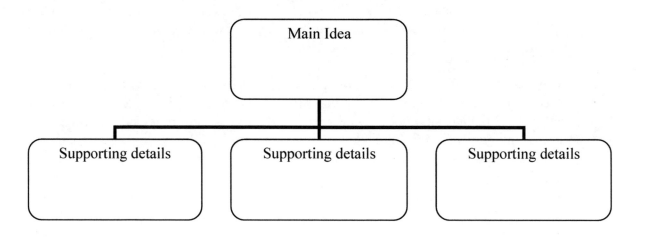

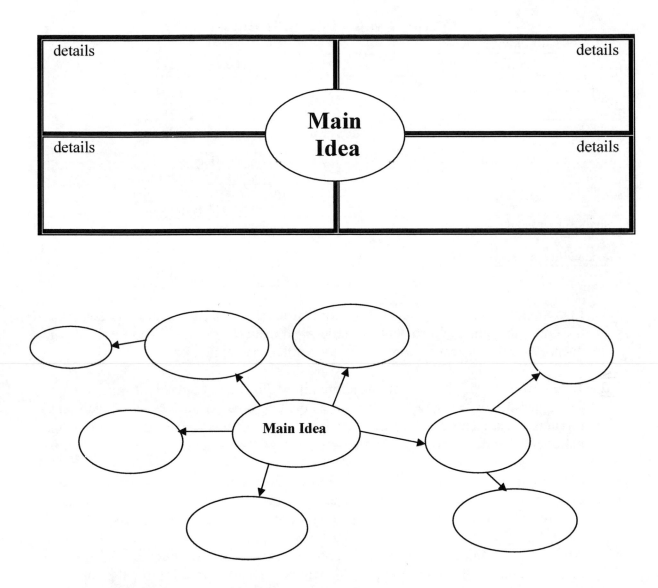

569. When presenting information in chronological order, provide the student with a timeline. Include the starting and ending points. For some students, additional reference points will need to be included.

570. Timelines may be either horizontal or vertical. **Form #95, Timeline,** is a vertical timeline. With a vertical timeline, the dates are written in the center column and the events can be listed on one or both sides. The following timeline example lists major events in U.S. history from 1990–1995. This timeline lists the political events on the left and other notable events on the right.

Major Events in U.S. History

Political Events	Date	Other Notable Events
Iraq invades Kuwait leading to Gulf War.	**1990**	Hubble Space Telescope is put into orbit.
Gulf War	**1991**	Oakland Hills firestorm
U.S. presidential election	**1992**	Los Angeles riots
		Hurricane Andrew hits FL and LA.
Bill Clinton becomes president.	**1993**	World Trade Center bombing kills 6.
		Branch Davidians' standoff in Waco, TX
North American Free Trade Agreement	**1994**	Northridge earthquake kills 57 in LA.
Republicans gain control of house and senate.	**1995**	Oklahoma City bombing
		TWA flight explodes off Long Island.

571. Encourage students to jot down key words if there is not enough time to complete the entire thought. Help students to understand that they do not have to write down every word that is heard during the lecture or that is read in a book.

572. When providing a visual demonstration, allow the student sufficient time to copy the material into the notes. At the end of the class period, allow a few additional minutes for students to compare their information to the visual aid. For complex material, provide handouts of the transparencies to the students.

573. If the student is unable to take notes, allow a peer to use carbon paper to create a copy, or make a photocopy. The student should still attempt to take notes during the presentation and actively participate in the lesson to the extent possible.

574. Allow time at the end of oral presentations for students to compare and discuss their notes in small-group settings. This will help students to reinforce the concepts learned and to clarify the points that were not fully understood.

575. At the end of each presentation, summarize the lesson. Place closure on the lesson by asking students to list or verbalize the main points of the lecture. Ask the students to look for and highlight this important information in their notes.

576. When using an overhead, allow the student with low vision to look directly into the overhead projector while the transparency is projected onto the wall.

577. An overhead projector also helps students with hearing impairments. It allows the student to see the presentation and read the teacher's lips simultaneously.

578. When presenting material orally, simultaneously record the presentation. This will assist students who may need additional reinforcement of the current lesson. It also benefits any students who are absent.

579. For students who are unable to take notes, provide hard copies of the major points discussed during lectures. These notes can be used as a study guide.

580. Allow students who are able to take *some* notes to preview notes received from the teacher or a peer. Have the students list any other information they may recall on the note page(s) after the lesson.

581. Allow students who are capable of taking notes to work in small, cooperative groups and discuss their lecture notes with peers. Students may adjust their notes at this time.

582. If the lecture has been recorded, allow students to check out audiocassettes of the lecture to listen to at home. Some students learn best by listening without the distractions of the school setting—and it helps to hear something more than once.

Chapter Ten Conclusion

This chapter has been about giving and receiving instruction. On the giving side of the equation, good teachers will do their best to make it as easy as possible for their students to learn and remember the material they teach. To that end, this chapter presents ideas for giving both oral and written instructions to improve their clarity and enhance the receptivity of the students. It points out the importance of self or peer evaluation to ensure that presentations are well organized and presented in a memorable way.

On the receiving side of the equation, students need to be guided to learn good listening and note-taking skills so they can best take advantage of those careful presentations. While some students may have little trouble, others need help focusing and distilling information. Structure, reminders and cues are aids for these students. Extra support in the form of outlines, discussion questions, small-group review or audiotapes can make the difference between forgetting and absorbing the information presented.

The reproducible Appendix forms listed on the next page will help give some structure to the processes of give and take mentioned in this chapter.

"The man who makes hard things easy is the educator."

Thomas Edison

Appendix Forms for Chapter Ten

#46	Chain of Events Organizer
#47	Compare and Contrast Organizer
#48	Fact or Opinion
#93	Self-Evaluation Worksheet
#94	Outline
#95	Timeline

"Ability is what you're capable of doing. Motivation determines what you do. Attitude determines how well you will do it."

Lou Holtz

"When grades become the substitute for learning, and when they become more important than what is learned, they tend to lower academic achievement."

William Glasser

Chapter Eleven

Classroom Assessments

For many students, the word *test* creates immediate anxiety. In a society where testing is often the major form of evaluation, it is important that students understand how assessments actually affect their overall grades. If the test is weighed relatively lightly in relation to projects, daily assignments and class participation, make sure students are aware of this. To help relieve test anxiety, provide practice tests and assessments for students. Simple strategies such as showing students how to eliminate answers on multiple-choice tests and finding key words on essay tests will help students become better test takers. If appropriate, allow students an opportunity to retake tests.

Some students require alternate forms of assessment due to difficulties with reading and written language. When developing alternate forms of assessment, there are two areas to keep in mind. First, be sure the accommodations used on daily assignments are incorporated into the assessment. For example, if the textbook is read aloud or taped for the student, this same accommodation should be used in a testing situation. Secondly, keep the objective of the assessment in mind. If the goal is to measure the student's knowledge of the curriculum, it is important to assess only the curriculum and not penalize the student by focusing on the student's limitations.

> **Chapter Note:**
> On page 191, you will find a complete list of the reproducible forms referred to throughout this chapter. The reproducible forms are located in the Appendix.

Many students with special needs have difficulty with short- and long-term memory. Often assessments become memory tests, as the student is asked to recall facts, figures and specific data presented during class presentations. When developing or using specific tests, read the test and determine whether the test measures the student's ability to memorize specific data or whether it measures true learning of information.

Traditional assessments fall into four basic categories: tests, products or projects, performance and skill assessment. Paper/pencil tests are the most common assessments for students. For students with IEPs, **Form #34, Testing Accommodations,** or **Form #35, Accommodations – Blank Template** should be filled out so that the accommodation list is readily available.

Essay Test Strategies

583. For students with IEPs, additional modifications and support may be provided to the student. The guidelines will be noted in the IEP or on the Accommodations Forms.

584. For special students, consider providing the essay questions in advance.

585. Provide the entire class with a set of questions, and explain that they will be required to select a specific number of questions for their final essay exam.

586. Common words used in essays include *analyze, assess, evaluate, classify, compare and contrast, define, identify, discuss, illustrate, evaluate, prove* and *review*. Make sure the student understands what these words mean.

587. When giving essay tests, explain the criteria that will be used for grading.

588. Ask the student to read the essay questions aloud and paraphrase them. Check for understanding before the student begins.

589. Provide students with blank outlines before beginning to write. This will help them to structure their thoughts and ideas. **Form # 94, Outline,** can be used.

590. Some students may need to write their ideas first and then formulate them into an essay format. Tell students who work in this manner not to worry about handwriting, spelling or the mechanics, as these can be corrected on their final papers.

591. Once the student has generated ideas, he or she should reread them to see if anything can be added. When complete, the student can begin to write the final product.

592. Some students will not be able to take essay tests due to the inability to write or organize ideas on paper. Allow these students to tape record their responses or orally discuss their responses with you.

Multiple-Choice Test Strategies

593. Read the directions with the students to check for understanding. For students with IEPs, **Form #34, Testing Accommodations,** or **Form #35, Accommodations – Blank Template,** should be filled out so that the accommodation list is readily available. Following are some strategies to discuss with students.

594. Students should review the entire test quickly and answer the easy questions first.

595. Once the easy questions are answered, students should read through the test a second time and mark the questions they believe they know. Sometimes they will notice clues within the test.

596. For some students, it will help to cover the possible answers. They can read the question and try to answer it without looking at the choices. After determining a response, they can look for a choice that most closely reflects their answer.

597. For more difficult questions, students should read the question more carefully. Place a line through the answers that they know are incorrect. Usually the answers can be narrowed to a 50/50 chance.

598. Explain to students that if the answer is totally unfamiliar, cross it off. Odds are, if it's not familiar, it hasn't been discussed in class.

599. If the test includes "all of the above" and the student knows that two of the answers are correct, "all of the above" is probably the answer.

600. Teach students how to rephrase a double negative so it becomes a positive statement.

Matching Test Strategies

601. Read the directions with the students to check for understanding. For students with IEPs, **Form #34, Testing Accommodations,** or **Form #35, Accommodations – Blank Template,** should be filled out so that the accommodation list is readily available. Following are some strategies to discuss with students.

602. Read each question carefully, along with the matching responses. The students should answer the questions they know first.

603. Have students use a pencil so a light line can be placed through incorrect responses. The student can erase the line when the response has not been used.

604. Instruct students to read the question and try different responses. Usually the question and the answer will be grammatically correct. Some questions and their matching responses will not match up, so these can be eliminated.

605. After all incorrect choices have been eliminated, the student should make the best choice with the answers that remain.

True and False Test Strategies

606. Read the directions with the students to check for understanding. For students with IEPs, **Form #34, Testing Accommodations,** or **Form #35, Accommodations – Blank Template,** should be filled out so that the accommodation list is readily available. Following are some strategies to discuss with students.

607. Read the sentence carefully. If any part of the sentence is false, the answer will be false.

608. If the sentence includes words such as *never, none, always* or *every,* it implies that the sentence must be true 100% of the time.

609. If the sentence is true, by changing it to a negative, it will be false.

610. The good news for students is that they have a 50% chance of getting a true and false statement correct, so if they aren't certain of the answer, they may as well make an educated guess!

Short-Answer Test Strategies

611. Read the directions with the students to check for understanding. For students with IEPs, **Form #34, Testing Accommodations,** or **Form #35, Accommodations – Blank Template,** should be filled out so that the accommodation list is readily available. Following are some strategies to discuss with students.

612. Look for grammatical clues. The statement should agree with the response.

613. If the student has narrowed the response to several answers, have the student pencil in the answers and read the remainder of the test and look for clues.

General Assessment Strategies

614. Read all test directions orally. Ask students to repeat the test directions to either a teacher or peer. Frequently students do not follow—or perhaps misunderstand—the instructions, which results in poor test scores.

615. Circle, underline or ask the student to highlight key words within the directions.

616. Some students will need tests to be read aloud and will need to test individually with the special education teacher or paraprofessional.

617. Allow the student to test orally with a peer, the general or special education teacher, or the paraprofessional.

618. If answers need to be written for the student, the scribe should transcribe the student's answers verbatim.

619. Allow students additional time to complete the test. If extra time cannot be provided, consider grading the student only on the items completed.

620. If the test permits, allow students to respond only to the even or odd numbered problems.

621. Permit the student to demonstrate the concept or illustrate what was learned.

622. Tape record the test and allow students to tape record their answers.

623. Test frequently to monitor progress. Give short daily quizzes. The student's progress can be easily monitored, and a determination can be made as to whether additional teaching or reinforcement is needed.

624. Maintain a record of the pretests and posttests. Give a final grade on individual progress and improvement. A student who fails a pretest and receives 50% on a posttest has made great strides in comparison to the student who has 80% on a pretest and 90% on a posttest.

625. When administering final grades, make sure you are aware of the mastery criteria on the Individualized Educational Plan.

626. Use recognition of facts rather than factual recall on tests. Delete the trick questions on commercially made tests.

627. If the district requires the student to take standardized tests, order consumable tests. This eliminates the need for the student to transfer their response to a computer score sheet. Errors often occur when transferring information.

628. Most standardized tests rely heavily on the student's ability to read the material. If the student's reading level is several years below grade level, this will be a frustrating experience. Address this issue during the IEP meeting. If the student does not participate in standardized testing, it must be addressed in the Individual Education Plan.

629. If students are required by law to take standardized tests, compare the test results to the individualized testing records in the special education folder. If the results on standardized testing are severely discrepant, you may want to place a note on the standardized test indicating that individual ability and achievement scores are listed in the Individual Education Plan.

Teacher-Created Tests

Formal and informal assessment occurs daily in the classroom setting. When creating teacher-made or curriculum-based assessments, use the following guidelines.

630. Divide the test into segments. Each segment should have an individual set of directions. Grade each segment of the test individually. This will help determine the areas that may need re-teaching.

631. Begin each assessment with several easy questions.

632. Write directions in a clear, precise format.

633. Include one direction per sentence. For example: *Read each sentence. Select the word that best completes the sentence.*

634. Limit the number of concepts presented on each test.

635. Separate the directions from the remainder of the text by boxing them.

636. Provide examples of correct responses. This will act as a visual aid for the student.

637. Use large bold print whenever possible.

638. Leave ample space between problems. Avoid making tests that have a cluttered appearance. Include white space on each page.

639. The terminology used on assessments is important. The goal of the assessment is to determine the student's knowledge.

- Avoid using words such as never, not, sometimes and always.

- When creating multiple-choice tests, exclude statements such as *all of the above* or *none of the above*. For some students, a modified multiple-choice test may include only two or three options instead of the standard four choices.

- When creating true and false tests, eliminate words such as *all* or *never*. Test only one fact per question. Avoid using double negatives, as they are easily misinterpreted.

640. When creating matching tests, organize both columns so the students' choices are clear and concise. Present the matching statements and answers in blocks of five. Double space between the blocks of information.

641. Create fill-in-the-blank tests by placing the choices under the blank space instead of at the end of the sentence. Keep statements short.

Thomas Edison invented the first _____ in 1819.
phonograph   car   light bulb

642. When giving essay tests, provide the student with a blank outline format, so the student may organize ideas before beginning to write. Highlight or underline key words in the essay questions. **Form #94, Outline,** in the Appendix is a standard outline that students may use to list a main idea with three supporting details. If essay tests require a student to compare and contrast, **Form #96, Compare and Contrast – Two Items**, may be used.

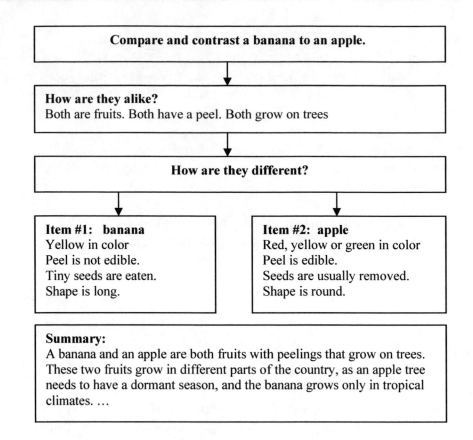

643. Provide students with a selection of essay questions before the actual test. Let the students select the question(s).

644. Some students will not be able to take essay tests due to the inability to write or organize ideas on paper. Allow these students to tape record their responses or orally discuss their responses with you.

645. Provide individual portfolios in which students can collect and save their work. All portfolio selections should be in the final format. Students, teachers and parents can easily note the progress the students have made over a period of time. This portfolio collection may be used as an alternative form of assessment.

646. Allow students to demonstrate knowledge by demonstrating the key concepts in some way. The assessment should test the students' knowledge base, not their ability to read or their ability to write and spell correctly. Following are several examples to assess math or science skills.

Math

- In place of paper and pencil tests, ask them to show their knowledge in real-life situations. Provide younger students with grocery store advertisements. Ask them to purchase items and list the cost for their total purchases.

- Collect old catalogs. Provide the student with a specific amount of money to purchase gifts for a family of six, furnish a room or buy school supplies.

- Older students may balance a checkbook, calculate gains given a savings amount and bank interest rates, or calculate the amount deducted from a paycheck given the percentage of taxes. Also of interest to older students are batting averages, clothing store discounts and sales tax. Depending upon the skill assessed, the directions may be simple or complex.

Science

- Following are types of performance assessments for environmental units. For example, during a weather unit, the student can document temperatures, explain high- and low-pressure areas from newspaper weather maps and document types of clouds present.

- Students can collect samples of simple and compound leaves. The leaves can then be labeled and categorized into groups.

- Students may collect different types of insects and label body parts. The insects may be categorized into groups.

- Science experiments can be completed in cooperative groups and the results of the experiments explained to the class.

647. Allow the student to create an audiocassette or video demonstrating knowledge of the content area. This is especially good for those students who have difficulty speaking or sharing in front of the entire group.

648. The following chart lists additional ideas that may be used to assess students. Provide some of the following suggestions to students and ask them to select how they would like to demonstrate their knowledge. **Form #97, Assessing Assessments,** can be used to list a student's strengths and weaknesses. Once the student's levels of performance have been listed, select the assessments that may be most appropriate for the student. **Form #98, Choose Your Own Assessment,** includes the following list of activities that students may use when given the option of demonstrating their knowledge in alternative ways. Students may also add their own ideas to the list.

Project Ideas	**Performance Activities**	**Processing Ideas**
Autobiographies	Acting	Checklists
Book reviews	Character sketches	Concept mapping
Brochures	Commercials and ads	Computer generated activities
Cartoons	Dance	Informal assessments
Collages	Debates	Interviews with students
Puzzles	Demonstrations	Journals
Displays	Discussions	Learning logs
Games	Experiments	Observations
Handbooks	Interviews	Portfolios
Illustrations	Music	Questionnaires
Maps and diagrams	News reports	
Models	Oral reports	
Portfolios	Plays	
Posters	Presentations	
Projects	Role play	
Trivia	Reports	
Questionnaires	Simulations	
	Speeches	

Alternate Grading Systems

Several grading alternatives may be considered for students with special needs. Many educators use a traditional percentage grading system. This system may not be appropriate for all students.

649. The student's IEP will provide the framework for grading. Be sure you are aware of the criteria.

650. If the test includes various sections testing multiple areas, grade each section individually. For example, if the test includes true/false, multiple-choice and essay sections, provide an individual grade for each section. This helps determine the preferred testing style of the student. The student will also be able to determine the area that needs more practice or additional reinforcement. If a student continually fails a specific type of assessment, such as multiple-choice, the student can be taught strategies to improve performance in that specific area. **Form #99, What Works Best?** can be used to document student performance on various types of assessments. By recording the student's test grades from the various types of assessments, a pattern will begin to emerge indicating what assessment methods are most appropriate for the student. Use the example below in filling out your form.

Student: Mary Smith

Type of Assessment: TRUE/FALSE

TOPIC	DATE	SOCIAL STUDIES	SCIENCE	MATH	READING
plant life	10/08		60%		
pioneers	10/08	65%			
leaf identification	10/08		65%		
main events	10/08				70%

Type of Assessment: SHORT ANSWER

TOPIC	DATE	SOCIAL STUDIES	SCIENCE	MATH	READING
plant description	10/08		80%		
pioneer life events	10/08	78%			
leaf classification	10/08		82%		
main events	10/08				75%

651. When testing various skills, for example in math, determine the specific skill area in which the student experiences difficulty. Re-teach these specific skills and allow the student to retake the test.

652. Contract grading is often used in inclusive settings. The student and teacher determine the quantity and quality of work the student must complete to receive a specific grade in a subject area.

653. Change the criteria for a student's grade according to how the particular student is best assessed. For example:

   Class Criteria: Exams 50%, Homework 25%, Class participation 25%.
   Modified Criteria: Exams 20%, Homework 40%, Class participation 40%

654. Combination grading can reward students for their performance and help individualize the grading process. In combination grading, the grade is based on the student's ability, effort and achievement. The ability grade is based on the expected amount of improvement in the subject area. The effort grade is based on the amount of time and effort the student puts into the assignment to master the concept. The achievement grade is related to the student's mastery in relation to others in the class. These three individual grades can be averaged for the final grade.

655. Shared grading is frequently used in inclusive settings. With shared grading, the regular and special education teachers collaborate to assign the grade. The final grade is based on the grades and observations of both teachers.

656. A pass/fail system may be appropriate for some students. This system acknowledges that the student has completed the required assignments as determined by the teachers and the IEP.

657. If the report card does not correspond to the student's individual goals and objectives on the IEP, write descriptive comments. List the skills that have been mastered. This is an appropriate time to review the IEP and discuss the goals and objectives that have been determined for the student.

Chapter Eleven Conclusion

Just as students learn in different ways, they may have preferred ways to demonstrate what they've learned, or they may not be able to take the kinds of tests the other students are given. This chapter offers strategies to help all students with various kinds of test questions, such as essay, multiple choice and short answer, as well as ideas for providing appropriate, individualized means of assessment and grading for special education students, considering their IEPs. The point is to use students' strengths and provide strategies to help them do well on assessments and accurately show what they know. Appendix forms for this chapter help you decide what types of assessment to give a student and help you determine how well the student is doing with each type of assessment. A form is also provided for a Compare and Contrast test question that helps determine thinking, organizing and writing skills.

Ready . . . set . . . test!

Appendix Forms for Chapter Eleven

#34	Testing Accommodations
#35	Accommodations – Blank Template
#94	Outline
#96	Compare and Contrast – Two Items
#97	Assessing Assessments
#98	Choose Your Own Assessment!
#99	What Works Best?

"The real contest is always between what you've done and what you're capable of doing. You measure yourself against yourself and nobody else."

Geoffrey Gaberino

Notes:

_____

_____

_____

_____

_____

_____

_____

_____

_____

_____

_____

_____

_____

_____

Chapter Twelve

Student Behavior

"I just don't know what to do anymore! The student is always out of his seat or walking around the room!" "The student is so disruptive in the classroom that it's affecting the other students." "The student seems to be in a dreamland. Even though she is looking at me, she doesn't seem to be able to focus on what I am saying or follow through on the assignments."

These are common concerns heard regularly by professionals and parents. Many students have difficulty sustaining attention. For some, it is an issue of maturity, and for others, the classroom structure may not be conducive to their individual learning styles. For some of these students, changing the environment by providing more—or perhaps less—structure is beneficial. Perhaps some students in your classroom are medically diagnosed as having Attention Deficit Disorder (ADD) or Attention Deficit Hyperactivity Disorder (ADHD). As indicated by the names of these disorders, such students have difficulty sustaining attention—and attention is an important prerequisite for all learning and success in the school environment.

> **Chapter Note:**
> On page 206, you will find a complete list of the reproducible forms referred to throughout this chapter. The reproducible forms are located in the Appendix.

For all of the above students, accommodations need to be made within the classroom setting if the student is to experience success in school. If a student is diagnosed as ADD and is on medication, it is important to obtain a Release of Information from the parent and speak directly with the doctor or psychologist. Also, meet with the parents. Both the parents and doctor will be able to provide valuable information about the student. If possible, adapt the strategies used in the home to the classroom setting. For the majority of the students, the accommodations discussed in this book will assist the student in achieving success in the classroom.

Students with attention difficulties misbehave for many different reasons. Some students are frustrated with the curriculum because the material is too difficult for them. Others may need more structure, or perhaps there are too many distractions in the classroom environment. Still other students may feel misunderstood or overwhelmed, or they may simply be hungry, which can interfere with concentration.

The strategies in this section pertain directly to the student who experiences difficulties with attention or staying on task, or who is impulsive or easily distracted.

General Tips for Student Discipline

School violence and the accompanying necessary discipline have increased in schools today. Often, there is a lack of respect for the authority of teachers and school personnel as well as for the rights of other students. Before discussing the specific areas of student behavior, following are general tips for actions you can take to help establish and maintain order.

658. Greet the students as they enter the classroom. This helps you to pick up early signs of possible trouble, such as arguments, angry students, students who may not be feeling well, etc. You will also provide a courteous role model for your students.

659. When the students arrive, provide an activity to get them started, once they have put their items into their desks AND turned in homework assignments. The activity may include journal writing, five-minute quiet conversation while in their seats, reading and copying an assignment on the board or any other quiet, settling-down activity.

660. Be sure that the established rules include workable consequences. Have students help make the rules. Never make consequences you cannot follow through with consistently.

661. Plan the arrangement of your classroom. Ease the traffic flow so that students are not bumping into each other or too close to each other. Students need their space.

662. Learn the students' names within the first two days of school, and learn as much as you can about each of them.

663. Maintain a daily schedule and be sure the students understand it. Often, student anxiety causes classroom disruption.

664. Avoid both verbal and physical confrontations with students. If you feel an interaction is headed in this direction, walk away.

665. Use "I" statements instead of "you" statements. For example, "I need you to…," "I expect you to…," "I need it quiet now …," etc.

666. Use positive discipline statements. Instead of telling the students "no chewing gum, no running in the halls, no yelling," rephrase these statements as "gum should be left at home, walk in the halls, use quiet voices," etc.

667. Avoid tactics that rarely work. Some include raising your voice, insisting on the last word, sarcasm, preaching, bribing, making comparisons to others, etc. If you find yourself in a situation where you are doing this, stop and take a deep breath and begin again. If appropriate, apologize to the student and explain that the example was not acceptable, or apologize for losing your cool.

Avoiding a Crisis

As an educator, there are ways you can respond to a student and help ease a situation before it escalates to a crisis. Try some of the following strategies.

668. Try to catch the student doing something positive throughout the school day. **Form #100, Reinforcement Cards,** includes cards that can be reproduced and placed on the student's desk as you see the student implementing the behaviors you want to see in your classroom. Often a simple strategy such as this will greatly improve behavior.

669. Choose your battles wisely. Ignore as much of the inappropriate behavior as possible. Provide a list of behaviors that will not be tolerated under any circumstance.

670. Provide alternatives to the student. Instead of making demands, provide choices. Often small choices during the day will help a student feel in control. Choices such as using a pencil instead of a pen, taking a short break before completing the assignment or writing a paper in manuscript instead of cursive will make a difference in the student's day.

671. When correcting a student, do so without criticizing.

672. Let the student know when a behavior is bothering you. Be consistent. A behavior that is not allowed today should not be allowed tomorrow.

673. Avoid conflict and de-escalate the situation by changing the subject or walking away from the student.

674. Try to ease tension with the use of humor.

675. Appropriate behavior may have to be modeled to the student.

676. Keep rules and guidelines to a minimum, but reinforce them consistently.

677. If any of the following behaviors are noted, they should immediately be reported to the school administration: signs of drug and alcohol abuse, physical abuse, physical neglect, sexual abuse, suicidal threats or threats to harm others.

Structuring the Environment

Daily structure needs to be provided for all students, but for students with behavior issues, it is especially important. Transition times are difficult and should be closely monitored. A well structured school day will decrease many unacceptable behaviors.

678. Establish your classroom rules at the beginning of the year. Limit the number of rules, and be sure the student understands each rule and the reason for the rule. These rules need to be reviewed and reinforced consistently. Students should keep a copy in their folders, and a copy should be sent home also.

679. Praise the student when the rules are followed. Be sure that you are praising other students also, so the student does not feel singled out.

680. If a student is having difficulty with a specific rule, write the rule for the student. Provide the student with specific examples of following the rule and breaking the rule. Not all students can (or want to) generalize the rules. For example, "Do not run in the hall!" does not necessarily mean do not run in the classroom or lunchroom, etc. Some students will push every rule to the limit. Therefore, the rule could be restated as: "Walk in the school building."

681. Encourage all students in the classroom to set individual goals. Every student can find one behavior or skill that needs improvement! A student may have a goal to raise his hand more frequently and participate in class discussions, whereas another, very talkative student may have a goal of sitting quietly and paying attention during lectures or instruction. Goals can be academic, social or behavioral. When incorporating goal setting for all students in the classroom, students with behavior plans will not 'stand out' from the other students. **Form #101, Student Goals,** can be used for all students in the classroom.

682. Plan your daily schedule and post a copy of the daily schedule on the board.

683. Discuss the schedule daily with the students and alert the students in advance to changes that will occur.

684. Indicate when transitions will occur by using a signal, such as turning the light off/on, ringing a bell or playing music, as a gentle reminder that the activity is coming to a close.

685. Provide extra structure and support during transition times. Often a student needs a few additional minutes to adjust and organize materials before beginning a new subject.

686. Some students need to move. Make a simple red and green flip card. When the red side is posted, it indicates that all students must be in their seats. When the green side is showing, the students may quietly move about the room.

687. Always state what the student should do, instead of what the student should not do. For example, you could say, "It's time to work quietly now," instead of "Why aren't you working?" or, "You shouldn't be playing with that now."

688. Schedule the strong academic subjects in the morning when students are most alert.

689. Check-in and check-out times are important for the student. Enlist the support of the special education teacher or paraprofessional if the student has special needs. If not, obtain the support of the school social worker or counselor. **Form #102, Check-in / Check-out,** may be used.

690. Encourage the student to keep a homework notebook. If a telephone is available, allow the student to call and leave a reminder for him/herself. For younger students, a laminated "No Homework" card can be inserted into the student's book bag to communicate with the parent that all work is complete. Whatever system is used, be sure to hold the student responsible for all assignments.

691. A three-ring notebook with pocket folders will help keep all supplies, materials and assignments in one place. Instruct the student not to remove an assignment unless it is time to turn it in.

692. Allow the student to check out extra copies of all of the textbooks for home use.

Behavior and Attention Difficulties

From time to time, all students are inattentive, impulsive and overly active. This chapter is related more to students where inattentive, impulsive behavior is the rule and not the exception to the rule. This chapter provides strategies for students who consistently have trouble focusing and maintaining attention, who are easily distracted by extraneous stimuli, who blurt out answers, and perhaps spend more time out of their seat than in it or tend to act before thinking.

Reasons for inappropriate behaviors are many. It is best not to jump to the conclusion that the student is intentionally rude or disruptive. The student may simply not know or understand what they are to do at a given moment. The student may be entering a developmental stage that is different from that of peers. For some students, oftentimes, ignoring the behavior will simply eliminate it.

When dealing with difficult students, one needs to think and respond rather than react. By remaining calm, positive and upbeat, it is apparent to the student that you are in control of the situation. It is important to avoid debating or arguing, as when strong emotions increase, thinking skills and listening comprehension decreases. The student will read more from your body language and the tone, cadence and volume of your words than from your actual words. Keep your words short and simple. Make sure your body language and voice are providing the same message!

Help students to realize they do have choices! Providing specific examples and role-playing situations helps some students realize the type of choices they have. Keep a list of consequences for misbehavior and always administer the consequences consistently and immediately. Praise the student immediately for good behavior and try to "catch" the student in positive situations.

An effective management system concentrates on only a few behavior goals at one time and adds additional goals as the student is able to master the first ones. Young children will need more immediate rewards whereas older students should be encouraged to work towards a long term goal.

693. Seat students in the front row or near the teacher's desk

694. Maintain frequent eye contact with the student.

695. Provide a work area for the student where there are minimal distractions.

696. Provide clear and consistent transition times between subjects. Allow the student time to get up and move around.

697. Provide a structured environment with a specific place for materials and books.

698. Ask the student to use prearranged signals or words, such as one finger raised means "I need help" and two fingers means "I need permission to get up and move around."

699. Make sure you have the student's attention when talking to him or her. Eye contact is important. Use private visual cues. Touching your eye means "look at me," your ear, "time to listen" and the side of your mouth, "no talking."

700. Provide small-group instruction as much as possible. A small group provides more opportunity for participation, thus increasing the student's chance to be actively involved and stay on task.

701. Allow ample time for hands-on instruction. This will help actively engage the student in the learning process. Active participation is extremely important for a special education student. It will assist the student in remaining focused.

702. Provide only one- and two-step directions. Check for understanding of each direction. Ask the student to repeat what he/she has just heard.

703. Give one assignment at a time. Be sure the student writes it down. Keep a daily list of assignments with due dates on the board. Ask students to copy the assignments into their assignment book. Check the student's assignment book at the end of the day.

704. Modify daily assignments to alleviate frustration. (See Chapter Five, Daily Assignments.)

705. Use computer programs for academic reinforcement when appropriate. This allows the student to receive immediate feedback. It also allows the student to self-pace the instruction and may help to increase motivation.

706. Use a timer to help the student stay focused. Set the timer to coincide with the amount of time you perceive the student is able to remain on task. Tell the student what you expect to be completed during the allotted time. Once the student has adjusted to using a timer, play "Beat the Clock!" Gradually increase the time and the length of the task. Challenge the student to complete the assignment before the timer rings.

707. Allow time during the day for the student to get up, walk around and stretch. Provide a list of appropriate times.

708. Use random strategies when calling on students during large- and small-group activities. Place the students' names in a basket and randomly draw a name, or use a deck of index cards and randomly select one. Since the students do not know who will be called on next, their attention increases.

709. Provide forms of immediate feedback for the student. Self-correctors are appropriate for daily assignments. Many students benefit from the immediate feedback.

Impulsivity and Distractibility

"She just doesn't think!" "He always blurts out the answer before he is called on!" "She is always daydreaming." Some students tend to act without thinking and are easily distracted.

710. Stand by the student when giving directions.

711. Use simple, clear words to explain a concept.

712. Place creative artwork in the back of the classroom to avoid cluttering walls with excessive amounts of materials that may distract the student.

713. Check seating arrangements. Students who are easily distracted should not be seated near doors, windows or high traffic areas. The student should be seated near the front or near the teacher.

714. The easily distracted student may need additional time to complete assignments, even if the assignments have been modified. For some students, earplugs help block out background noise. For others, listening to soft music with earphones will block out some of the distracting stimuli.

715. Avoid timed activities and tests. Some students become frustrated when they notice others have finished an assignment that they have barely started. The student often will guess or simply quit working. When giving group assessments, ask all students to remain in their seats and read quietly until everyone has finished. Collect the tests at the end of the session.

716. Ask the student to stop and think before responding. Create a visual signal between the adult and student. An example of a visual signal would be to place your finger aside your nose. When the student observes this, he/she will know it is time to slow down and think about the action.

717. Ask the student to whisper the directions and quietly read assignments to him/herself. This helps the student focus, as he/she not only sees the material but also hears it. This also is helpful when completing assignments with multiple steps. By verbalizing the steps, students often become more conscious of the procedure. Some students are able to stay on task longer if they verbalize the entire assignment while working.

718. Create seating charts. Seat the student near students who are both quiet and independent workers. Provide good role models. Do not seat disruptive students or students that are easily distracted together.

719. Allow the student to keep only the necessary materials for the current assignment on top of the desk. Toys and play objects should remain at home.

Aggressive or Noncompliant Behavior

720. Listen to the student with genuine interest and respect. Allow the student time to share problems as they arise

721. Try to spend time one-on-one with the student and discover the student's likes and dislikes.

722. Involve the student in small groups with activities in which the student has a special interest.

723. Create tasks you know the student will be able to complete successfully.

724. Provide a safe place for the student to go if he/she needs time away.

725. Use behavior contracts. When creating behavior contracts, do the following:

    - Define the behavior and be specific.
    - Select the reinforcers with the student.
    - Negotiate with the student what must be done to receive the reward.
    - Fill in the contract and sign it.

    If a student begins by working toward the goal and loses interest, check to be sure the student is receiving consistent reinforcement and that the rewards are still motivating for the student. If not, readjust the criteria.

    Keep the rewards simple. The student may be happy to have 10 minutes of free time to talk with friends, play on the computer or simply do nothing. The rewards should be easy to implement and not too time-consuming for you.

    Form #103, Behavior Contract, and Form #104, My Way to Change, are two contracts in the Appendix that may be reproduced.

726. If you need to reprimand the student, do so in private. Explain the reason for the reprimand, and give the student an alternative to the behavior.

727. Make sure the student knows the class rules. Provide the list of the rules to keep in the student's notebook or folder for the student to refer to, if necessary.

728. Report any severe changes in personality or self-injurious threats or intimations to the school counselor or administrator.

Poor Social Skills

729. Be positive, and encourage all attempts at age-appropriate behavior. Praise the student as often as you can for positive behaviors that occur.

730. When working in small groups, start with a group of only two. As the student becomes more comfortable working with one other person, increase the group size to three and so forth.

731. Teach conversation skills in small group settings so the student receives ample opportunity to participate and generous positive feedback. Gradually increase the group size.

732. Point out appropriate behavior when observed in other students by providing positive reinforcement to these students.

733. Model the desired behavior to the student. Practice and role-play social situations with another student.

734. Praise and reward all positive group participation.

735. Provide opportunities to participate in group activities and take turns.

736. If the student does not have friends, pair the student with a friendly study partner.

737. Assign a monitoring friend to help the student during free-time, such as recess, lunch and transition. Encourage the student to model behaviors after the peer.

738. Help students to make friends. Talk about some of the simple rules for friendship.

   - Be nice and be kind.
   - Care about the feelings of others.
   - Remember that listening is just as important as talking.
   - Tell the person that he/she is your friend.
   - Share!
   - Notice how your friend looks. When your friend looks sad, ask how he/she is feeling.
   - Think about what you are going to say.
   - Think before you talk!

Reinforcement and Discipline

Students with special needs and those with ADD are often more dependent on external reinforcement than other students in the classroom environment. These students also may need more encouragement. Try to reward more than punish. When you see a positive behavior, praise the student immediately. Always avoid ridicule and criticism.

A number of students have difficulty controlling their behaviors. These students may respond to a reward system. If you decide to incorporate a reward system, be sure the student participates in the development of the reward list. For many, an appropriate reward is simply allowing a few extra minutes to socialize with a friend, as often these students are the last to finish their work and rarely have extra time.

739. Help students increase their emotions-related vocabulary. For example, the student who is angry actually may be frustrated. Students need to understand and be able to verbalize their feelings.

740. If the student consistently needs to be disciplined during a specific academic block, it is important to check to see if the current adaptations are appropriate. If the

majority of acting out behaviors occur when the assignment is too difficult, perhaps the assignment needs to be modified.

741. Develop a reward system. Since the student will need continuous and frequent feedback, break the educational day into time blocks. Some students need feedback every five to 10 minutes during the initiation of the program. This can easily be done by placing a chart on the student's desk and putting a check or a sticker onto the chart or index card as you walk around the room. Gradually increase time to cover the entire academic block.

742. **Form #105, Reward Chart – Subject Area,** is a simple grid that students can use to chart behavior and achieve a reward. A subject chart will help the student see what behaviors occur during which class times. Is math more difficult than reading? Does the student's behavior reflect this? Does the student's behavior decrease before lunch and get better after lunch?

743. **Form #106, Reward Chart – Puzzle,** is an alternative way to track behavior when working towards a reward. It can be used instead of the standard check-off charts. The puzzle is copied and cut into pieces. This allows the teacher to determine how long it will take to receive the reward by adjusting the number of puzzle pieces. The student gets to add a piece to the puzzle every time a goal is met. When the puzzle has been completed, the student receives a predetermined award. [Any drawing can be used for this type of reward chart. Some teachers coordinate this with a reward the student is to receive at home. For example, if the student is working towards a reward such as a computer game, the cover of the game can be reproduced and used as the puzzle. When the student completes the puzzle, the parents provide the reward.

744. **Form #107, Reward Chart Grid,** is a standard grid that the student can color in, or the student can cut apart the small icons, which can be glued into place as goals are accomplished.

745. **Form #108, Reward Chart – Morning/Afternoon,** works well for students who are working on specific goals that need to be documented both in the morning and at the end of the day. This also can be used for daily check-in and check-out.

746. The class discipline plan is not always an appropriate plan for all students in the class. The student may need a supplemental discipline plan with extra warnings, coupled with a reward system. Whatever discipline plan is used, it is important for the plan to remain consistent for the student throughout the school day.

747. Time-outs are often used in response to behavioral difficulties or as proactive measures when problems are about to surface. A time-out allows the student to regroup, have some personal space for a few minutes or recover from a temper outburst. It may also allow time for the teacher and the class to regroup and refocus. The goal of the time-out is to allow the student time to calm down and

rethink the situation. Adults often take a time-out when experiencing a stressful situation. An adult may get a drink of water or cup of coffee or simply walk out into the hall to regroup. Time-outs should be viewed as a legitimate way to cope with a situation before it reaches crisis level.

If using time-outs, post a specific sequence, such as the following common sequence of steps. Frequently, Steps 1 and 2 can be used as preventive and proactive strategies.

TIME-OUT

Step 1 – Time-out in a designated classroom area
(Some teachers call this place the "Thinking Area." This area, usually located in the classroom, is appropriate for all students who need a few minutes to think something through without interruption.)

Step 2 – Time-out outside of the classroom area
(Sometimes a student needs to leave the classroom environment. Often teachers work collaboratively to provide a supervised location in a separate classroom.)

Step 3 – Time out with a counselor or principal
(This allows the student to cool down and work through the situation with a person who was not directly involved with the situation.)

Step 4 – Telephone call home

748. A token system is appropriate for some students. Tokens may consist of small laminated paper shapes, buttons or beads. You may choose to make your own. With a token system, students are responsible for keeping the tokens in their desks and redeeming them for rewards. In the beginning, students tend to work for rewards that can be easily obtained. Encourage them to set more challenging goals and work towards larger rewards.

749. With the student, create a list of reward objects or activities. The student may choose from these activities when an individual goal has been met. What motivates an adult probably will not motivate the student. Create the list together, and keep the rewards simple. Some suggestions include: stickers, pencils, pens, basic school supplies, 10 extra minutes on the computer, five minutes of free-choice activity with a friend, a coupon for one "excused" homework assignment, the student's photo on the "photo recognition board," an extra gym pass or a celebration conference with the parents where only positive events are reported.

750. An inexpensive way to obtain trinkets for elementary students is to attend garage sales. Many small items can be purchased for five cents or less. Another option is

to send form letters to large companies asking for donations. Often companies have promotional items they will send to you free of charge.

751. Keep the parents informed when the student has shown improvement during the day. Create a list of positive sayings such as:

> Awesome Day!
> I discovered the secret to success today!
> Super Star!
> I'm a Great Student!
> Wow!

(If you like, you can use **Form #100, Reinforcement Cards,** as a start.) Photocopy the sayings onto fluorescent paper and laminate them. Cut them into strips and put the strips in an envelope. When the student has a good day, he or she may choose a laminated saying to take home. If proper guidelines are set, the older student will be able to monitor his or her own progress. This is also an easy way to communicate good news to parents.

752. Keep parents informed about the reward system used in class. Parents often will provide additional reinforcement in the home.

753. A daily report can be used to monitor behavior and academic goals. An easy way to create a daily report is to tape an index card to the student's desk. Subjects can be added to the card as they are presented during the day. For younger students, a happy face may be placed on the card if the student has reached the expected goal during the time block. For older students, a rating scale of 1-5 may be used. This report may be sent home daily to increase communication between the school and home.

754. A daily log has proven successful for coordinating home and school communication. Both parents and teachers can use this log to write comments, concerns and suggestions. The student is rewarded by the parent(s). As valuable as it can be, do not begin a narrative log unless you are sure you will have the time to complete it daily. A daily log is very time-consuming, especially when comments usually need to be written at the end of the day or class period, when there can be more confusion than usual. If you decide to write a daily log, keep your entries short, as you will be more likely to keep it up.

755. Negative reinforcement or self-talk includes consistent remarks such as, "I can't do this!" "I don't know how!" or "I'm not good at anything." Teach the student to use positive self-talk, such as "I can do this!" "I can handle this!" or "I'm good at this!" When you hear a student using negative self-talk or putting him- or herself down, stop the student and help the student to rephrase the comments positively.

Chapter Twelve Conclusion

This chapter provides many options for dealing with behavior difficulties. Some strategies are appropriate for all students in the classroom, and others are specifically meant for special education students, who may need more support and structure. Often behavior problems can be prevented by reducing confusion and stress for these students. Other options accommodate the various needs of the students, such as the need to move about periodically or the need to be accepted, have friends and understand their own feelings. A creative reward system provides motivation for the students and reinforces good behavior, and in cases where discipline is necessary, it should be fair and understood. The specific strategies offered in this chapter are designed both to help teachers maintain order in the classroom and their own "cool," and to help students improve behavior and thus learn more effectively.

Appendix Forms for Chapter Twelve

#100	Reinforcement Cards
#101	Student Goals
#102	Check-in / Check-out
#103	Behavior Contract
#104	My Way to Change
#105	Reward Chart – Subject Area
#106	Reward Chart – Puzzle
#107	Reward Chart Grid
#108	Reward Chart – Morning /Afternoon

"Children need love, especially when they don't deserve it!"

Harold Hulbert

Appendix

Form #1.1

Planning for Inclusive Education: The Special Education Team

How many special education students are currently in our program? Approximately how many students are at each grade level or subject area?

_____
_____
_____
_____
_____
_____

As a team, what is our preference? Should the program be implemented with a small group of selected students, or would it be better to transition students by grade level? Should the entire special education population transition at the same time? Is there a target group of students that we would like to transition first? Do we have a choice?

_____
_____
_____
_____
_____
_____

What is our rationale for selecting the previous transition method?

_____
_____
_____
_____
_____
_____

Do we have sufficient support staff (paraprofessionals) in the classroom environment? For the upcoming school year, do we anticipate a growth or decrease in support staff?

_____
_____
_____
_____
_____
_____

Form #1.2

Considering the amount of support staff we currently have, are we using these vital members to the fullest extent? Do the support staff have blocks of downtime in the current schedule? Does the support staff arrive too early or too late in the day to maximize student support? Are the schedules flexible so support staff can be staggered, with some paraprofessionals arriving earlier and others later in the day to maximize student contact?

_____

_____

_____

_____

_____

As a team, how can we provide a continuum of services for students? Do we have a sufficient special educator staff to provide service to students both in a pull-out program (if needed) and in the general education setting?

_____

_____

_____

_____

_____

If the decision is made to transition a percentage of the students, which special education teachers would like to work in an inclusive classroom the upcoming year? Do we have a choice?

_____

_____

_____

_____

_____

After discussing the previous questions, what are the biggest obstacles we will encounter?

_____

_____

_____

_____

_____

Additional comments and concerns:

_____

_____

_____

_____

_____

Leadership Goals

What is our vision of the ideal inclusive program?

_____
_____
_____
_____

Leadership Team Goal #1:

_____
_____
_____
_____

Leadership Team Goal #2:

_____
_____
_____
_____

Leadership Team Goal #3:

_____
_____
_____
_____

Leadership Team Goal #4:

_____
_____
_____
_____

Form #3

Sample Benefits and Barriers

Benefits of Inclusion

* Students receive service in the classroom to the greatest possible extent.

* Students are no longer labeled because they leave the classroom to attend a special class.

* More students will be able to participate in all instructional activities with proper accommodations, even though the outcome may be different.

* Students do not lose valuable academic learning time transitioning between regular education and special education classrooms.

* Students no longer need to work within two fragmented educational systems.

* Students are not pulled in so many directions. Related services are provided within the classroom setting as much as possible.

* The special education teacher develops a better understanding of the classroom curriculum. Strategies that meet the needs for the student in one academic area may be transferred to other academic areas.

* Students become more accepting of one another regardless of the limitations.

* The special education staff can assist other students within the classroom setting if needed.

* Communication increases between regular education and special education.

* General education teachers have more flexibility. They do not have to wait for students to return from their special class in order to begin a new lesson.

Barriers to Inclusion

* Scheduling difficulties

* Need time to communicate and work together

* Need to group students due to number of special education teachers/assistants

* Money

Form #4

Benefits and Barriers

Benefits:

Barriers:

Sample Goals and Objectives

Goal: To implement the inclusive education program by the upcoming school year

Objectives:
- Determine target group of students by April of current school year.
- Group students into classrooms by May.
- Select general and special education teachers to participate.
- Include all special education teachers in end-of-year student placement.

Goal: To develop guidelines for student placement

Objectives:
- Form a committee to establish guidelines for student placement.
- Discuss possible options for grouping students.
- Include all special education teachers in student placement meetings.

Goal: To develop structured communication times for general and special education teachers involved in inclusive settings

Objectives:
- Design and implement additional time for teachers to meet.
- Incorporate a rotating schedule for team planning time.
- Analyze current preparation periods, and coordinate general and special education planning times.

Goal: To develop individualized curricula

Objectives:
- Research materials to supplement current textbook materials, including high interest/low vocabulary reading materials, consumable materials and prerecorded materials.
- Create lists of curriculum adaptations that are easy to implement.
- Create lists of modified curricula to share between grade/subject areas.

Goal: To increase awareness of inclusive education

Objectives:
- Survey the staff to determine needs.
- Plan and implement staff development from compiled survey results.

213

Form #6

Goals and Objectives

Goal:
_____

Objectives:
_____
_____
_____
_____

Goal:
_____

Objectives:
_____
_____
_____
_____

Goal:
_____

Objectives:
_____
_____
_____
_____

Goal:
_____

Objectives:
_____
_____
_____
_____

Form #7.1

Learning Styles Checklist
Students 10 and Older

This following checklist can be distributed to students age 10 and up. Ask the student to check off all that apply. The characteristics have been divided into four separate sections.

Section A – The student shares characteristics with people who have an abstract-random style of learning.

Section B – The student shares characteristics with people who have an abstract-sequential style of learning.

Section C – The student shares characteristics with people who have a concrete-sequential style of learning.

Section D – The student shares the characteristics with people who have a concrete-random style of learning.

Photocopy and ask students to complete all sections of the Learning Styles Checklist. Tally the total number of checks per area.

More checks in an area indicate that the child may have a preference for that style of learning. If the student profile indicates an area with a large number of checks (in comparison to the other three areas), it may indicate that the learning style is dominant for the student and the student may function best in a classroom where the teacher has a similar style of teaching.

If the checks are scattered throughout all areas, it usually means the student is able to work in a variety of classroom settings.

Learning Style Checklist

A. I see myself as someone who:

- ☐ likes to be with people
- ☐ is sensitive to how others feel
- ☐ is creative
- ☐ likes to learn things that are meaningful to me
- ☐ likes to collect things and save them
- ☐ likes to have a lot of information about something
- ☐ likes to work on my own time schedule
- ☐ makes decisions because they feel right
- ☐ enjoys learning in a group
- ☐ needs to balance time between work and play
- ☐ does not like conflict or disagreements
- ☐ likes to have time to think about things

____ **TOTAL**

B. I see myself as someone who:

- ☐ likes to work with ideas and thoughts
- ☐ likes my work to be organized and neat
- ☐ prefers to work alone
- ☐ likes to have enough time to learn something thoroughly
- ☐ likes to debate or argue about ideas
- ☐ likes finding answers
- ☐ likes books
- ☐ likes things to be predictable
- ☐ likes to have things right
- ☐ judges the value or importance of something
- ☐ takes learning seriously
- ☐ is good at integrating information to form a new idea
- ☐ likes a quiet environment in which to work

____ **TOTAL**

Learning Style Checklist (cont.)

C. I see myself as someone who:

- ☐ learns best through practical, hands-on ways
- ☐ likes to have rules to follow
- ☐ likes everything to be in its place and organized
- ☐ likes to work one step at a time
- ☐ wants to know what is expected of me
- ☐ likes to have a specific time for doing things
- ☐ likes to have a finished product for my efforts
- ☐ likes to work with details
- ☐ likes approval for my work
- ☐ likes to have a consistent way of doing things
- ☐ wants to create practical products
- ☐ likes things to be accurate and precise
- ☐ thinks about what I am going to do before I do it

___ **TOTAL**

D. I see myself as someone who:

- ☐ likes change
- ☐ sees the world as a laboratory to explore
- ☐ is curious
- ☐ thrives on new experiences
- ☐ likes to be "on the go"
- ☐ likes to do several things at one time
- ☐ likes choices
- ☐ likes to do things on my own
- ☐ gets more involved in the process of doing than the outcome
- ☐ is independent
- ☐ is flexible in how I do things
- ☐ likes to do the unusual
- ☐ gets so involved in what I am doing that I forget about time
- ☐ prefers to construct a model by looking at its picture rather than by reading the directions

___ **TOTAL**

Form #8

Student Data Sheet Example

#	Student's Name	Disability	Paraprofessional Time	Minutes of Service in Accordance with the Student's Individualized Education Plan						
				Reading	Written Language	Math	Social/ Emotional	Speech/ Language	OT/PT DAPE	Other
1	Mary	LD		300	150	300			OT 60	
2	John	MMI	1500	300	300	300		90	DAPE 60	
3	Lynn	LD		150	150					
4	Jake	LD				300		60		
5	Joey	LD		300						
6	Heidi	OHI	600	300	300	300		90	OT 60 PT 60	Health 300
7	Amy	LD		300						
8	Mike	LD		300						
9	Steve	BD	300				300			
10	Frank	VI	300	300	150					Enlargement 60
11	James	LD			300				OT 60	
12	Alicia	LD				300			OT 60	
13	Mark	BD					300			
14	Tim	LD		300	300	300		90		

Form #9

Student Data Sheet

| Student's Name | Disability | Paraprofessional Time | Minutes of Service in Accordance with the Student's Individualized Education Plan | | | | | | |
			Reading	Written Language	Math	Social/ Emotional	Speech/ Language	OT/PT DAPE	Other
1									
2									
3									
4									
5									
6									
7									
8									
9									
10									
11									
12									
13									
14									

Sample Student Groups

This form demonstrates how the information derived from Form #7 is used to group the students in the classroom environment. Form #11 is a blank copy that can be used to experiment and group your students.

Classroom #1 – 5 students

Lynn, Brandon and Paul (LD)   **Steve (BD)**   **Aaron (HI)**

Services provided:
☒ Consultation: <u>10 min. daily with Spec. Ed.</u>
☒ Paraprofessional: 1 hour per day for LD students
☒ Paraprofessional: 1 hour per day for BD student

These five students were grouped together, as the students needed minimal academic support. All of the students in this classroom receive their direct instruction from the general education teacher. Steve has a student behavior support paraprofessional written into his IEP for approximately one hour per day. The LD students also have academic support for one hour. The two paraprofessionals should be scheduled into the classroom at separate times, allowing for additional support throughout the day. Brandon also receives language service. If the language specialist is able to schedule time in the classroom, this person may also lend support to the other students if needed.

Classroom #2 – 5 students

Joey, Mary, Mike, Amy (LD)   **Heidi (OHI)**

Services provided:
☒ Paraprofessional: 2 hours per day
☒ Special Education Teacher: 1-2 hours per day, including related support

This group of students requires more direct service than the students placed into Classroom #1. Three of the students receive support only for reading. The special education teacher provides this support. Heidi and Mary have the greatest academic needs. Heidi receives support from a paraprofessional for two hours per day. This paraprofessional will be able to provide some support to the other students as well. Heidi also receives support from the occupational and physical therapist. The occupational therapist could provide service during the written language block, as the special education teacher is in the classroom only during reading. This teacher can provide service to Heidi and monitor the other students if needed.

Form #10.2

Classroom #3 – 3 students

Frank (VI)   **Mark (BD)**   **John (MMI)**

Service provided:
☒ Paraprofessional: Full time in the classroom
☒ Special Education Teacher: 1-2 hours per day, including related support

This is the only classroom that includes a full-time paraprofessional. This paraprofessional is assigned to John. Mark was placed into this classroom so his behavior goals could be monitored throughout the day by the paraprofessional. Frank will need many accommodations due to his low vision. The special education teacher is involved on a daily basis. Both John and Frank receive service from related service providers. The paraprofessional will need lunch and a break scheduled into the day. These breaks can be scheduled while the special education teacher and related service providers are providing service to the students.

Classroom #4 – 4 students

Tim, Jake, James, Alicia (LD)

Service provided:
☒ Special Education Teacher: 1 hour per day, plus related services

The services in this group vary. Tim is the only student who receives services for reading, written language and also math. Therefore, the other students will also have access to some additional support, if needed, in these subject areas, even though it is not in their IEPs. Several of the students receive OT services, speech and language and some additional related services. By grouping these students, service will be able to be provided throughout the day.

The groupings shown here are only examples. The students may be grouped in various ways. Since three of the classrooms in this hypothetical situation receive pupil support from paraprofessionals, the students could possibly be grouped into three classrooms, depending upon the behavior and how well the students work together. This would allow for additional coverage throughout the school day. The students who receive service in only one academic area, such as math, could be grouped into a different classroom.

The scheduling process will take time. Keep in mind that no matter how many times the students are grouped and regrouped, there will never be a perfect group. The key is to look for a group that will be manageable for both general and special education teachers.

Student Groups

This form may be used to help group the students. You may reproduce as many copies as needed.

Classroom #___

Students: _____ _____ _____

_____ _____ _____

☐Consultation:_____ ☐Special Education:_____
☐Paraprofessional:_____ ☐Related Services:_____
☐Other:_____

_____
_____
_____
_____
_____
_____
_____
_____
_____

Classroom #___

Students: _____ _____ _____

_____ _____ _____

☐Consultation:_____ ☐Special Education:_____
☐Paraprofessional:_____ ☐Related Services:_____
☐Other:_____

_____
_____
_____
_____
_____
_____
_____
_____
_____

Student Groups

This form may be used to help group students by learning styles, problem solving or related services.

Learning Styles

Students: _____   _____   _____

_____   _____   _____

❑Consultation:_____   ❑Special Education:_____
❑Paraprofessional:_____   ❑Related Services:_____
❑Other:_____

_____

_____

_____

_____

_____

_____

_____

Math and Problem Solving Skills

Students: _____   _____   _____

_____   _____   _____

❑Consultation:_____   ❑Special Education:_____
❑Paraprofessional:_____   ❑Related Services:_____
❑Other:_____

_____

_____

_____

_____

_____

_____

_____

_____

Student Groups

Related Services

Students: _____   _____   _____

_____   _____   _____

❏Consultation _____   ❏Speech and Language_____
❏PT Services _____   ❏Occupational Therapy_____
❏Other _____   ❏Other _____

_____
_____
_____
_____
_____
_____
_____
_____
_____
_____

Final Classroom Groups

Classroom	Classroom	Classroom	Classroom	Classroom
Student's name	Student's name	Student's name	Student's name	Student's name

Form #12

Paraprofessional Minutes

Copy one form for each class that has a paraprofessional. Calculate the number of minutes of paraprofessional time carefully. Paraprofessionals assigned to specific students should be listed separately from those who provide program support. Build in a minimum of 15 minutes per day for consultation.

Classroom #	Minutes	Total Program Minutes
Paraprofessional (assigned to a specific student)		
Student contact minutes:		
Consultation time:		
Lunch:		
Break:		
TOTAL minutes:		
Paraprofessional (program support)		
Student contact minutes:		
Consultation time:		
Lunch:		
Break:		
TOTAL minutes:		

225

Form #13.1

Sample Schedule for Special Education Teacher

This is a sample schedule for a grade level of 17 students. The students are cross-categorically grouped by reading abilities. The students in our hypothetical example will receive service from one, full-time special education teacher, with three hours of paraprofessional support. By dividing the morning into two different time blocks (one early morning and the second late morning), service can be easily provided. If the classroom teachers had not rearranged their schedules, two special education teachers and two paraprofessionals would have been needed to provide service to all the students.

In the afternoon, the special education teacher is available from 1:00 – 2:15 to support students. General education teachers may sign up in advance, if additional support time is needed. At 2:35, the students are grouped for a math class that is team-taught by both general and special education teachers. An additional 15-minute time block is allocated at the end of the day to check on individual students as needed.

Form #13.2

Morning Schedule:

8:00 – 9:00 a.m.   IEP meetings, preparation, collaboration and planning time for special education teachers.

9:00 – 9:30 a.m.   Check-in with general education teachers for changes in schedules, daily lesson plans or any other daily responsibilities

Classroom #1 4 students	Classroom #2 4 students	Classroom #3 5 students	Classroom #4 4 students
9:40 – 11:15 Language Arts **Special Education Teacher** Supplemental curriculum is provided by the special education department when assignments are inappropriate and when classroom material cannot be modified.	**9:40 – 11:15** Social Studies and Science block Movies, large-group instruction, story, snack or break. During this time, activities do not require the assistance of the special education department.	**9:40 – 11:15** Reading and Language Arts **Paraprofessional** This classroom has full-time support, as a paraprofessional is assigned to one of the students. Therefore, this person can re-teach, and the assistant can oversee the material provided by the general and special education teachers.	**9:40 – 10:40** Special Classes: Music, Gym, Art, Technology and Media **10:40 – 11:15** Large group instructions, spelling, break. Activities do not require the assistance of the special education department.

Classroom #1 4 students	Classroom #2 4 students	Classroom #3 5 students	Classroom #4 4 students
11:15 – 12:00 Special Classes: Music, Gym, Art, Technology and Media **12:00 – 12:30** Handwriting, spelling, prepare for lunch and recess. No special education needed.	**11:15 – 12:20** Reading and Language Arts **Special Education Teacher** Supplemental curriculum is provided by special education.	**11:15 – 12:20** Social Studies and Science block Movies, large group instruction, story, snack or break. During this time, activities do not require the assistance of the special education department.	**11:15 – 12:30** Reading and Language Arts **Paraprofessional** **10:40 – 11:15** Large-group instructions, spelling, break. Activities do not require the assistance of the special education department.

Form #13.3

Afternoon Schedule:
12:30 – 1:00 p.m. Lunch

Classroom #1 4 students	Classroom #2 4 students	Classroom #3 5 students	Classroom #4 4 students
1:00 – 2:15 Social Studies, Science and large-group activities	**1:00 – 1:45** Special Classes: Music, Gym, Art, Technology and Media	**1:00 – 1:45** Special Classes: Music, Gym, Art, Technology and Media	**1:00 – 2:15** Social Studies, Science and large-group activities
1:00 – 1:45 Special education teacher is available on a sign-up basis. This occurs two days in advance.	**1:45 – 2:15** Special education teacher is available on a sign-up basis. This occurs two days in advance.	**1:45 – 2:15** Special education teacher is available on a sign-up basis. This occurs two days in advance.	**1:00 – 1:45** Special education teacher is available on a sign-up basis. This occurs two days in advance.

1:00 – 2:15 Flexible Time Block

This period of time is a "flexible time" block for the special education teacher. General education teachers can sign up in advance for additional student support. This daily time block will allow special education teachers to provide additional support across the curriculum. Suggestions for this time block may include: alternative forms of assessment; planning time for teachers, support for additional curriculum areas, drill and practice activities and supplemental support. The special education teacher is also able to use this time for individual assessments and student observations as needed.

2:35 – 3:35 Math

In this schedule, there are seven students who receive math service according to their IEPs. All of the students are placed into one math class, and the class is team taught.

3:35 – 3:50

This period of time is available to check with students with regard to assignment books, contracts and progress charts, if necessary.

Form #14

Schedule for
Special Education Teacher

Classroom # ___ ____ students	Classroom # ___ ____ students	Classroom # ___ ____ students	Classroom # ___ ____ students
Time:_____ Subject:_____ Support:_____	Time:_____ Subject:_____ Support:_____	Time:_____ Subject:_____ Support:_____	Time:_____ Subject:_____ Support:_____

Classroom # ___ ____ students	Classroom # ___ ____ students	Classroom # ___ ____ students	Classroom # ___ ____ students
Time:_____ Subject:_____ Support:_____	Time:_____ Subject:_____ Support:_____	Time:_____ Subject:_____ Support:_____	Time:_____ Subject:_____ Support:_____

Form #15

Staff Survey of In-Service Needs

This form will help us to determine upcoming staff development and in-service workshops. Please fill this out and return it to the Special Education Department. Thank you!

I understand the concept of inclusive education.
       ❑ Yes   ❑ No   ❑ I still have questions.

I am willing to participate in the inclusive program.
       ❑ Yes   ❑ No   ❑ I'm not sure.

I would like to have an inclusive classroom in the upcoming year.
       ❑ Yes   ❑ No   ❑ I am not sure.

I will need additional training and in-service before I would feel comfortable participating in the program.
       ❑ Yes   ❑ No

I would like to receive further information or attend an in-service on the following area(s). (Please check all that apply.)

    ❑ Inclusive education (general information)
    ❑ Collaboration and teaming
    ❑ Accommodations and modifications
    ❑ Working with support staff
    ❑ Disability awareness _____
    ❑ Other: (Please write in below.)

_____

_____

_____

_____

Comments or suggestions:

_____

_____

_____

_____

_____

_____

_____

_____

_____

Student Survey

1. How do you feel about your classroom placement?

   _____
   _____
   _____

2. How do you feel you are doing academically in school?

   _____
   _____
   _____

3. Are you able to follow the class schedule? Class rules?

   _____
   _____
   _____

4. Do you feel you are able to meet the class expectations?

   _____
   _____
   _____

5. Do you feel you will need more, less or about the same amount of classroom support next semester?

   _____
   _____
   _____

6. How do you feel about the current homework? Is it too little or too much, or is it manageable?

   _____
   _____
   _____

7. Are you comfortable in the classroom social situations?

   _____
   _____
   _____

8. Are you involved in any after-school activities? If not, would you like to be?

   _____
   _____
   _____

Form #16.2

9. **If you could change one thing about school, what would it be?**

_____

_____

_____

10. **What do you need from me to help you succeed?**

_____

_____

_____

Comments or suggestions:

_____

_____

_____

_____

_____

_____

_____

All about School!

I like school.	☺	😐	☹
I prefer to stay at home.	☺	😐	☹
I like my teacher.	☺	😐	☹
My teacher likes me!	☺	😐	☹
I have friends.	☺	😐	☹
I like to play by myself.	☺	😐	☹
I like to do art projects!	☺	😐	☹
I like math!	☺	😐	☹
I like to read!	☺	😐	☹
I love computers!	☺	😐	☹
School is easy for me.	☺	😐	☹
I can follow the rules.	☺	😐	☹

I would like help with the following:

Homework   ☺   😐   ☹
- -

Classwork   ☺   😐   ☹
- -

Making new friends   ☺   😐   ☹
- -

Following school rules   ☺   😐   ☹
- -

                             ☺   😐   ☹
- -

                             ☺   😐   ☹
- -

                             ☺   😐   ☹
- -

My favorite things at school are:

_____
_____
_____
_____
_____
_____
_____
_____

Form #18

Parent Survey

1. What are your feelings about your child's new placement?

_____

_____

_____

2. How does your child feel about the new placement?

_____

_____

_____

3. How is your child coping with the academic demands of the classroom?

_____

_____

_____

4. How would you rate your child's self-esteem? Does your child feel more confident or less confident in this setting?

_____

_____

_____

5. How do you feel your child interacts with his/her peers?

_____

_____

_____

6. Have you noticed changes in your child (either positive or negative) since this new placement? If so, please explain.

_____

_____

_____

7. Can you suggest any ideas or strategies that will help us when working with your child?

_____

_____

_____

Please list additional comments, questions and concerns on the back side of this paper.

235

Paraprofessional Survey

1. **How do you feel the students that you work with directly are performing?**

_____
_____
_____

2. **Do you have any specific concerns about individual students? If so, please explain.**

_____
_____
_____

3. **Do you feel you have the support you need to do your job? If not, what are your needs?**

_____
_____
_____

4. **Do you feel you have adequate time to talk and plan with both general and special education teachers? Do you have suggestions about this time?**

_____
_____
_____

5. **Do you have suggestions to help the program run more smoothly?**

_____
_____
_____

6. **Do you feel a need for training in specific areas that have not been addressed? If so, what type of training would be beneficial?**

_____
_____
_____

Additional comments, questions and concerns:

_____
_____
_____
_____
_____

Form #20.1

Staff Survey

1. How do you feel the students are performing academically in your classroom?
   _____
   _____
   _____

   If there are specific students you would like to discuss, please list the student(s) and the specific area(s) of concern.

   Student: **Area of Concern:**
   _____   _____
   _____   _____
   _____   _____

2. Do you feel the students in your classroom are interacting appropriately with their peer group?
   _____
   _____
   _____

   If there are specific students you would like to discuss, list the student(s) and the area(s) of concern.

   Student: **Area of Concern:**
   _____   _____
   _____   _____
   _____   _____

3. Are the students in your classroom completing the daily class and homework assignments?
   _____
   _____
   _____

4. How do the students' work and study habits compare to their peers'?
   _____
   _____
   _____

5. How do your students respond to your behavior management system?
   _____
   _____
   _____

237

6. How do you feel the current placement has affected the students' self-esteem?

_____
_____
_____

7. Do you feel you have adequate time for collaboration with the special education department?

_____
_____
_____

8. Are you satisfied with the progress the students have made?

_____
_____
_____

9. Do you feel that you had too many students with special needs in your classroom this year? Too few? Was it a manageable group?

_____
_____
_____

10. What changes would you like to see for the upcoming semester (or school year)?

_____
_____
_____

Additional comments, questions and concerns:

_____
_____
_____
_____
_____
_____

Form #21

Daily Lesson Activities and Objectives

Circle one: M   T   W   Th   F

Lesson	Student Needs	General Educator's Role & Responsibilities	Special Educator's Role & Responsibilities
Subject:	**Type of Teaching:** ❑ #1 Team teaching ❑ #2 Supportive ❑ #3 Supplemental ❑ #4 Parallel		
Lesson with objectives:	**Student / Specific lesson accommodations**		
Subject:	**Type of Teaching:** ❑ #1 Team teaching ❑ #2 Supportive ❑ #3 Supplemental ❑ #4 Parallel		
Lesson with objectives:	**Student / Specific lesson accommodations**		

Form #22.1

Discussion Questions: Planning and Teaching

1. **When and how much time do we need to allocate for planning? Daily? Weekly?**
_____
_____
_____

2. **Do we prefer formal or informal sessions?**
_____
_____
_____

3. **What is the best time to schedule these sessions within our current schedules?**
_____
_____
_____

4. **What will our individual roles be in lesson planning?**
_____
_____
_____

5. **How will the teaching be structured in the classroom? Will classes be team taught? Will supportive teaching, supplemental teaching or parallel teaching better serve the students in the classroom?**
_____
_____
_____

6. **If we will be co-teaching the majority of the day, how should we communicate this to parents?**
_____
_____
_____

7. **When problems occur, how will we solve them?**
_____
_____
_____

Form #22.2

8. What do we see as personal, individual strengths that will contribute to the classroom teaching structure?

_____
_____
_____

9. What are the strengths we see in each other?

_____
_____
_____

Additional discussion questions:

_____
_____
_____

_____
_____
_____

_____
_____
_____

_____
_____
_____

_____
_____
_____

Discussion Questions: Discipline

1. What is the classroom discipline plan? Is the discipline plan posted in the classroom?

_____
_____
_____

2. Will all students be expected to follow the same plan?

_____
_____
_____

3. Are rewards and consequences part of the classroom discipline plan?

_____
_____
_____

4. Who will be responsible for classroom discipline? Who will deal with specific behaviors—and how?

_____
_____
_____

5. Will all students be expected to follow the same rules?

_____
_____
_____

6. If rules are different for different students, how do we work out issues of fairness in the class, and how do we explain the different standards for different students to the class?

_____
_____
_____

Additional discussion questions:

_____
_____
_____

Form #24

Discussion Questions: Grading

1. **Who will be responsible for grading the students?**

_____

_____

_____

2. **What type of grading system will be used?**

_____

_____

_____

3. **Will adaptations and modifications affect the students' grades?**

_____

_____

_____

4. **If modified grading is used, what guidelines should be used?**

_____

_____

_____

5. **Will we be able to evaluate a student's progress using a variety of ways in addition to testing?**

_____

_____

_____

6. **Will students receive credit for participation?**

_____

_____

_____

Additional discussion questions:

_____

_____

_____

_____

_____

_____

Discussion Questions: Classroom Environment

1. What is the daily classroom routine? What about pencil sharpening, bathroom breaks and moving around the classroom?

_____
_____
_____

2. Are there designated areas in the classroom to turn in assignments and store home/school notes, assignment books, curriculum materials, etc.?

_____
_____
_____

3. Does sharing a space include sharing supplies and materials?

_____
_____
_____

4. What are your greatest concerns about sharing a teaching space?

_____
_____
_____

Additional discussion questions:

_____
_____
_____

_____
_____
_____
_____

_____
_____
_____

_____
_____
_____

Form #26

Discussion Questions: Working with Parents

1. When problems arise, who will be responsible to contact the parents of the shared students?

   _____

   _____

   _____

2. How will parent/student conferences be handled?

   _____

   _____

   _____

3. How should we introduce ourselves to the parents and students on the first day of school?

   _____

   _____

   _____

Additional discussion questions:

_____

_____

_____

_____

_____

_____

_____

_____

_____

_____

_____

_____

My Profile as an Inclusive Teacher

	No	Sometimes Maybe	Yes
Organization			
I have detailed lesson plans for each classroom.			
On my lesson plans, I list the accommodations for specific students.			
I keep accurate records and documentation for individual students.			
I arrive on time to the general education classroom.			
I have a detailed plan in case of my absence.			
I meet the due process deadlines for the IEP and review meetings.			
Classroom Environment			
I follow the classroom rules for each individual classroom.			
I am flexible in my teaching and have developed a range of strategies.			
I have a well stocked work area so I do not have to continually ask the classroom teacher for materials and supplies.			
I am ready and prepared when working in a co-teaching situation.			
I lend support not only to the students with special needs but to other students who may need support periodically.			
I am patient and supportive with all students in the classroom.			
I deal with discipline effectively, according to the predetermined discipline plan.			
I respect the teachers with whom I work, and I treat information confidentially.			
I seek help from others if needed and provide information if needed.			
I continually check to be sure that I am providing the correct amount of service to students and following their IEPs.			
Working with Parents			
Parent meetings and conferences are constructive and positive.			
I try to understand the parents' points of view and try to offer positive, practical solutions if they are frustrated, angry or upset.			
I try to use minimal special education "jargon" when working with parents.			
I take the time necessary to meet with parents, and if parents have additional questions, I arrange for a follow-up meeting.			
I am not afraid to admit when I do not know the answer to a parent's question. I offer to find out and follow up with the parent.			
I am honest when dealing with parents and students.			
Professional Development			
I set short- and long-term goals for my own personal development.			
I keep up-to-date on current research in education.			
I try to learn as much as I can about the students I teach.			

Form #28

My Profile as a Paraprofessional

	No	Sometimes Maybe	Yes
Organization			
I keep the lesson plans provided by the teacher close at hand.			
I know which accommodations are appropriate for my assigned students.			
I arrive on time to the classroom.			
I keep good notes and documentation when asked.			
I have my daily schedule and notes prepared in case I am absent.			
Classroom Environment			
I follow the classroom rules for each individual classroom.			
I know from whom to take direction.			
I have a well stocked work area so I do not have to continually ask the classroom teacher for materials and supplies.			
I lend support not only to the students with special needs but other students who may need support periodically.			
I am patient and supportive with all students in the classroom.			
I look for strengths in the students.			
I help students to develop friendships and learn new things.			
I know when to step back so the student is able to become more independent.			
I follow the classroom teacher's lead.			
I know with whom and when to share my frustrations and concerns.			
I respect the teachers, students and peers with whom I work and I treat all information confidentially.			
I seek help from others when needed.			
I continually check to be sure that I am providing the correct amount of service to students.			
Working with Parents			
I know what my role is in relation to parents.			
When parents ask me questions, I am positive and refer the parent to the teacher if questions are related to the student's progress or IEP.			
I try to understand the parents' points of view, and I am a good listener.			
I maintain confidentiality if parents ask me about others in the classroom.			
When I meet parents outside of the school setting, I maintain a high standard of confidentiality.			
Professional Development			
I continually try to learn and apply new strategies when working with students.			
I attend all required meetings.			
I try to learn as much as I can about the students with whom I work.			

Form #29

Emergency Back-Up Plan

Student: _____

Time block: _____

Classroom Teacher: _____

☐ Student behavior plan is attached.

The behavior plan for this student includes:

_____

_____

_____

_____

_____

_____

_____

Listed below are the names of the people to contact regarding this student. Also listed are the extensions where the people can be reached.

1st Contact: _____

_____

2nd Contact:

_____

_____

3rd Contact: _____

_____

Additional information:

_____

_____

_____

_____

_____

_____

248

Curriculum Accommodations

Date: _____

Student:_____   **Grade Level:**_____

Team Members:

_____   _____

_____   _____

Student's Strengths:

_____   _____

_____   _____

_____   _____

Suggested Strategies and Accommodations:

Textbook:

_____

_____

_____

Daily Assignments:

_____

_____

_____

Written Language:

_____

_____

_____

Spelling:

_____

_____

_____

Mathematics:

_____

_____

_____

Form #30.2

Organization:

_____
_____
_____

Information Processing:

_____
_____
_____

Large and Small Groups:

_____
_____
_____
_____

Assessments:

_____
_____
_____

Social/Emotional/Behavioral:

_____
_____
_____

Additional Areas of Concern:

_____
_____
_____

_____
_____
_____

List the person responsible to create or implement the accommodations:

Textbook:_____   **Daily Assignments:**_____
Written Language:_____   **Spelling:**_____
Math:_____   **Organization:**_____
Assessments:_____   _____

_____   _____
_____   _____

Form #31

Textbook Accommodations

Student's name:_____   **Date:**_____
Subject:_____   **Grade:**_____

Team Members
Name and Title:

_____   _____
_____   _____
_____   _____
_____   _____

Check all that apply:

❑ The student will need the following accommodations for classroom textbooks.
   ❑ The student should read textbooks aloud with a peer or in a small group setting.
   ❑ Audiocassettes of textbooks will be provided for the student.
      ❑ Full recorded version. Subjects: _____
      ❑ Alternate pages recorded
      ❑ Paraphrased textbook
   ❑ _____
   ❑ _____
   ❑ _____

Person responsible: _____

❑ The student will need the following support with classroom material.
   ❑ Pre-teaching or previewing of textbook material
   ❑ Outline of the required reading material
   ❑ List of vocabulary words and definitions
      ❑ Modified list of vocabulary _____
   ❑ Assignment sheet of required assignment with due dates listed
   ❑ Study guide or contract for assigned materials
   ❑ Set of textbooks for home use. Subject areas: _____
   ❑ _____
   ❑ _____
   ❑ _____

Person responsible: _____

❑ The student will require direct support from the special education department.
   ❑ Supplemental textbooks required.
   Service provider:_____
   Minutes of direct daily service:_____
   Additional information: _____
_____

Form #32

Textbook Accommodations – 2

Student's name:_____   **Date:**_____
Subject:_____   **Grade:**_____

Team Members

Name and Title:

_____   _____
_____   _____
_____   _____
_____   _____

Student Goal: _____ _____ _____ Modification:_____ _____ _____ _____ Person Responsible: _____ _____ _____	Review date: _____ Comment:_____ _____ Review date: _____ Comment:_____ _____ Review date: _____ Comment:_____ _____ Review date: _____ Comment:_____ _____
Student Goal: _____ _____ _____ Modification:_____ _____ _____ _____ Person Responsible: _____ _____ _____	Review date: _____ Comment:_____ _____ Review date: _____ Comment:_____ _____ Review date: _____ Comment:_____ _____ Review date: _____ Comment:_____ _____

Form #33.1

Daily Assignments

Student's name:_____   **Date:**_____

Subject:_____   **Grade:**_____

Team Members

Name and Title:

_____   _____
_____   _____
_____   _____
_____   _____

Check all that apply:

❑ The student will need the following support with daily assignments.
   ❑ Modify the length of the assignment _____
   ❑ Allow additional time for assignment completion. _____
   ❑ Use cooperative groups when possible. _____
   ❑ Complete written assignments orally. _____
   ❑ Use a scribe to help with written assignments. _____
   ❑ Partner with a peer to read assignments._____
   ❑ Use an alternative form of grading for assignments. _____
   ❑ _____
   ❑ _____
   ❑ _____
   ❑ _____

Person responsible: _____

❑ The student will need the following supplemental services.
   ❑ A checklist of assignments and due dates._____
   ❑ A complete set of textbooks for home use._____
   ❑ Photocopies or consumable textbooks._____
   ❑ Study guide or contract for assigned projects._____
   ❑ _____
   ❑ _____
   ❑ _____
   ❑ _____

Person responsible: _____

Form #33.2

❑ The student will require direct support from the special education department.
    ❑ Assignments with same content but lower readability level will be provided.
    ❑ Supplemental curriculum or adapted material will be provided covering the same skill areas.
    ❑ _____
    ❑ _____
    ❑ _____
    ❑ _____

    Service Provider:_____
    Minutes of direct daily service:_____
    Additional information:_____
    _____

❑ The student is unable to complete the assignments.
    ❑ Supplemental assignments will be provided as outlined in the student's IEP.

    _____
    _____
    _____

    Service Provider:_____
    Minutes of direct daily service:_____
    Additional information:_____
    _____

❑ Student will receive additional classroom support from a special education assistant.

    _____
    _____
    _____

    Service Provider:_____
    Minutes of direct daily service:_____
    Additional information:_____
    _____

❑ Student will receive special instruction in a separate special education placement.

    _____
    _____
    _____

    Service Provider:_____
    Minutes of direct daily service:_____
    Additional information:_____
    _____

Form #34

Testing Accommodations

Student's name:_____   **Date:**_____
Subject:_____   **Grade:**_____

Team Members

Name and Title:

_____   _____
_____   _____
_____   _____
_____   _____

Check all that apply:

❑   The student will need accommodations during tests.

    ❑ No accommodations are needed.
    ❑ Additional time will be needed.
    ❑ Tests should be read aloud.
    ❑ Student responses should be written or recorded for the student.
    ❑ The number of test items should be modified.
    ❑ Student is allowed to use notes during testing.
    ❑ Student is allowed to use calculators or manipulative material.
      Specify:_____
    ❑ Student is tested individually by classroom teacher or special education staff.

❑   The following tests are most appropriate for this student. Check all that apply. Include specific information if appropriate.

    ❑ computer generated   Comment_____
    ❑ demonstration   Comment_____
    ❑ essay   Comment_____
    ❑ fill-in-the blank   Comment_____
    ❑ group assessment   Comment_____
    ❑ matching   Comment_____
    ❑ multiple-choice   Comment_____
    ❑ open-book test   Comment_____
    ❑ oral exam   Comment_____
    ❑ projects   Comment_____
    ❑ portfolio   Comment_____
    ❑ short answer   Comment_____
    ❑ take-home test   Comment_____
    ❑ tape record response   Comment_____
    ❑ teacher observation   Comment_____
    ❑ true/false   Comment_____

Form #35

Accommodations—Blank Template

Student's name:_____   **Date:**_____

Subject:_____   **Grade:**_____

Team Members

Name and Title:

_____   _____
_____   _____
_____   _____
_____   _____

List academic area and appropriate accommodations.

❏ _____

    ❏ _____
    ❏ _____
    ❏ _____
    ❏ _____

Person responsible: _____

❏ _____

    ❏ _____
    ❏ _____
    ❏ _____
    ❏ _____

Person responsible: _____

❏ _____

    ❏ _____
    ❏ _____
    ❏ _____
    ❏ _____

Person responsible: _____

Form #36

Accommodations Log Sheet

Student: _____

Start Date	End Date	Strategy #	Comments and Results

The First 50 Instant Words
Group #1

the	of
and	a
to	in
is	you
that	it
he	was
for	on
are	as
with	his
they	I
at	be
this	have
from	

The First 50 Instant Words
Group #2

or	one
had	by
word	but
not	what
all	were
we	when
your	can
said	there
use	an
each	which
she	do
how	their
is	

My Personal Reading List – Genre and Topics

❑ Autobiography

_____

❑ Biography

_____

❑ Comic

_____

❑ Drama

_____

❑ Fantasy

_____

❑ Health

_____

❑ How-To books

_____

❑ Hobby

_____

❑ History

_____

❑ Inspirational

_____

❑ Just-for-fun

_____

❑ Legends

_____

My Personal Reading List—Genre and Topics

❑ Magazine

_____

❑ Mystery

_____

❑ Myths

_____

❑ Nature

_____

❑ Newspapers

_____

❑ Poetry

_____

❑ Religion

_____

❑ Science Fiction

_____

❑ Self-Help

_____

❑ Short Stories

_____

❑ Sports

_____

My Personal Reading List

★ _____

_____

★ _____

_____

★ _____

_____

★ _____

_____

★ _____

_____

★ _____

_____

★ _____

_____

★ _____

_____

Recommended Reading List

Title	Author	I recommend this book because:
		☆ ☆ ☆
		☆ ☆ ☆
		☆ ☆ ☆
		☆ ☆ ☆
		☆ ☆ ☆

Compare and Contrast – Book /Video

Area	Book	Video
Characters:	_____ _____ _____	_____ _____ _____
Setting:		
Main Event #1		
Main Event #2		
Main Event #3		
Occurred in only one form of media.		

Tips for Reading with Your Children

📖   **Spend time with your children talking, telling stories and singing songs.** These are fun and important activities that help children get ready for reading.

📖   **Read to and with your children every day.** This shows that daily reading and spending time together is important.

📖   **Let your children help choose the books you read together.** This will help keep your children's interest.

📖   **Find a comfortable place to read, and sit close to your children.** This helps create a special feeling at reading time.

📖   **Change your voice and the pace that you read to fit the story.** This makes the story more interesting for your children.

📖   **After reading a book, talk about the story.** Discussing the pictures and the main ideas in a book helps develop understanding.

📖   **Let your children see you reading books, newspapers and magazines.** This sets an example for children that you enjoy and value reading.

📖   **Take your children to the library regularly.** Libraries are a wonderful place to find books and so much more.

Tips for Reading with your Children is available in multiple languages:
www.thinkmhc.org/literacy/tips.htm

Common Prefixes

Prefix	Meaning	Examples
auto	self	autobiography, autograph
bi	two	biweekly, bicycle, biculturalism
de	opposite	defrost, decode, deport
dis*	opposite of	disapprove, disagree, disbelief
fore	before	foretell, forecast, forewarn
in, im	not	impossible, incredible
hyper	over	hyperactive, hypersensitive
inter	between or among	intertwine, interact, intervene
mis*	wrongly	misunderstood, misguide, misspell
non	not or without	nonfiction, nonsense, nonexistent
over*	too much	overwork, oversleep, overdo
pre	before	pretest, preview, preheat, prepay
re*	again	redo, remake, rewrite, replace, resend
semi	half	semisweet, semicircle, semiprivate
super	above	supersonic, superstar
sub	below	subway, substandard. submarine
tri	three	triangle, tricycle
un*	not or opposite of	unhappy, unnecessary, unusual, unsure

* indicates the most common prefixes

Common Suffixes

Suffix	Meaning	Examples
-able	to give or to be	acceptable
-ed*	past tense	walked, bumped, shoveled
-en	made of, to become	wooden, broken, taken
-er*	comparative or doer	bigger, sweeter, faster teacher, writer
-est	comparative	largest, smallest
-ful	full of or enough to fill	beautiful, wonderful, joyful
-ing*	verb ending	walking, running, jumping
-less	without	tireless, relentless, penniless
-y or -ly	characteristic of	quickly, slowly, evenly, gently
-ness	state of	kindness, sadness, happiness
-ous	full of	dangerous
-s or -es	more than one	cars, toys, boxes
-y*	in a certain way or characterized by	easy

* indicates the most common suffixes

Chapter Summary

Subject:

_____

Chapter or Page Numbers_____

Main Idea:

_____

_____

_____

Supporting Details:

_____

_____

_____

_____

Main Idea:

_____

_____

_____

Supporting Details:

_____

_____

_____

_____

Main Idea:

_____

_____

_____

Supporting Details:

_____

_____

_____

_____

Chain of Events Organizer

First Event

Second Event

Third Event

Final Event

Form #47

Compare and Contrast Organizer

Attribute	#1	#2

Form #48

Fact or Opinion

Fact	Opinion

Story Map

What is the setting of the story?

Who are the major characters?

1.	2.

Who are the secondary characters?

1.	2.	3.	4.

What are the main events of the story?

Event #1

Event #2

Event #3

How does the story end?

Story Map #2

Where does the story take place?

_____

_____

Who are the main characters?

_____

_____

_____

What happens first?

_____

_____

_____

What happens next?

_____

_____

_____

How does the story end?

_____

_____

_____

_____

My Reading Words

Word I Read (said)	Correct Word

Form #52

Word Analysis Chart

Prefix	Base Word	Suffix	Compound Word

Vocabulary

Directions: Write your new vocabulary words and their definitions. Create a sentence that relates to the story and uses the vocabulary word. Create a sentence that does not relate to the story using the word. Check the box by the sentence that relates to the story.

Vocabulary Word and Definition:

_____
_____
_____

❑ Sentence #1_____
_____

❑ Sentence #2 _____
_____

Vocabulary Word and Definition:

_____
_____
_____

❑ Sentence #1 _____
_____

❑ Sentence #2 _____
_____

Vocabulary Word and Definition:

_____
_____
_____

❑ Sentence #1 _____
_____

❑ Sentence #2 _____
_____

Study Buddies

Today is _____

Morning Study Buddy!

Classwork: _____

Recess: _____

Lunch: _____

Afternoon Study Buddy!

Classwork: _____

Break: _____

End of day: _____

Weekly Study Buddies
Subject Area:

Monday:_____

Tuesday:_____

Wednesday:_____

Thursday:_____

Friday:_____

Monthly (Fill in the dates.)

Monday	Tuesday	Wednesday	Thursday	Friday

Required Class Materials

Don't Forget!

The following items must be brought daily!
Take a minute to check before coming to class!

❑ _____

❑ _____

❑ _____

❑ _____

❑ _____

❑ _____

Special Items!

❑ **Item:** _____

Date needed: _____

❑ **Item:** _____

Date needed: _____

Cooperative Groups

Assignment_____

Group members and roles:

Reader:_____
My role is to:

_____

Recorder:_____
My role is to:

_____

Note taker: _____
My role is to:

_____

Observer:_____
My role is to:

_____

Timekeeper:_____
My role is to:

_____

Scorekeeper:_____
My role is to:

_____

Encourager:_____
My role is to:

_____

Material handler:_____
My role is to:

_____

Material storage helper:_____
My role is to:

_____

Form #57.1

World War II Supplemental Project Sheet (Example)

Following is an example of a project sheet that can be used to individualize the curriculum, allowing all students to meet the minimum requirements for the unit. The project sheet is appropriate for middle and high school students that have completed a unit on World War II. This type of project sheet is often used after the unit has been taught. The project sheet is handed out to all students, and the guidelines can be predetermined for the individual students. For the student who needs extension activities, several projects of interest may be selected. For students who struggle, the one required activity may be sufficient.

The classroom teacher may provide a selection of books with various reading levels. Simple activities may be included for students with severe discrepancies—such as the last two activities, flag etiquette and illustration and the illustration of basic vocabulary words. These items were intentionally placed at the end of this project sheet, but when distributing the sheet to the class, items may be ordered randomly or listed from simple to difficult.

For the students who struggle and need additional time to reach the basic goal of completing the class requirements, a simple project may be selected so the student participates in additional activities but still has time to master the required material. The student may select an activity that does not involve a vast of amount of time and energy, such as creating flags for the countries involved in World War II or viewing a video and writing a short review.

For the student who completes the basic requirements of the unit quickly, several extension projects may be selected, such as additional research on famous World War II figures, creating a newspaper of the time or delving into a portion of the history that has great interest to the student.

For the student who has difficulty reading, the student may view a video and give an oral review or create drawings of the various warships and airplanes used at the time.

For the student who has a severe discrepancy between his or her achievement level and that of peers, the student may make a booklet and illustrate simple related words, such as *airplane, boat* and *flag.*

For the ESL student who has recently arrived to the United States, it may be an appropriate time to learn the basic flag etiquette for the U.S. flag and focus on the vocabulary portion of the unit.

By providing project sheets for separate units, it is easy to individualize the curriculum for all students in the classroom and meet their needs.

Form #57.2

World War II Supplemental Project Sheet

Directions: In class, we have been studying World War II. To better understand this era of history, select at least one of the following activities to complete. Once you have chosen your project(s), please see your teacher to discuss the guidelines for your proposed project.

Required: (Choose one.)

☐ Select a book about World War II to read, such as *The Diary of Anne Frank, On the Other Side of the Gate, Dangerous Spring, The Upstairs Room, Children of the Resistance, Don't Fence Me In, The Hiding Place,* or *Milkweed.* If you select another book, please bring it to class for approval. Read the book and give an oral report, or write a report on the book. (If you choose to write your book report, a form will be provided.)

☐ View a movie about World War II, such as *The Diary of Anne Frank, Schindler's List, Bridge Over the River Kwai,* or *The Sound of Music,* and write a review about the movie. If there is another movie of interest, please bring it to class for approval. A movie review form will be provided.

☐ Read the book *The Diary of Anne Frank,* and then view the movie *The Diary of Anne Frank.* Compare and contrast the book and the movie. How are they similar? How are they different?

Projects:

☐ Draw a map of Europe and show the countries Adolf Hitler controlled.
☐ Create a World War II Timeline from 1939-1945.
☐ Research the impact of World War II on the advancement of women in society.
☐ Interview a person who lived during World War II and find out how their life changed during the war.
☐ Create a World War II game of trivia. Create 20 questions to ask the class.
☐ List at least five famous people who lived during World War II. Determine why the person is important and the contribution the person made to the world.
☐ Make a vocabulary book using each letter of the alphabet. For example: *Anti-Semitism* – prejudice against Jews. *Badge* – a Nazi-ordered symbol that those targeted by the Nazi regime were forced to wear for easy identification.
☐ Use an atlas or other resources to locate at least five concentration and death camps. Either describe the locations in writing or map them in a drawing.
☐ Watch a movie produced during the World War II era. Compare and contrast the homes, clothing, food and transportation to that of your own lifestyle.
☐ Imagine that you are a newspaper editor during World War II. Taking into consideration the emotions and feelings of the times, write an editorial either in support of or in opposition to the use of the atomic bomb.
☐ Listen to music produced during the World War II era. What are the general themes of the music? How does it differ from the music of today?
☐ Draw pictures of aircraft and sea vessels used during World War II.
☐ Research the etiquette surrounding the flag of the United States of America. Make a list of the "do's and don'ts," and share it with the class. Draw pictures of the flags of the major countries involved during World War II.
☐ Make a booklet and illustrate the following words: *airplane, ship, boat, flag* or others related to World War II. Write a sentence for each word.

Incomplete Assignments

Missing Assignment!

Student:
_____

Date Assigned:
_____

Due Date:
_____

Comments:
_____
_____
_____
_____
_____
_____

Plan:
_____
_____
_____

Student signature:_____
Parent signature: _____
Teacher signature: _____

Missing Assignment!

Student:
_____

Date Assigned:
_____

Due Date:
_____

Action Required:

☐ Assignment must be completed at home and returned to class by
_____(date).

☐ Assignment may be completed together with parent at home.

☐ Student was not able to complete this assignment at home.
_____ (Parent's initials)

☐ Other: _____

Student signature:_____

Parent signature: _____

Teacher signature: _____

Form #59

Assignment Sheet

Name:_____**Date:**_____

Date	Subject	Assignment	Due Date	✓ Complete

Daily Assignments

Name:_____Date:_____

Date	Teacher, Subject, Assignment	Due Date	Teacher / Parent Initials
Upcoming test, projects			
Comments			

Date	Teacher, Subject, Assignment	Due Date	Teacher / Parent Initials
Upcoming test, projects			
Comments			

Daily Homework Log

Student _____ Week of: _____

Monday	☑		☑
Tuesday			
Wednesday			
Thursday			
Friday			

Additional Notes:

_____

_____

_____

Form #62

Priority Checklist

Directions: List the high priority assignments first. High priority assignments are those that must be completed for the next school day. Low priority assignments may be listed in the second section.

Priority	Due Date	Assignment or Task	Complete ☑
#1 is top priority!		List the assignment and the approximate amount of time it will take to complete.	
Low Priority Assignments			

286

©Peytral Publications, Inc

Form # 63

Weekly Planner

Week of _____

Name:_____

Time Slot	MONDAY	TUESDAY	WEDNESDAY	THURSDAY	FRIDAY
3:00					
3:30					
4:00					
4:30					
5:00					
5:30					
6:00					
6:30					
7:00					
7:30					
8:00					
8:30					
9:00					
9:30					

Curriculum Modifications

Date of Implementation:_____

IEP Goal:_____

Time Block	Date and Activity	Student Expectations	Additional Information and Notes

Form #65

Alphabetical Chart

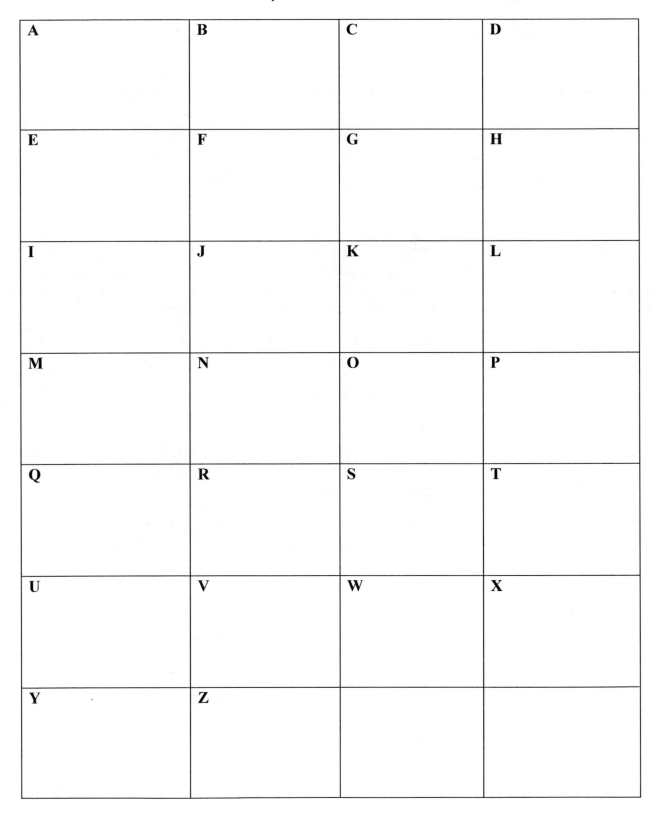

A	B	C	D
E	F	G	H
I	J	K	L
M	N	O	P
Q	R	S	T
U	V	W	X
Y	Z		

Skip-a-Line Paper

Form # 67

Story Frame

Story:

I was late! I ran home from _____.

Just as I opened the _____ I heard the

☎ _____. I ran to answer it! It was

the _____! "Just a minute," I said, as I

quickly found my ✍ , a ✏ and a piece of 📄 to

take a message. The _____ said,

_____

_____.

I didn't know what to do! So I quickly _____

_____

_____.

That's how I solved the problem!

Story Starters

Sally was so bored!

He stared out of the window into the rain.

The train raced down the tracks at full speed!

John saw the footprints leading across the freshly fallen snow.

Mark ran as fast as he could without looking back.

Her eyes were glazed with fever, and she was trembling.

I rubbed my eyes again, as I couldn't believe what I saw!

I remember the day I decided I would never go home again.

I looked around, and everyone looked identical.

School was called off for the day!

It was my lucky day!

All of a sudden, the house started shaking!

Story Map

Title:

_____

Describe the setting:_____
_____
_____
_____

Who are the characters in your story? First list and describe the main characters. If you have additional characters, name and describe two of them here.

_____
_____
_____
_____
_____
_____
_____
_____
_____
_____

List the main event(s) of the story. You may include up to three events, but only one is required.

_____
_____
_____
_____
_____
_____
_____
_____
_____

How does the story end?

_____
_____
_____

Story Map - 2

Title:

Character #1:	Character #2:

Where does the story take place?

What is the major event of the story?

Is there another event that is important?

Is there additional information that you would like to include?

How does the story end?

Compare and Contrast - Attributes

Attribute to Compare	#1	#2	#3

Transition Words and Phrases

Addition	Comparison	Consequence
also	in comparison	accordingly
besides	in the same way	as a result
in addition	likewise	consequently
as well as	similarly	so
		then
		therefore

Contrast	Generalization	Restate
another point of view	as a rule	in essence
although	for the most part	in other words
but	generally	
by contrast	usually	
however		
instead		
otherwise		
on the other hand		
rather		

Result	Time	Summary
as a result	afterward	in brief
because	at the end	in closing
consequently	at the same time	in conclusion
therefore	during	in summary
	earlier	to sum up
	finally	
	first	
	lastly	
	later	
	next	
	second	
	then	
	third	

Proofreading Checklist

I have looked for the following:	
Capital Letters	☐ All sentences begin with a capital letter. ☐ Names of people begin with a capital. ☐ Places begin with a capital letter. ☐ The title has capital letters.
Ending Punctuation	☐ Periods ☐ Question marks ☐ Exclamation marks
Spelling	☐ I have checked the spelling. ☐ When a word does not look right, I look it up.
Additional Strategies	☐ I have looked for overused words. ☐ I have read my paper out loud. ☐ A friend has read my paper. ☐ Someone has read my paper out loud to me.

Proofreading Checklist – 2

<u>S</u>pelling	☐ **I have checked spelling:**
	    ☐ **by examining each word carefully**
	    ☐ **using a dictionary**
	    ☐ **asking a peer to read the paper and look for errors**

<u>P</u>unctuation	☐ **I have checked the punctuation:**
	    ☐ **apostrophes**
	    ☐ **commas**
	    ☐ **ending punctuation**
	    ☐ **quotation marks**

<u>A</u>ppearance	☐ **I have checked the appearance for:**
	    ☐ **margins**
	    ☐ **paragraph indentation**
	    ☐ **legibility and neatness**

<u>C</u>apitalization	☐ **I have checked the capitalization:**
	    ☐ **first word of the sentence**
	    ☐ **proper names**
	    ☐ **within quotes**
	    ☐ **title**

<u>E</u>xtra Areas to Analyze	☐ **I have analyzed the paper for:**
	    ☐ **fragmented and run-on sentences**
	    ☐ **topic sentence for each paragraph**
	    ☐ **transition words to connect ideas**
	    ☐ **the common errors that I typically make**
	    ☐ **I have read the paper aloud to determine left-out words.**

Word List Chart

Word	Date	#1	#2	#3	#4	#5	Mastery

Sound Chart

Initial Sound	Medial Sound	Ending Sound

Initial Sound	Medial Sound		Ending Sound

Alphabet Chart – Vowels

a	a	a	e	e
e	e	i	i	i
o	o	o	u	u
A	A	A	E	E
E	E	I	I	I
O	O	O	U	U

Alphabet Chart – Consonants

b	c	d	f	g
h	j	k	l	m
n	p	q	r	s
t	v	w	x	y
z	B	C	D	F
G	H	J	K	L
M	N	P	Q	R
S	T	V	W	X
Y	Z			

Spelling Usage Card

Place a check each time you use your spelling word while speaking or writing! Try to use each word three times!

_____ ☐ ☐ ☐ ☐

_____ ☐ ☐ ☐ ☐

_____ ☐ ☐ ☐ ☐

_____ ☐ ☐ ☐ ☐

_____ ☐ ☐ ☐ ☐

_____ ☐ ☐ ☐ ☐

_____ ☐ ☐ ☐ ☐

_____ ☐ ☐ ☐ ☐

_____ ☐ ☐ ☐ ☐

_____ ☐ ☐ ☐ ☐

_____ ☐ ☐ ☐ ☐

_____ ☐ ☐ ☐ ☐

_____ ☐ ☐ ☐ ☐

_____ ☐ ☐ ☐ ☐

_____ ☐ ☐ ☐ ☐

_____ ☐ ☐ ☐ ☐

_____ ☐ ☐ ☐ ☐

Study Methods for Spelling

Study Method #1

Step 1: Write each of your spelling words on note cards.
Step 2: Look at the word while the teacher (or a Study Buddy) reads it out loud.
Step 3: Study the word. Read it! Spell it! Read it again!
Step 4: Close your eyes. Spell the word two times without looking.
Step 5: Write the word on paper. Compare your word to the note card.
Step 6: If it is correctly written, select another word. If it is incorrect, repeat Steps 1–5.

Study Method #2

Step 1: Watch your teacher while she reads, writes and spells the new word out loud.
Step 2: Now it's your turn. Read the word, write the word and spell the word out loud while looking at it.
Step 3: Watch your teacher again as she reads, writes and spells the word out loud.
Step 4: Now it's your turn. Spell the word out loud.
Step 5: If you spelled it correctly, it is time to try the next word! If not, repeat Steps 1–4.

Study Method #3

Step 1: Write the spelling words on note cards.
Step 2: Read each word and spell it out loud.
Step 3: Cover the word and write it.
Step 4: Compare the word to the model note card.
Step 5: Did you spell it correctly? If so, write it three more times. If not, repeat Steps 1–4.

Form #80

Spelling Contract
Example

Spelling can easily be individualized for students by creating spelling contracts. A contract such as this example can be individualized by checking off the items that each student is to complete.

Name: Date:
Staple your spelling list to this sheet. If you have a pretest, staple that also so you know which words you need to pay special attention to during practice sessions.
❑ Practice reading and clapping each syllable of each word.
❑ Write each word five times on the following days: M__, T__, W__, Th__, Fr__.
❑ Write each word in a complete sentence.
❑ Create a crossword puzzle with your spelling list to share with others.
❑ Write a poem and include as many spelling words as possible.
❑ Use a thesaurus to find synonyms or antonyms for each word.
❑ Practice writing your words using rainbow colors.
❑ Write and illustrate a short story with your spelling words.
❑ Make a list of five words that rhyme with each of your spelling words.
❑ Make a set of flashcards for daily practice.
❑ Make up short songs that spell out each letter in the word. Record the songs.
❑ Develop silly sentences using your words and draw pictures to go with them.
❑ Use a tape recorder to practice spelling your words orally. Listen to the recording, and check the words against your master list.

Error Analysis Chart – Math

❑ **Addition**
    ❑ Student knows addition facts.
    ❑ Student understands place value.
    ❑ Student works problem from right to left.
    ❑ Student regroups correctly.

❑ **Subtraction**
    ❑ Student understands the concept of subtraction.
    ❑ Student knows subtraction facts..
    ❑ Student understands place value.
    ❑ Student works problem from right to left.
    ❑ Student regroups correctly.

❑ **Multiplication**
    ❑ Student understands the concept of multiplication.
    ❑ Student knows multiplication facts.
    ❑ Student understands the concept of place value.
    ❑ Student regroups correctly.

❑ **Division**
    ❑ Student understands the concept of division.
    ❑ Student knows multiplication facts.
    ❑ Student is subtracting correctly.
    ❑ Student understands the concept of place value.
    ❑ Student regroups correctly.
    ❑ Student follows the steps for division.
    ❑ Student regroups correctly.

Teacher Observation
Addition:_____
_____
_____
_____
_____
_____
_____
_____
_____

Subtraction:_____
_____
_____
_____
_____
_____
_____
_____
_____
_____

Multiplication:_____
_____
_____
_____
_____
_____
_____
_____

Division:_____
_____
_____
_____
_____
_____
_____
_____
_____

Form #81.2

Error Analysis Chart – Math

❑ **Decimals**

❑ **Decimals – Addition**
    ❑ Student understands place value.
    ❑ Student adds correctly.
    ❑ Student lines up decimals correctly to perform operation.

❑ **Decimals – Subtraction**
    ❑ Student understands place value.
    ❑ Student subtracts correctly.
    ❑ Student lines up decimals correctly to perform operation.

❑ **Decimals – Multiplication**
    ❑ Student understands that decimals do not need to be lined up for multiplication.
    ❑ Student correctly counts decimal places and inserts decimal in the correct location.

❑ **Decimals – Division**
    ❑ Student understands how to make the divisor a whole number by moving decimal in both the divisor and the dividend.
    ❑ The student places the decimal point for the answer aligned with the decimal point in the dividend.

❑ **Converting Decimals to Fractions**
    ❑ The student understands the place value of decimals: tenths, hundredths, thousandths, etc.
    ❑ The student is able to read decimals correctly. (E.g., 1.75 is one and 75 hundredths; 1.2 is 1 and 2 tenths.)
    ❑ The student is able to write the fraction correctly. (1 75/100 and 1 2/10)

Teacher Observation

Decimals: Addition
_____
_____
_____
_____

Decimals: Subtraction
_____
_____
_____
_____
_____

Decimals: Multiplication
_____
_____
_____
_____
_____
_____
_____

Decimals: Division
_____
_____
_____
_____
_____
_____
_____

Decimals to Fractions:
_____
_____
_____
_____
_____
_____
_____
_____
_____
_____

307

Addition and Subtraction Charts

Addition Chart

1	1+0								
2	1+1	2+0							
3	1+2	2+1	3+0						
4	1+3	2+2	3+1	4+0					
5	1+4	2+3	3+2	4+1	5+0				
6	1+5	2+4	3+3	4+2	5+1	6+0			
7	1+6	2+5	3+4	4+3	5+2	6+1	7+0		
8	1+7	2+6	3+5	4+4	5+3	6+2	7+1	8+0	
9	1+8	2+7	3+6	4+5	5+4	6+3	7+2	8+1	9+0
10	1+9	2+8	3+7	4+6	5+5	6+4	7+3	8+2	9+1	10+0

Subtraction Chart

10	10-0								
9	10-1	9-0							
8	10-2	9-1	8-0						
7	10-3	9-2	8-1	7-0					
6	10-4	9-3	8-2	7-1	6-0				
5	10-5	9-4	8-3	7-2	6-1	5-0			
4	10-6	9-5	8-4	7-3	6-2	5-1	4-0		
3	10-7	9-6	8-5	7-4	6-3	5-2	4-1	3-0	
2	10-8	9-7	8-6	7-5	6-4	5-3	4-2	3-1	2-0
1	10-9	9-8	8-7	7-6	6-5	5-4	4-3	3-2	2-1	1-0

Multiplication Charts

Multiplication

×	1	2	3	4	5	6	7	8	9	10
1	1	2	3	4	5	6	7	8	9	10
2	2	4	6	8	10	12	14	16	18	20
3	3	6	9	12	15	18	21	24	27	30
4	4	8	12	16	20	24	28	32	36	40
5	5	10	15	20	25	30	35	40	45	50
6	6	12	18	24	30	36	42	48	54	60
7	7	14	21	28	35	42	49	56	63	70
8	8	16	24	32	40	48	56	64	72	80
9	9	18	27	36	45	54	63	72	81	90
10	10	20	30	40	50	60	70	80	90	100

Multiplication

×	1	2	3	4	5	6	7	8	9	10
1	1	2	3	4	5	6	7	8	9	10
2	2	4	6	8	10	12	14	16	18	20
3	3	6	9	12	15	18	21	24	27	30
4	4	8	12	16	20	24	28	32	36	40
5	5	10	15	20	25	30	35	40	45	50
6	6	12	18	24	30	36	42	48	54	60
7	7	14	21	28	35	42	49	56	63	70
8	8	16	24	32	40	48	56	64	72	80
9	9	18	27	36	45	54	63	72	81	90
10	10	20	30	40	50	60	70	80	90	100

Menu Card

Sunshine Cafe

Daily Lunch Menu

SANDWICHES

Hamburger	$2.50
Cheeseburger	$3.00
Tuna	$2.25
Grilled Cheese	$2.25
Ham Sandwich	$2.00
Grilled Chicken	$3.00

SIDES

French Fries	$1.50
Potato Salad	$1.50
Side Salad	$1.50
Soup of the Day	$1.50

DESSERTS

Hot Fudge Sundae	$1.75
Apple Pie	$1.50
Ice Cream or Sherbet	$1.00

BEVERAGES

Milk	$1.00
Soda	$1.00
Juice (Apple / Orange)	$1.25
Coffee / Tea	$ .75

Student Activity Card
Sunshine Cafe

Lunchtime! What would you like? Order a maximum of four items from the menu!

Item:	Price:
#1_____	_____
#2_____	_____
#3_____	_____
#4_____	_____

What is the total cost of the food? _____

The tax is 6%. How much is the tax for your order? _____

Do you want to leave a tip? How much?   10%   15% Calculate the tip. _____

What is the total bill? _____

Check your answers with a calculator!

Numerals and Math Symbols

1	2	3	4	5
6	7	8	9	10
11	12	13	14	15
16	17	18	19	20
0	0			
+	−	=	<	>

One-to-One Correspondence

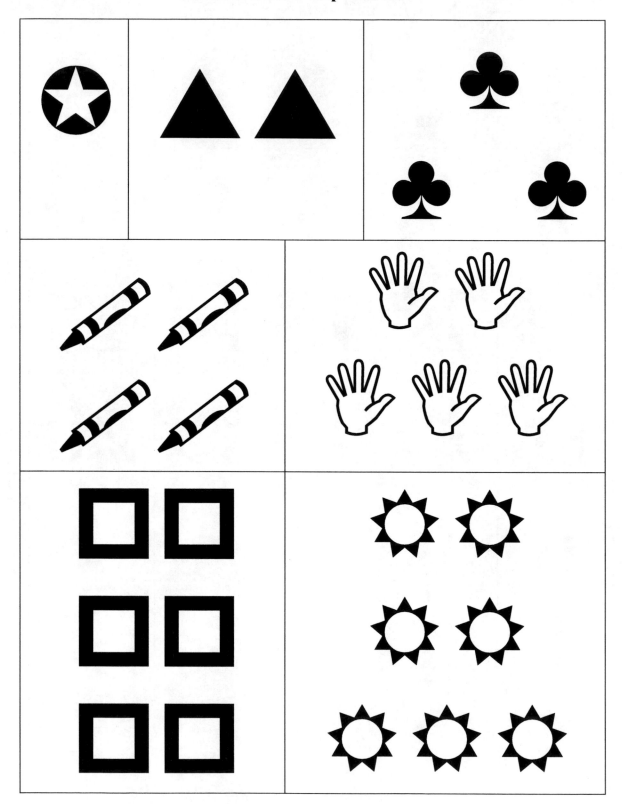

Form #86.2

One-to-One Correspondence

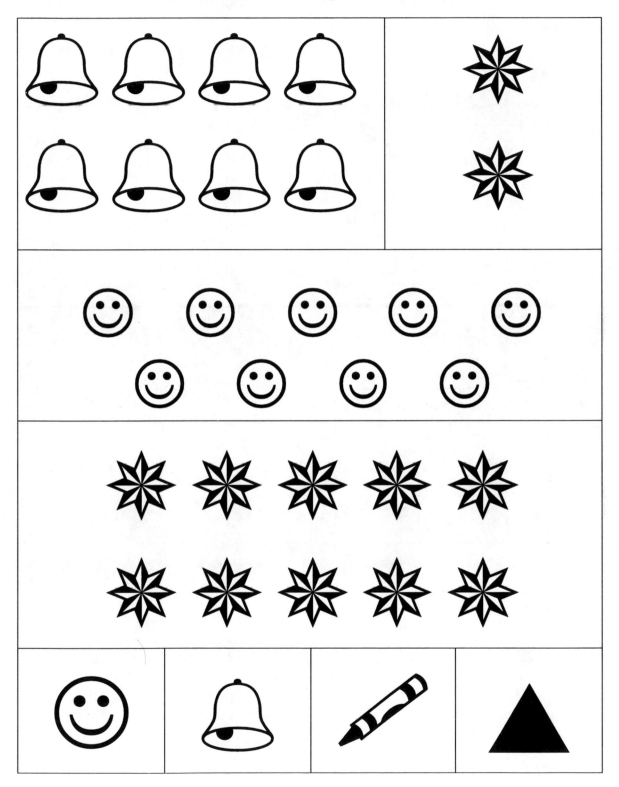

Take Two Playing Cards
(Instructions for the card game are listed in Strategy #422)

one	two	three	four
1	2	3	4
☆	☆☆	☆☆☆	☆☆☆☆

five	six	seven	eight
5	6	7	8
☆☆☆ ☆☆	☆☆☆ ☆☆☆	☆☆☆☆ ☆☆☆	☆☆☆☆ ☆☆☆☆

nine	ten	zero	zero
9	10	0	0
☆☆☆☆ ☆☆☆☆☆	☆☆☆☆☆ ☆☆☆☆☆		

314

Form # 88

Classroom Managers

Student Name	Assignment Book	Board Manager	Classroom Manager	Computer Manager	Line Leader (L) End of Line (E)	Homework Manager	Paper Manager	Substitute Helper			

Form #89

Class Homework Log

Student ID #												
1												
2												
3												
4												
5												
6												
7												
8												
9												
10												
11												
12												
13												
14												
15												
16												
17												
18												
19												
20												
21												
22												
23												
24												
25												
26												
27												

Schedule Pictures

Photocopy and cut apart. Space is available below pictures to write in subjects.

☺			1, 2, 3
♫	A, B, C		

Schedule Pictures

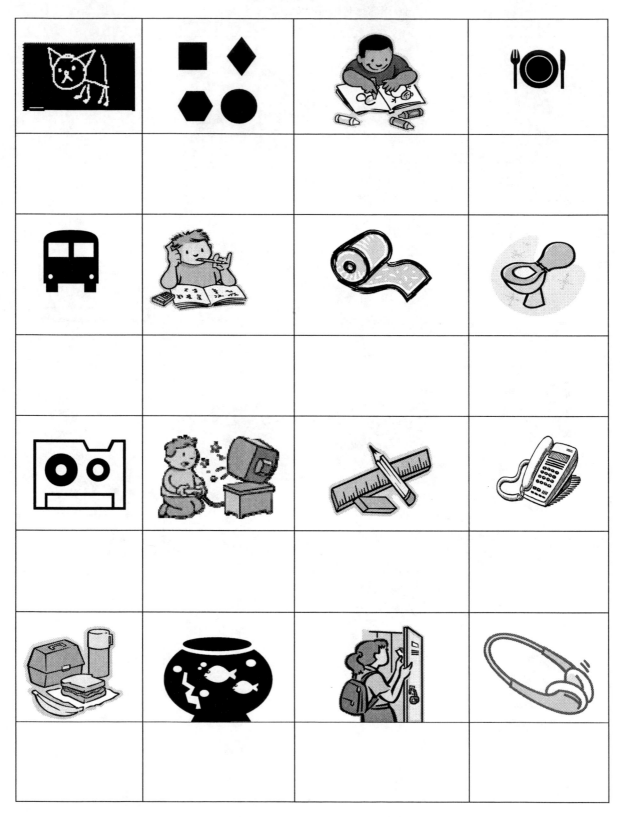

How Organized Are You?

	No	Sometimes	Yes
School			
I arrive to class on time.			
I am prepared for class.			
I have the necessary supplies for class.			
I complete my homework.			
I usually have projects completed the day before they are due.			
I can find materials in my locker or desk.			
I have lunch money or a lunch daily.			
I feel that I am organized.			
Home			
I have a scheduled study time.			
I complete my homework in the evening.			
I keep a calendar of assignments and their due dates.			
I pack my backpack in the evening.			
I have time to do things I enjoy.			
I have enough time in the morning to have breakfast.			
I arrive to school on time.			

Look at your responses to the questions above. If you answered "yes" to all of the above, you are extremely organized! Congratulations! Perhaps you can share your techniques with other students in the class!

If your scores are scattered or most of the checks fall in the "no" category, it is time to think about and develop a self-improvement plan! Select one or two areas you would like to improve, and list several actions you could take to help yourself.

Area #1: _____

Action:

_____
_____
_____

Area #2: _____

Action:

_____
_____
_____

My Personal Goals!
Use this simple chart to monitor your progress.

Directions: Fill in the following chart. Here is an example:

My Old Behavior: I forget to turn in my homework assignments.
My New Behavior: I will pack my homework into my backpack as soon as it is complete.
Monitor your progress daily: ☑

My Old Behavior	My New Behavior	Daily Monitoring				
		M	T	W	Th	F

Choose one or two behaviors to change at first. Do not choose more than two, as you want to be sure you can follow through and monitor each goal daily. Bad habits take a long time to develop—and also take time to correct.

After two to three weeks of using a new behavior every day and monitoring your progress, the behavior will become a natural part of your daily routine, and you will have achieved your goal.

Once you are comfortable with a new behavior, consider adding another to the list. If you begin to slip into your old ways, make another copy of the monitoring chart and start again. Keep at it, and you will succeed!

Self-Evaluation Worksheet

	Yes	No	NA
The classroom arrangement is conducive to the lesson.			
I provide a purpose for learning the lesson.			
I state the goals and objectives of the lesson.			
I review previously learned material.			
I provide an anticipatory set and summarize the lesson.			
I add humor to my lessons.			
My rate of speaking is appropriate to the lesson.			
My speech is clear and understandable.			
My thoughts are organized.			
My lessons follow a logical pattern.			
I frequently monitor for student understanding.			
I incorporate supplemental visual material into the lesson.			
I provide sufficient wait time for students to process the information.			
I provide sufficient time for students to take notes.			
I provide both verbal and visual examples.			
I stay on the topic and avoid irrelevant information.			
I use vocabulary that is at an appropriate level for the students.			
I highlight important material on the board and on transparencies.			
I pause frequently when teaching to check for understanding.			
I consistently cue students to important information.			
I vary the level of questioning so all students can participate.			
I encourage active participation during the lesson.			

Outline

I. _____

      a._____

      b._____

      c._____

      d._____

II. _____

      a._____

      b._____

      c._____

      d._____

III. _____

      a._____

      b._____

      c._____

      d._____

IV. _____

      a._____

      b._____

      c._____

      d._____

Form #95

Timeline

	Date	

Compare and Contrast – Two Items

Items:

How are they alike?

How are they different?

Item #1:	Item #2:

Summary:

Form #97

Assessing Assessments

Student: _____

Date: _____

Strengths: **Weaknesses:**

_____   _____

_____   _____

_____   _____

_____   _____

_____   _____

Standard Assessments

☐ Essay   ☐ True / False   ☐ Matching   ☐ Multiple Choice

☐ Short Answer   ☐ Project (below)   ☐ Performance (below) ☐ Processing (below)

Project Ideas		Performance Ideas		Processing Ideas
autobiographies		acting		checklists
book reviews		character sketches		concept mapping
brochures		commercials and ads		computer activities
cartoons		dance		informal assessments
collages		debates		interviews with students
puzzles		demonstrations		journals
displays		discussions		learning logs
games		experiments		observations
handbooks		interviews		portfolios
illustrations		music		questionnaires
maps and diagrams		news reports		
models		oral reports		
portfolios		plays		
posters		presentations		
projects		role play		
trivia		reports		
questionnaires		simulations		
		speeches		

Form #98

Choose Your Own Assessment!

Student: _____

Date: _____

Subject Area: _____

Additional Information/Assignment: _____

_____

_____

_____

Check the box (or boxes) that indicate how you would like to demonstrate your knowledge for the assignment listed above.

Standard Assessments

☐ Essay ☐ True / False ☐ Matching ☐ Multiple Choice

☐ Short Answer ☐ Project (below) ☐ Performance (below) ☐ Processing (below)

Project Ideas	Performance Ideas	Processing Ideas
autobiographies	acting	checklists
book reviews	character sketches	concept mapping
brochures	commercials and ads	computer activities
cartoons	dance	informal assessments
collages	debates	interviews with students
puzzles	demonstrations	journals
displays	discussions	learning logs
games	experiments	observations
handbooks	interviews	portfolios
illustrations	music	questionnaires
maps and diagrams	news reports	
models	oral reports	
portfolios	plays	
posters	presentations	
projects	role play	
trivia	reports	
questionnaires	simulations	
	speeches	

326

Form #99

What Works Best?

(See the example in Strategy #650 to help you in filling out this form.)

Student: _____

Type of Assessment: _____

TOPIC	DATE				

Type of Assessment: _____

TOPIC	DATE				

Type of Assessment: _____

TOPIC	DATE				

Reinforcement Cards

Great Job!	Way to Go!
Awesome!	Congratulations!
WOW!	**You are #1!**
Be Proud!	Perfect!

Student Goals

Student's Name:	M	T	W	TH	F
My Goal:					
List what needs to be done to meet the goal.					

Student's Name:	M	T	W	TH	F
My Goal:					
List what needs to be done to meet the goal.					

Check-in / Check-out

☑	Morning	☑	Afternoon
	I brought my homework to school..		My assignments are written into my assignment book.
	I have a lunch or lunch money.		My books are packed.
	I am prepared for school.		

☑	Morning	☑	Afternoon

Behavior Contract

I would like to change the following:

_____
_____
_____
_____

It is important to change this behavior because:

_____
_____
_____
_____

My goal is:

_____
_____
_____
_____

The steps I will take to meet my goal include:

_____
_____
_____
_____

If I meet my goal, my reward will be:

_____
_____
_____
_____
_____

_____   _____
Student Signature / Date   Teacher Signature / Date

_____   _____
Signature / Date   Signature / Date

My Way to Change

My New Goal

The new goal I would like to obtain is:_____

_____

This will happen when:_____

_____

Positive Reinforcer

My reward is:

_____

_____

_____

_____

I can earn my reward by:

_____

_____

_____

_____

Negative Reinforcer

If I choose not to work toward my new goal, then:

_____

_____

_____

_____

Progress Tracker!
Check a box each time you meet your goal!

_____

Student Signature

_____

Teacher Signature

_____

Signature

Form #105

Reward Chart – Subject Area

Subject: _____

Subject: _____

Subject: _____

Reward Chart – Puzzle

Photocopy the picture and cut it into pieces. The student gets to add a piece to the puzzle every time a goal is met. When the puzzle has been completed, the student receives a predetermined award.

Reward Chart Grid

My Goal:

Color a box on the reward chart each time you make your goal,
or cut out the pictures below and glue one onto your chart each time
you make your goal!

Reward Chart – Morning /Afternoon

Week	Goal #1	Goal #2	Goal #3	Goal #4	Goal #5
Monday AM					
Monday PM					
Tuesday AM					
Tuesday PM					
Wednesday AM					
Wednesday PM					
Thursday AM					
Thursday PM					
Friday AM					
Friday PM					

Directions: Write your goals below. When you achieve a goal, place a check mark under that goal across from the time and day you achieved it. If you get ___ checks for the week under a goal, you receive a reward.

(Decide with your teacher how many checks will earn a reward.)

My Goals:

1._____

2._____

3._____

4._____

5._____

Resources

Books

This section includes resources referenced in this book plus additional useful resources available from Peytral Publications, Inc.

Bender, W. *Differentiating Instruction for Students with Learning Disabilities*. Thousand Oaks, CA: Corwin Press, 2003.

Bender, W. *Differentiating Math Instruction. Strategies that Work for K-8 Classrooms*. Thousand Oaks, CA: Corwin Press, 2005

Cramer, S. *The Special Educator's Guide to Collaboration: Improving Relationships with Co-Teachers, Teams and Families*. Thousand Oaks, CA: Corwin Press, 2006

Dieker, Lisa. *Demystifying Secondary Inclusion*. Port Chester, NY: Dude Publishing, 2007.

Fry, Edward. *Dr. Fry's 1000 Instant Words – The Most Common Words for Teaching Reading Writing and Spelling*. Westminster, CA: Teacher Created Press, 2004.

Gardner, Howard. *Frames of Mind: The Theory of Multiple Intelligences*. City: Academic Internet Publishers, 1993

Greene, Lawrence. *Winning the Study Game*. Minnetonka, MN: Peytral Publications, Inc., 2002

Giangreco, Michael. *Ants in His Pants. Absurdities and Realities of Special Education*. Minnetonka, MN: Peytral Publications, Inc. 1998

Giangreco, Michael. *Flying by the Seat of Your Pants. More Absurdities and Realities of Special Education*. Minnetonka, MN: Peytral Publications, Inc. 1999

Giangreco, Michael. *Teaching Old Logs New Tricks. More Absurdities and Realities of Education*. Minnetonka, MN: Peytral Publications, Inc. 2000

Hammeken, Peggy A. *Inclusion: 450 Strategies for Success*. 2nd ed. Minnetonka, MN: Peytral Publications, Inc., 2000.

Hammeken, Peggy A. *Inclusion: An Essential Guide for the Paraprofessional*. Minnetonka, MN: Peytral Publications, Inc., 2003.

Hannell, Glynis. *Dyslexia Action Plans for Successful Learning.*. Minnetonka, MN: Peytral Publications, Inc., 2004.

Hannell, Glynis. *Let's Learn about Language! Teacher's Toolbox of Instant Language Activities*. Minnetonka, MN: Peytral Publications, Inc., 2007.

Hannell, Glynis. *The Teacher's Guide to Intervention and Inclusive Education*. Minnetonka, MN: Peytral Publications, Inc., 2007.

Heacox, Diane. *Differentiating Instruction in the Regular Classroom*. Minneapolis, MN: Free Spirit Publishing, 2002.

Henrikson, Peggy and Lorraine O. Moore, Ph.D. *Creating Balance in Children: Activities for Optimizing Learning and Behavior*. Minnetonka, MN: Peytral Publications, Inc., 2005.

Horstmeier, DeAnna. *Teaching Math to People with Down Syndrome and Other Hands-On Learners*. Bethesda, MD: Woodbine House, 2004.

Kelly, Karen. *The Power of Visual Imagery*. Minnetonka, MN: Peytral Publications, Inc., 2006.

Lee, Patty. *Collaborative Practices for Educators – Six Keys to Effective Communication*. Minnetonka, MN: Peytral Publications, Inc., 2006.

Le Messurier, Mark. *Cognitive Behavior Training:* A How-to Guide for Successful Behavior. Minnetonka, MN: Peytral Publications, Inc., 2005.

Le Messurier, Mark. *Parenting Tough Kids*. Minnetonka, MN: Peytral Publications, Inc. 2007

Moll, Ann. *Differentiated Instruction Guide for Inclusive Teaching*. Port Chester, NY: National Professional Resources, 2003.

Moore, Lorraine O. *Inclusion: A Practical Guide for Parents*. Minnetonka, MN: Peytral Publications, Inc., 2000.

Scott, Victoria Groves. *Phonemic Awareness: Ready-to-Use Lessons Activities and Games*. Minnetonka, MN: Peytral Publications, Inc., 2005.

Scott, Victoria Groves. *Phonemic Awareness: The Sounds of Reading. Staff Development Training Video*. Minnetonka, MN: Peytral Publications, Inc., 2002.

Sliva, Julie A. *Teaching Inclusive Mathematics to Special Learners, K-6*. Thousand Oaks, CA: Corwin Press, 2004.

Tilton, Linda. *The Teacher's Toolbox for Differentiating Instruction.* Minnetonka, MN: Covington Cove, 2003.

Thorne, Beverly. *Hands-On Activities for Exceptional Children.* Minnetonka, MN: Peytral Publications, Inc., 2001.

Villa, R., Thousand, J. and Nevin, *A. Guide to Co-Teaching. Practical Tips for Facilitating Student Learning.* Thousand Oaks, CA: Corwin Press, 2004

Winebrenner, Susan. *Teaching Kids with Learning Difficulties in the Regular Classroom.* Minneapolis, MN: Free Spirit Publishing, 2005

Websites

This section includes resources from the chapters plus additional resources, grouped by subject area.

Disability Information

American Brain Tumor Association: http://hope.abta.org/site/PageServer

American Council of the Blind: www.acb.org

American Society for Deaf Children: www.deafchildren.org

American Speech-Language-Hearing Association (ASHA): www.asha.org

Autism Society of America: www.autism-society.org

Best Buddies – Disability awareness and community inclusion: www.bestbuddies.org

Children and Adults with Attention Deficit/Hyperactivity Disorder (CHADD): www.chadd.org

Council for Exceptional Children (CEC): www.cec.sped.org

DB-LINK – National Information Clearinghouse on Children who are Deaf-Blind: www.dblink.org

Fetal Alcohol Spectrum Disorders (FASD) Center for Excellence: www.fascenter.samhsa.gov/index.cfm

HRSA Information Center – for publications and resources on health care services for low income, uninsured individuals and those with special health care needs: www.ask.hrsa.cov

International Dyslexia Association: www.interdys.org

Kids on the Block – Disability awareness and community inclusion: www.kotb.com

LDOnline: www.ldonline.org

Learning Disabilities Association of America: www.ldaamerica.org

National Center for Learning Disabilities (NCLD): www.ld.org

National Center on Secondary Education and Transition: www.ncset.org

National Dissemination Center for Children with Disabilities (NICHCY): www.nichcy.org

National Down Syndrome Society: www.ndss.org

National Fragile X Foundation: www.fragilex.org

Recording for the Blind and Dyslexic: www.rfbd.org

Spina Bifida Association of America: www.sbaa.org

TASH (formerly Association for Persons with Severe Handicaps): www.tash.org

Inclusive Education Program Information

Family Village: www.familyvillage.wisc.edu/

IDEA – NICHCY provides up-to-date information: www.nichcy.org/idea.htm

KidsSource: www.kidsource.com/kidsource/content2/inclusion.disab.k12.3.1.html

Kids Together, Inc.: www.kidstogether.org

National Association of Special Education Teachers – Great site. Membership required: www.naset.org/799.0.html

National Information Center for Children and Youth with Disabilities – Planning for Inclusion website: www.kidsource.com/kidsource/content3/inclusion.disab.k12.3.1.html

NICHCY Disability Fact Sheets: www.nichcy.org/disabinf.asp

University of Northern Iowa: http://www.uni.edu/coe/inclusion/

U.S. Department of Education: http://idea.ed.gov

Teacher Resources

Alphabet strip – Colorful, illustrated and printable alphabet strip:
www.abcteach.com/ABC/alphaline3.htm

alphaDictionary – A site that provides commonly misspelled and confused words:
www.alphadictionary.com/articles/misspelled_words.html
www.alphadictionary.com/articles/confused_words.html

AOL at School – Resources for parents, teachers and students. Games, activities, lesson plans, tutorials and more! Click on Educators on the main site: www.aolatschool.com

Book Notes – Comprehensive guide to free book notes, summaries, literature notes and study guides: www.freebooknotes.com

Books on Tape – Site with a large inventory of books on tape for purchase:
www.school.booksontape.com

Cliffs Notes – Summaries of stories and novels: www.cliffsnotes.com

Disney – Games and activities: http://disney.go.com

edHelper – This site contains many teaching resources for educators at all levels and all subject areas; $19.95 yearly membership: www.edhelper.com

Education World – Lesson planning, professional development and more:
www.education-world.com

Educational Teacher Software Download Center – Membership fee:
www.teach-nology.com/downloads/

Fun Brain – Math games, facts and more: www.funbrain.com

Geoboards: http://mathforum.org/trscavo/geoboards/

Homework Help! SCORE! Educational Center provides math tutoring for a fee:
www.escore.com

Improving Education, Inc. – Free online worksheets to help students grade K-4. All subject areas: www.onlineworksheets.org/math_worksheets.htm
www.onlineworksheets.org/language_arts_worksheets.htm

Innovative Learning Concepts, Inc. – A site for Touch Math: www.touchmath.com

Learning Styles - Gregorc, Anthony. *An Adult's Guide to Style.* http://idea.ed.gov

Learning Styles and Multiple Intelligences – Students quickly assess their personal learning styles and determine their individual strengths. Interactive site for both students and teachers: www.ldpride.net

Math Activity – A site of math activities: www.yourlearning .net

Math Activities K-12 – Interactive lessons and activities for teachers and students: www.shodor.org

Math Centers – Membership required: www.teacherfilebox.com/index.aspx

Math Dictionary – Great site if you are looking for definitions and examples: www.teachers.ash.org.au/jeather/maths/dictionary.html

Math Fact Café – Math fact sheets and flashcards. Math worksheets. Grades K-5: www.mathfactcafe.com

Math Help – Math support for students: www.helpingwithmath.com

Math Stories – Boost math problem solving and critical thinking skills. Some free material, but membership is required for much of the site: www.mathstories.com

Math Vocabulary – Thousands of math vocabulary words listed alphabetically: www.mathwords.com/a_to_z.htm

Minnesota Humanities Commission – Tips for Reading with Your Children in 24 languages. Great for Book Backpacks: www.thinkmhc.org/literacy/tips.htm

Paper – Therapro – Various widths, raised line. Various widths of paper for written language: www.theraproducts.com

Paragraphs – This site is an interactive, online paragraph-writing site: www.paragraphpunch.com

Parent Support – Pacer Center: www.pacer.org

Picture Sequence Cards – Sequence card activities and more: www.dotolearn.com

Pocket Full of Therapy – Materials to purchase for fine- and large-motor control: www.pfot.com

Posters – Letter-size, full-color phonics posters for the wall or student folders created by Adrian Bruce. Free, but donations are accepted! www.adrianbruce.com/reading/posters/
The National Institute on Drug Abuse also offers free posters and material for educators and parents: www.nida.nih.gov/parent-teacher.html

Recording for the Blind and Dyslexic – Textbooks and books on audiotape; 4000 new books each year. Membership required: www.rfbd.org

Resources for Christian Teachers – Large amounts of free materials plus links to hundreds of sites. All curriculum areas: www.teacherhelp.org

School Express – 9000 + free worksheets; all areas: www.schoolexpress.com

Spark Notes – Study guides to classic novels; secondary level: www.sparknotes.com

SuperKids – A collection of easy-to-use, free educational resources for home and school. You may also create your own: www.superkids.com/aweb/tools/

Tangrams – For information, examples and printable tangrams: http://tangrams.ca/
Work a virtual tangram puzzle online: http://pbskids.org/cyberchase/games/area/tangram.html

Teacher File Box – Math Centers. Membership required: www.teacherfilebox.com/index.aspx

Teachers Helping Teachers – Site for all teachers but has good basic skills materials for special educators: www.pacificnet.net/~mandel/

Teacher Timesavers – Resources for Christian Teachers:
www.teacherhelp.org/teacher_timesavers.htm

Teacher Views – Free online resources for teachers: www.teacherview.com

Timelines – Create your own timeline of events: www.ourtimelines.com

Tools for Teachers – Microsoft has many templates and organizational tools:
http://office.microsoft.com/en-us/workessentials/FX101996731033.aspx

Vocabulary University – Free vocabulary puzzles and activities: www.vocabulary.com

Word of the Day sites – www.wordcentral.com   www.superkids.com/aweb/tools/words
www.dictionary.reference.com/wordoftheday

yourDictionary.com – Lists the 100 most commonly misspelled words in English and provides some mnemonics and other information to help students spell the words correctly:
http://yourdictionary.com/library/misspelled.html

Peytral Publications

Peytral Publications, Inc. is here to help you. If you have questions, comments, would like to place an order, or request a catalog, please contact us by mail, telephone, fax, or online. We will be happy to assist you!

Peytral Publications, Inc.
PO Box 1162
Minnetonka, MN 55345

To place an order call toll free: 1-877-PEYTRAL(739-8725)
All other questions or inquiries
Telephone 952-949-8707
FAX 952-906-9777
E-mail help@peytral.com

For the most current listing of new titles and
perennial best sellers,
we encourage you to visit our web site at:
www.peytral.com